Ancient, Medieval and Modern Philosophy

A Historical Introduction
(500 BC-1800 AD)

This volume acknowledges the invaluable contribution of Prof Cyril Desbruslais, S.J., to Jnana-Deepa Vidyapeeth, Pune on his 80th birthday (*Dec 21, 1940). His colleagues, students and well-wishers have contributed to this project.

JDV Philosophy Series - 17

Ancient, Medieval and Modern Philosophy

A Historical Introduction
(500 BC-1800 AD)

Cyril Desbruslais, S.J.
(Prof Emeritus, Jnana-Deepa Vidyapeeth, Pune, India)

Edited by
Valerian Mendonca, S.J.

Jnana-Deepa Vidyapeeth

&

Christian World Imprints

First Published in 2021 by

Jnana-Deepa Vidyapeeth
Ramwadi, Nagar Road, **Pune-411014**
jdvoffice@jdv.edu.in
www.jdv.edu.in
Phone: +91 20 41036111

&

Christian World Imprints
Christian Publishing & Books from India
C-3, Shop No. 14, Ground Floor
Wazirpur Industrial Area, **Delhi-110052**
cwidelhi2017@gmail.com
www.ChristianWorldImprints.com
Phone: +91 11 41526079

ISBN: 978-93-5148-519-3

"Published with the help of the Institute of Missiology – Germany"

Printed in India.

CONTENTS

JDV PHILOSOPHY SERIES - 17

Since 1893 Jnana-Deepa Vidyapeeth has been pioneering philosophy discussion and debate inspired by prominent personalities like Richard De Smet, Jean de Marneffe, Salvino Azzopardi, Cyril Desbruslais, Noel Sheth, John Vattanky, etc. It has been in the forefront of promoting Indian philosophy and making philosophical thinking relevant for contemporary times. In its effort to reach out to like-minded scholars, JDV Philosophy Series has been visualized as a catalyst for interdisciplinary thinking and contemporary exploration on social issues fostering holistic liberation, integral development and creative engagement.

JDV Philosophy Series

1. Salvino Azzopardi: ***Epistemology and Phenomenology of Religions*** (2018)
2. Kuruvilla Pandikattu & Thomas Karimundackal (eds): ***Melodies from the Flute***: For Prof Noel Sheth SJ (2018)
3. Kurien Kunnumpuram: ***Freedom and Joy*** (2018)
4. Cyril Desbruslais SJ: ***Postmodernity: An Indian Christian Philosophical Appraisal*** (2019)
5. Cyril Desbruslais SJ: ***Metaphysics: Philosophy of Be-ing for Today*** (2019)
6. John Peter Vallabadoss: ***Indian Thinkers: Modern and Contemporary Period*** (2019)
7. Thomas Karimundackal & Kuruvilla Pandikattu (eds): ***Logic and Love***: For Prof John Vattanky SJ (2019)
8. Fabian Jose UMI: ***Relevance of Thomas Merton's Spirituality for the Consecrated Life in India*** (2019)
9. Kuruvilla Pandikattu & PT Mathew (eds): ***Committed to the Church and the Country***: For Prof Kurien Kunnumpuam SJ (2019)
10. Cyril Desbruslais SJ: ***The Philosophy of God*** (2019)
11. Thomas Karimundackal & Kuruvilla Pandikattu: ***Fully Spiritual, Fully Human:*** For Dr Stephen Chundanthadam SJ (2020)
12. Kuruvilla Pandikattu: ***Fully Human and Fully Alive:*** For Dr Cyril Desbruslais SJ (2020)
13. Thomas Karimundackal SJ & Dolichan Kollareth SJ (eds) ***Reason: Faithful and True: For Dr. George Karuvelil SJ*** (2020)
14. Kuruvilla Pandikattu SJ, Sebastian Vazhapilly SJ & Prasad Lankapilly SJ (eds) ***Serving the Church and the Nation: Gratefully and Faithfully***
15. Kuruvilla Pandikattu (ed) ***Befriending the Other: Other Religions***
16. Gargi Mukherjee: ***Emancipation of the Wretched of the Earth***
17. Cyril Desbruslais: ***Ancient, Medieval and Modern Philosophy***
18. Cyril Desbruslais: ***Contemporary Philosophy***

AUTHOR'S INTRODUCTION

> "It is far easier to point out the errors and faults in the work of a great mind, than to give a distinct and clear exposition of its values."
> –Arthur Schopenhauer, 19c German Philosopher

A.1. Why this Survey?

We have already had occasion to mention, during our "Introduction to Philosophy" sessions together, that Philosophy should be a team-work, an ongoing process of dialogue. This is because, among other reasons, reality is too rich, the mystery of being too vast for any one human mind to be able to grasp it exhaustively - even from a select stand-point. In addition, each one of us is more or less conditioned by his past experiences- even by the language he speaks! It is only through contact with Others who belong to other cultures, other times, or who don't quite think as we do, that we might be made aware of deficiencies and oversights in our approach to reality. A true philosopher or 'lover of wisdom', then, will always be open to others-but critically, of course! - for he recognises that even these with whom he cannot quite agree may have some message for him. After all, as we have seen, an error is nothing but an exaggerated (or, if you prefer, a distorted) truth.

A.2. Fellow-Pilgrims

We shall be meeting with a selection of great thinkers who, after all, were only trying to do for their times what we are struggling to do for ours: attempting to make some sense of this "complicated business of existence", offering to their fellows a "reason for living and hoping." Many of them, whether we realise it or not, have left a profound mark on the modern mind - which includes us, too. Sometimes they have inspired man, have helped him better understand the mysteries of existence. At times, they have crippled human thought — but only when men have followed them blindly, uncritically, taking them for Oracles, rather than fellow-pilgrims on the path to Truth. We can as much profit from their insights as from their mistakes as we try, in our turn, to respond to the same basic and challenging questions concerning God, man, knowledge, the world... questions that will invigorate the mind of man as long as he is man... questions that have no final, exhaustive "once-and for-all" type of answers, but are humble responses that help us advance yet another step on that unending pilgrimage to Truth. It will be an even more exciting pilgrimage as we realise that Truth has spoken to us a Word, that his Word has willed to share in our quest and walks by our side, even though we take him for just another fellow-pilgrim as did those trekkers to Emmaus.

A.3. Confusion Confounded

All this is not to deny that the jumble of conflicting views bandied about, concerning the apparently most basic facts of knowledge, could very well produce in us the contrary effect. The "philosophical scandal", far from aiding us in our quest, might give us a disgust for these men and their books who, in Erasmus' telling phrase, "speak sentences more than sense." Even Descartes almost fell into despair when he noted that though "philosophy had been cultivated for many years by the most distinguished men there is not a single matter within its sphere which is not under dispute." And Kant remarked in nigh despair, "metaphysics has become rather to be regarded as a battle-field quite particularly suited for those who desire to exercise themselves in mock combats, and in which no participant has ever succeeded in gaining so much as an inch of territory, at least in a manner as to secure its permanent possession." Each of these men tried to get philosophy started again on a surer, securer footing. But things are no better today; witness the number of "-isms" floating about. Besides, they also added to the confusion by leaving behind them new (sometimes false) problems for others to solve!

A.4. Take Your Pick

One solution to all this would be to give up, to despair of reaching any Truth, to retire from the task. After all, if such eminent thinkers could not agree, what chance have I, with my mediocre intelligence? This is the temptation of scepticism.

Or one could seek refuge in the naive over-simplification of the eclectic: the man who tries to make a hotch-potch of the whole business, ignoring basic differences and incompatibilities (not to say outright contradictions), dishonestly forcing a pseudo-agreement. "They are all saying the same thing in different ways," he boldly asserts.

Or one could have a more sober, humbler understanding of the limits and capacities of human knowledge. He could say that knowledge can be obtained only with difficulty. He could proceed with more caution, less dogmatism, greater openness to others, to correction. Yet he would be critical in all this. Instead of hastily condemning and refusing, he might try to concentrate more on understanding and listening (which is a whole life's work in itself). Finally, he may have to admit that a great part of our life must be prepared to base itself and its decisions less on metaphysical certitudes and irrefutable proofs, but on calculated risk and shared common endeavour.

If this survey will have helped to the formation of clear, critical and creative minds, it will be well worth the effort!

Cyril Desbruslais SJ
De Nobili College

1. ANCIENT PHILOSOPHY

1.1. Introductory

For the beginnings of Western Philosophy, as for most other disciplines, we must need to turn to Ancient Greece, the cradle of almost every branch of learning in the West.

Scholars have sometimes attributed this to mercantile contacts with India and with other Oriental cultures, such as that of Egypt and Babylon. and it is true that certain doctrines, such as transmigration of souls, seem to point to foreign and even Indian inspiration. However, there is precious little positive evidence to substantiate this view. On the other hand, there were several developments in Greece which could have facilitated the growth and development of philosophical speculation. A mere stable political life and the maturing of democracy made it possible for men to find the leisure and security to reflect on the mysteries of existence. In this, they had a good fund of myths to draw upon and interpret. Besides, the Greek mentality - especially at the time - was particularly religious and ethical preoccupations were very marked among the people. Whatever be the truth about the origins of the "Greek miracle", it is true that, even if the beginnings of Greek philosophy were imported, the Greeks soon gave a particular and original stamp and orientation to their research and reflection that differentiated it from the philosophy of other lands.

Let us not forget, at the outset, that 'ancient' is a very relative term. We use it to designate men and times that are removed from us in the past. In reality the word refers to people and cultures that stood at the beginnings of recorded history and who would leave their mark on our times which are, historically speaking, ancient with regard to their new, endeavours!

These remarks would be useful if and when we are inclined to smile indulgently at the apparent naivety of some of the views of, say, a **Thales** or even a **Plato.** Let us not forget that they were pioneers, venturing on a new territory. They did not have the centuries of experience and trial and error that we have to fall back upon. Indeed, sometimes the very freshness and simplicity of their vision can be a lesson to us - to us who are so accustomed to complex systems of thought and culture that we tend to lose that fresh, youthful, sense of wonderment when viewing the world and which is the foundation of all true philosophy.

1.2. The Pre-Socratics

1.2.1. The Name

These thinkers are called 'pre-Socratics' (people who came before Socrates), not just for reasons of convenient chronology. On the whole, their views and interests ran in another direction than that of Socrates, his illustrious successors and the Sophists among whom he must be originally numbered.

All these thinkers were mainly concerned with the outer, external world and the problems and issues raised from such an interest. With the Sophists, the focus of attention would be the 'internal world', that is the mystery of man. Aristotle dubbed the pre-Socratics the "physicists" because they had reflected so much on nature (Greek, physics). Two major issues command their attention:

(a) the search for the **arche**, the alleged primordial stuff out of which the universe was supposed to have been fashioned;
(b) the famous controversy of **change** (becoming) vs. **permanence** (being) or, to use a more precise philosophical vocabulary, the question of the **One** and the **Many**. Since they tended to view the universe as an organic whole, and even as a living whole, they are called *hylozoists*.

1.2.2. Sources

Our sources as regards the pre-Socratics are admittedly very scanty. We have only a handful of short passage written by them or purported to have been written by them. These are, for the most part, quotations from their writings, now no longer extent, taken from later writers as Aristotle. And we cannot be too sure of the objectivity and impartiality of these sources. But it is all we have!

To put you in touch with these primary sources the following bibliography is recommended:

K. Freeman, *Ancilla to the Pre-Socratic Philosophers*, Oxford Blackwell, 1956 (An English translation of the best collection of Pre-Socratic fragments assembled by H. Diels under the title Fragmente der Vorsokratiker, Berlin, 1934—35).

K. Freeman, *The Pres-Socratic Philosophers: A Companion to Diels*, Oxford Blackwell 1959 (adds to the texts cited also a commentary).

G. S. Kirk and L. E. Raven, *The Presocratic Philosophers: A Critical History with a Selection of Texts* (Texts given in the original Greek along with their English translation).

T. V. Smith, "Philosophers Speak for Themselves", Vol. I. *From Thales to Plato*, Chicago Univ. Press, 1957 (A good selection of texts but less than those found in the above).

1.2.3. The Sensualist Response: The Ionian School

The School: Ionia is a district on the West coast of present-day Turkey. Colonised by the Greeks in the 11th century B.C., it numbered among its more important commercial and literary with the exception of Heraclitus, perhaps the most celebrated of them all. He came from Ephesus. This school is called "sensualist" because in its attempt to answer the being-vs-becoming question, as well as in its effort to discover the arche of the universe, it relied rather on sense knowledge and sense observation and not on reason. Broadly speaking, their reply comes out heavily in favour of becoming. The Ionians tend to hold that becoming alone is real and that being is an illusion.

1.2.3.1. Thales (c. 585 BC)

Thales, a very versatile genius, is generally accredited to be the 'father of Greek philosophy'. He held that the arche was water - for a more profound reason than the mere fact that he lived in a place virtually surrounded by water! It was rather because he had noted how much water is necessary for life. He was beguiled by the wonderful properties of the magnet and wondered whether it had a kind of soul. In fact, he seems to have had the conviction that everything is fundamentally alive. This is probably how we should interpret his alleged view that "all things are full of gods."

1.2.3.2. Anaximander (c. 570 BC)

Anaximander, proposed the mysterious 'apeiron' as the arche. Now the whole problem consists in trying to decide how to translate this word. One could render it vaguely as "the indefinite". However, it could equally mean the "spatially infinite", the boundless as the qualitatively indefinite. Which did he mean? Most likely the second - which would show that his response was far more metaphysical than that of Thales!

1.2.3.3. Heraclitus (c. 500 BC)

Heraclitus was surnamed "the obscure" by his fellow citizens with whom he didn't seem to get on very well. Plato records of him the famous dictum that "all things are forever in flux, nothing ever remains the same". He is supposed to have explained this by the famous analogy of the river, saying that you cannot step into the same stream twice. However, though he did stress the constant "becoming" of things and their consequent impermanence – his reference to the arche as fire should be seen as having more of a metaphorical import – he did not quite seem to overlook the underlying element of order or permanence that seemed to rule this world of flux and change. This he did by drawing attention to the Logos, the principle of order or reason, the element of unity in diversity.

1.2.3.4. Critical Remarks

It is indeed interesting to note the gradual maturing and refinement of philosophical speculation and concepts from Thales to Heraclitus, by way of Anaximander and his *apeiron*. Heraclitus is certainly the most accomplished thinker of this school. He was greatly to influence the Stoics, especially as regards his doctrine of the Logos. Hegel saw in him a predecessor.

1.2.4. The Rationalist Response: The Eleatic School

The School: Elea, a town in Southern Italy, had been founded by Ionian refugees, fleeing from the Persian invaders in the mid-6th century BC. Since the men of this school, in responding to the controversial questions of their time, preferred to make use of their reason, rather than rely on the data of their sense, they are called rationalists. They tend to assert that Being alone is real, that Becoming is illusory.

1.2.4.1. Xenophanes (c. 530 BC)

Xenophanes, is the alleged founder of the school. He is noted for his attacks on the anthropomorphic Greek deities. He criticized the militarism and anthropomorphism of traditional Greek morality and religion, arguing that fundamental truth about the world is difficult to achieve. In this way he calls for a purification and deepening of religious language.

1.2.4.2. Parmenides (c. 500 BC)

Parmenides, as erstwhile political figure of Elea, was soon to become the leading light of the school. He exposes his basic philosophy that "It is." In other words, Reality ("It") exists, always existed and cannot 'not be'. His philosophy of the One is summarised as: "Being is ... single, indivisible and homogenous, timeless, changeless and, since motion is itself one form of change, motionless as well." Parmenides knew fully well that his views were in flagrant contradiction with what his senses told him. He dismissed the latter testimony as illusory. Change, he argued, is impossible for reason shows that it involved a contradiction. For it implies that something new must come to be. Now this something new must be either being or non-being. If it is non-being, it is nothing and so can bring about no change. If it is being, this is nothing new for that to which it is added is already being!

1.2.4.3. Zeno (c. 450 BC)

Zeno was contemptuously dubbed by Aristotle as "the Father of Dialectic," by which he meant specious arguments which lead men astray under their appearance of truth. The title seems to be well-merited, for Zeno worked out a whole series of astute but bogus arguments to prove that multiplicity and change (including movement) are impossible. He thus sought to bolster up the thesis of his Master, Parmenides. Whether he did it deliberately or not, Zeno misleads us by confusing the actual with the potential!

1. *The Dichotomy*: It is impossible to move around a racetrack since we must first go halfway, and before that go half of halfway, and before that half of half of halfway, and… If space is infinitely divisible, we have infinitely many partial distances to cover, and cannot get under way in any finite time.
2. *The Arrow*: If, on the other hand, motion occurs in discrete intervals, then at any given moment during its flight through the air, an arrow is not moving. But since its entire flight comprises only such moments, the arrow never moves.

1.2.4.4. Critical Remarks

Monism will ever be the great temptation of the synthetic mind, the mind which loves order, discipline and symmetry and is ever seeking to relate and connect the apparently divided. On the contrary, it is something very human and praise worthy, but care must be taken to see that this "passion for harmony" doesn't become a kind of blinker, forcing us to block out whole areas of experience that don't quite square with our prejudice. If the unified, monistic vision of Parmenides will keep on appearing in various forms in diverse cultures over the ages, is it not but a moving testimony to that human longing to make sense and meaning of the complicated business of life? Actually, the thesis of Parmenides stems from an as yet unresolved question in Metaphysics which the Aristotelian notion of act and potency as well as the Thomistic elaboration of the theory of participation would go a long way to resolving.

1.2.5. An Attempt at Synthesis: The Mediating Atomist School

The School: Man, rather than admit defeat, rather than let himself remain confounded and despairing over apparent contradictions, tries to find a way to reconcile conflicting opinions and harmonise all the data. Thus, it was with the Atomists. They noted the clash of views between the first two great schools of Greek philosophy, concerning even so elementary a datum of experience as movement and change. In their response they seem to have saved both the Being so beloved of the Eleatics as well as the Becoming championed by the Ionians. Reality, according to the Atomists, then, would be a heap of atoms tumbling about in a void. The indivisible atom, itself unchanging, is the element of permanence whereas its incessant motion provides the element of change.

1.2.5.1. Leucippus (c. 440 BC)

Leucippus founded the school at Abdera near the Black Sea. His view:
1. The reality of empty space or void.
2. The plurality of things and their motion.
And this is about all we know of him for sure!

1.2.5.2. Democritus (c. 440 BC)

Democritus was Leucippus' fellow-citizen and his most eminent disciple. He travelled extensively and wrote widely on various topics. It is to him that we owe the elaboration of the ancient atomic thesis, as it has come down to us. Where Parmenides postulated one, indivisible and unchanging Being, Democritus would divide it into an infinite number of infinitely small but ultimately indivisible particles called atoms (Greek *a-tomos*: *un-cut*, *un-cuttable*). Each of these atoms is complete and eternal, though they may admit of different shapes. They are surrounded by a total void, a real non-being, which is the theatre of' their constant movement. In course of their tumbling about, they come to interlock. Thus, forming the various beings of experience. At times they come apart and thus we have the phenomena of death and decay. A couple of unresolved questions remain though: where did the atoms come from and what set them in motion? Little thought is given to the first question. As to the second, the reply is but vague, inadequate and embarrassed. It is but a matter of fate or chance, we are told. But these "answers" are a mere matter of hiding behind words!

1.2.5.3. Empedocles (c. 430 BC)

Empedocles was obviously dissatisfied with such aspects of the atomic thesis. And so, he harnessed his poet's spirit to the mechanism of Democritus. In place of an infinite number of basic atoms, he proposed four ultimate elements: earth, air, fire and water. The various objects of experience are formed by the combination of these. Their diversity being accounted for by the different proportions of their combination. Their combination and dissolution takes place under the influence of two conflicting forces, *love and hate*. This is a poetically more satisfying explanation, but is it any better than the vague forces of fate and chance?

1.2.5.4. Anaxagoras (c. 425 BC)

Anaxagoras was one of the first great philosophers who came to settle in Greece. Inevitably he became implicated in the political and social upsets of the city-state and had to do a spell of prison for having backed a loser! However, he was finally allowed to return to his native Asia Minor, to finish his days in relative peace. He felt that neither the atoms of' Democritus, nor the four basic elements of Empedocles could explain for instance, how hair can grow out of flesh or mighty oaks out of tiny acorns. Thus, he concluded that, "there is something of everything in everything." This is known as his theory of *homoemeries* (from two Greek words meaning similar or like parts), a word coined by Aristotle and which does not really express what Anaxagoras wanted to say unless we take it to mean that every reality has, hidden within itself, parts that are like unto parts of other realities. Finally, in place of the vague force of Fate or Love he proposed an ultimate principle of movement and order, which he called ***"Nous"*** (i.e., Mind). This Nous is infinite and autonomous, but it knows all and controls all that happens. In this he represents the first great attempt to break away from a simplistic, materialistic and mechanical vision of the universe. Though he has often been faulted for having a materialistic comprehension of his Nous (he describes it, for example as "the thinnest of all things" and "the same in all its parts"), this may be less a materialistic understanding of the Nous and more a stumbling, clumsy way to describe a reality perceived as super-material for which a more accurate technical vocabulary still remained to be found.

1.2.5.5. Critical Remarks

Atomism is, admittedly, a clever via media between the two mutually exclusive theses of the Ionians and Eleatics. It is a clever insight, the scientific basis of which is well known today - however, it is not too difficult to notice the essential differences between the atomism of Democritus and the theory of atomic particles (for one thing, the so-called "atom" is a misnomer. for it can be cut into smaller particles!). In any case, the brilliant hypotheses of Leucippus and Democritus would by no means be the last word in Greek philosophy: it was not long before later thinkers saw that the rich variety of the world could hardly be reduced to the mechanical interplay of atoms! Yet Democritus' vision provided the first working blue-print for a full-fledged materialistic system: there is even a trace of Democritus in the dialectic materialism of Marx.

We have seen how Empedocles and Anaxagoras were dissatisfied with the conclusions of atomism. Empedocles felt the need to bring in four basic elements and two forces to explain better the variety around us. But his "forces" still are conceived in a very materialistic way – one has only to' check the fragments. With Anaxagoras, however, "a light, if still a weak one, begins to dawn, because the understanding is now recognised as the principle" (Heller). Aristotle says of him that he "stood out like a sober man from the random talkers that had preceded him." Yet, even if we grant that his Nous was understood by him to be more supra-material than his vocabulary succeeded in making it out to be, we cannot but, in the last analysis, echo the disappointment of Socrates in the *Phaedo* when it becomes clear that Anaxagoras put to such poor use his original perception: "My extravagant expectations were all dashed to the ground," laments Socrates, "when I went on and found that the man made no use of Nous at all. He ascribed no causal power to it whatsoever in the ordering of things, but to airs, and aethers, and waters, and a host of other strange things."

1.2.6. The Pythagorean Brotherhood

The brotherhood: The first thing to note is that Pythagoras did not found a philosophical school, but a kind of religious community in the full sense of the term. There was a general "two-way drift" then in the Ionian civilisation: towards scepticism or towards the "mystery religions". This always happens when a civilisation is felt to be on the decline. It happened with the Romans, it was happening with the Greeks and it happens in our times.

It is rather difficult to separate the views taught by Pythagoras himself from those of others of the brotherhood. Since we are dealing here not with a school, a crowd of "disciples" more or less independent and isolated from one another, it does not matter. For they were a real community and it is to the community as a whole that we may ascribe the teachings.

We leave aside the list of quaint religious tabus and traditions that the Pythagoreans enjoined, which do not really concern us here. We might also not, in passing, that the Pythagoreans taught transmigration of souls (hence, perhaps, their vegetarianism - which even included a ban on the eating of beans!) and were the first to hold - long before Copernicus - heliocentrism (the view that the sun and not the earth is the centre of the universe).

1.2.6.1. Pythagorean Thought

But the doctrine for which they remain famous - and which it is rather difficult to understand - is the teaching that the arche is ***number*** and that things, ultimately, are *numbers*!

Before we try to understand just what all this means, let us remember that the Pythagoreans were very much interested in, as well as devoted to, the study of mathematics and music (two disciplines which are not so unrelated as they may appear to be at first sight). Indeed, they are the first to have taken these two subjects seriously. It did not take them long to note that there is a relationship between the quality or "pitch" of a note and the length of: say, the harp string, which produced it. If the transition between quality and quantity (length of harp string and pitch of musical note) could be provided by number, then perhaps numbers might be able to account for the qualitative diversity in the world at large!

The Pythagoreans held that nature can be 'unlocked' by mathematics. They believed, therefore, that mathematical structures underlie all things (substance). There were other arguments as well: things perish, but mathematical concepts do not. Mathematics, therefore is that which is *unchangeable* in nature. And mathematical knowledge is *certain* knowledge, since the subject matter does not change.

Although the Pythagoreans can rightly be called rationalists, they conceived of mathematics as something that, through reason, *points beyond reason* toward something mystical.

That might seem a fair enough conclusion, but when the Pythagoreans go on to attribute the number four to justice or six to animation, we may well begin to wonder if not a little of arbitrary dogmatism has come into the picture.

1.2.6.2. Critical Remarks

The Pythagoreans did not stop short at pointing out the importance of number in the constitution of things, they go on to say that things actually are numbers. No one seems to have taken their heliocentric views very seriously. It was only much later with Galileo, Copernicus and Kepler that man would take this theory seriously – some fifteen centuries after it was first proposed. But perhaps the greatest tribute we can pay to the Pythagoreans, as Copleston remarks, is to point out that they were one of the determining influences in the development and maturing of the thought of Plato!

1.3. The Golden Age

1.3.1. The Transition: The Sophists

A new orientation: Round about the beginnings of the 5th c. B.C, the focus of attention in Greek philosophical speculation begins to shift from the world around man to the world that is man himself, from the macrocosm to the microcosm or, to use a more precise philosophical vocabulary, from the Object to the Subject. No doubt the conflicts and contradictions that resulted from the efforts of the major thinkers among the Ionians and Eleatics to plumb the constituents of the world discouraged further work on that theme. Besides, as Greek democracy began to mature and as the 'common man' began to realise that he could play an important role in the affairs of the city-state, he wanted to equip himself with knowledge in practical affairs, especially in rhetoric and the art of persuading. In this he was aided by a band of self-appointed itinerant teachers who were ready to offer him the fruit of their expertise and their fruitful travels ... for a fee. This latter practice of dispensing knowledge for a fee was something wholly out of keeping with the Greek custom and earned the "Sophists", as they were called the epithet, "shopkeepers with spiritual wares" from Socrates.

As time went on, and the demands for the services of sophists tutors increased, not a few charlatans saw in the profession an opportunity to make "a fast buck". Rival teachers tried to out-do each other in their claims as encyclopaedists and didn't hesitate to dress up their speech with all manner of obscurisms to appear more profound. Further, in order to appear more original, they worked out various fine-sounding and specious arguments to attack established mores - which, as is always the case, - won for them, at the same time, the enthusiastic support of the younger generation and the hatred and alarm of the elder folk.

In no time, whatever their initial motives and ideals were, sophistry had acquired that connotation of quackery and fraud that it has today. In this, it was particularly the opposition and attacks of Socrates and Plato, that gained for them this reputation. And the word still has this implication today.

Let us not forget, though, that no less a man than Socrates could be, historically speaking, classed in this "school". But with a difference, of course. For in Socrates we can see the nobility and grandeur of what must have been the pristine sophist ideal. Both Socrates and the "sophists" gave much attention to virtue or arete. But whereas for the latter, this soon came to mean the acquiring of practical "know-how" - worse, the art of convincing and "getting-ahead" at all costs - for Socrates, it concerned the formation and development of the whole man. However, Socrates was seen by the State - as it was to regard many a Sophist - as a corrupter of the youth and a disturber of the peace and security of the nation. Thus, would die one of the first victims of power that brooks no criticism.

Sources: Once again, we are brought up short by the paucity of our resources. The nearest we have to direct sources are two well-known dialogues of Plato which you could read for your profit: *Thaetetus* and *Protagoras*. There are several copies available. Besides they touch upon an issue that is both relevant and interesting (i.e., what is knowledge?).

1.3.1.1. Protagoras (c. 450 BC)

Protagoras was a native of Abdera. He travelled widely and knew many of the important personnages of his time. Characteristically, he got into trouble with the authorities because of some of his views on the gods and died while fleeing a summons to trial. He is best remembered for his celebrated *homo-mensura* dictum:

> "Man is the measure of all things; of those that are, that they are, of those that are not, that they are not."

In spite of the controversy, it seems pretty clear that what Protagoras means here by "man" is the individual man and not the "species" as such! "Man is the measure of all things" can be interpreted as an epistemological thesis: things do not reveal themselves to people the way that the things are in themselves; but it is always only certain aspects or properties of the things that at any one time present themselves to man. E.g. a hammer in the hands of a carpenter, a physicist or a merchant.

This view implies a kind of epistemological *perspectivism*: Our knowledge is always conditioned by our perspective at any one time. This kind of perspectivism implies an epistemological *pluralism*: there is a plurality of ways of viewing things. This perspectivism also represents a *relativism*: our knowledge of things is determined by our activities or situations – knowledge is relative to our situation.

1.3.1.2. Gorgias (c. 450 BC)

Gorgias came from Lentini in Sicily and is the usual other Sophist selected to stand, along with Protagoras, as representative of the Sophist tradition. For while Protagoras asserted, in effect, that everything is true, he taught that, in the last analysis, nothing is true. He develops this last point along three steps, close examination of which provides a good example of sophist dialectics:

(a) Nothing exists.
(b) Even if something were to exist, it could not be known.
(c) Even if it could be known, this knowledge wouldn't be capable of being passed on.

There are people who think that Gorgias is only joking and doesn't expect to be taken seriously. But his development of the argument seems serious enough, though it is founded on much ambiguity and confusion which perhaps is not due so much to his ill-will as to the inadequacy of terminology and the lack of development of metaphysics at the time.

Georgias, in a way, concluded that philosophy itself was hopelessly self-contradictory and, therefore, meaningless. Georgias may then have gone over to the practice of rhetoric purely as a method of persuasion, because he no longer believed in the possibility of true knowledge.

1.3.1.3. Critical Remarks

Much as we might regret some of the attitudes and practices that the sophists brought into philosophy (it is due to people such as they that philosophy has gained a 'bad name, as a kind of nonsense tricked up in bombast and pedalled by men with cobwebs in their head), in all fairness, it should be admitted that they started some other praiseworthy trends in the discipline. First, there was the welcome shift of attention from the object (the thing known) to the subject (the knower). Then, as regards the method, there is also - naturally - a shift from the deductive to the empirico-inductive approach. Finally, even if the "virtue" they are interested in was of the cheapest pragmatic variety, it was a beginning all the same. Socrates would do full justice to this and thus would save and immortalise the best and noblest that there ever could have been in the early sophist spirit.

1.3.2. Socrates (c. 470 – 399 BC)

1.3.2.1. Life

As in the case of most great men of long age, it is very difficult to separate fact from legend, as regards the life of Socrates. Though his father Sophroniscus is alleged to have been a stone-cutter and his mother Phaenarete a mid-wife, it is little likely that we should conclude that he was of the humblest of origins.

Like the young men of his time - especially those whose youth, like that of Socrates, coincided with the full flowering of Athenian splendour, he had some fair share of military experience - and even quite distinguished himself in the bargain. But his speculative temperament became soon evident. He is reported to have, on an occasion (and during a military campaign at that), fallen into a fit of abstraction that lasted a whole day and night. This is not too unusual in the life of great thinkers. He claimed to be also in communication with a mysterious inner voice or *daimon* who would often counsel him.

When the Delphic Oracle told a friend of Socrates that none was wiser than the self-same Socrates, he construed this to mean that he was the wisest of men because he recognised his own ignorance. He then began a more or less itinerant life in Athens, gathering round about him groups of mainly young people and getting them to reflect and, at the same time, pointing out the humbug and hypocrisy in many a self-appointed scholar, or in various social structures. As might be expected, he won himself not a few enemies in powerful places and he was finally arrested and brought to trial on the grounds of corrupting the youth and attacking religion and the state. He was sentenced to death which in those pre-electric chair days, meant having to drink Hemlock (a deadly poison). The authorities, it seems would have allowed him to escape- - for everyone knows that a dead hero attracts more followers than one who runs away - and he did have his chance. But Socrates refused to shrug off the sentence of the law and so met a noble and inspiring death in 399 B.C.

1.3.2.2. Sources

There is not a single work extant that has come down to us from the hand of Socrates, himself. It is even quite probable that he did not leave behind any written work, preferring the style of the informal dialogue. Socrates is, however, the leading character in the famous dialogues of his most illustrious disciple, Plato. However, it was a literary device - a kind of cross between humility and publicity - to place one's own views on the lips of some great personage. Considering the reputation of Socrates, it is hardly likely that Plato would ascribe to him views that were totally at variance with his own personal teachings. But, at times it is often difficult to decide whether a certain theory (for example the Theory of Forms) is to be attributed to Socrates or to Plato. It is generally thought, though, that the Platonic dialogues on the last days of Socrates are - for obvious reasons - deliberately historical. These dialogues - copies of them are easily available in the library - include the *Apology*, *Crito* and *Phaedo*. There is an excellent commentary on these (together with the *Euthyphro*) to be found in Romano Guardini's *The Death of Socrates*, Lodon 1948. There is also a chapter on Socrates in T.V. Smith's *Philosophers Speak for Themselves*, Vol. I. Finally, in case you want to supplement the Platonic picture of Socrates with that of other ancient writers, you may consult

Xenophon whose writings to the point are found in A D Lindsay's *Socrates Discourses*, London: Everyman's, 1950. The comic poet Aristophanes used him as a figure for buffonery and vaudeville in his plays such as *Clouds*. As for literature on Socrates, that is immense. A few major works are mentioned here.

A. E. Taylor, *Socrates*, London, 1932 (A classic; Prof. Taylor has also several well-written columns on Socrates in the *Encyclopaedia Britannica*).

Gregory Vlastos, *The Philosophy of Socrates*, New York, 1971 (A collection of critical essays: for the major part, rather technical).

John Fergusson, *Socrates: A Source Book*, London, 1960

Laszle Versenyi, *Socratic Humanism*, New York, 1963.

Micheline Sauvage, *Socrates and the Human Conscience*, London, 1960.

Norman Gulley, *The Philosophy of Socrates*, London, 1968 (A very readable and thorough treatment from the stand-point of the topics we shall be studying).

1.3.2.3. His Doctrine

The "Socratic Method": Some years ago, an article in a popular periodical summed up Socrates' pedagogy as a way to "make people think straight by forcing them to talk in circles." And this, indeed, is what appears to be the case, as is borne out by a perusal of any of the dialogues where he is the central character. For his main contribution to the dialogue seems to be the clever question. His interlocuter gives an over-hasty and over-confident answer; Socrates reflects on this and puts another question that reveals the inadequacies of the reply. The other is forced to think more deeply and give a more careful response. And so, it proceeds. Thus, by seemingly making the person talk in circles (because one keeps coming back, as it were, to the same topic), he gets him to realise that his thinking was not so "straight" after all. This method is called "Socratic irony" because, though Socrates appears to be the pupil - since he is putting the questions - he is actually ("ironically") the one who is teaching by means of well-chosen questions. This is also referred to as the *"maieutic method"* (from the Greek verb, *maia*, meaning to serve as a midwife) because Socrates said that his role was but to help the student to give birth to knowledge, not to put it into him. In this, the mid-wife image is a very illuminating one and represents a whole new (?) approach to education.

1.3.2.3.1. His Philosophy of Man

Like his sophist colleagues, Socrates was interested in helping his fellows cultivate "virtue" (arête), except that, for him, the word meant no mere pragmatic "know-how" but all that the more contemporary ethical meaning of the word implies. However, in this regard, he has a rather startling phrase, "Virtue is knowledge". However, the "knowledge" spoken of over here is mere a question of a deep conviction (a real assent, rather than a notional assent, as Newman would say) - as is borne out by other remarks of Socrates such as the one in Protagoras, where he holds that "No one does evil willingly." An interesting conclusion that is often drawn from these observations is that sin arises from ignorance. If so, then it should be possible to "teach" virtue - even if it can't quite be taught as one teaches other disciplines. Or perhaps why not? Socrates also paved the way for a deeper reflection on the soul of man as the inner principle of thought and action - whereas before him thinkers had a rather corporeal understanding of it. For Socrates, philosophy was no more hair-splitting and intellectual conceptualising, but the sincere search for truth and the all-round betterment of the human person. That is why he felt he could never give up this quest or vocation, even if it meant having to suffer the death penalty for it. (Cf the *Apology*)

1.3.2.3.2. His Philosophy of God

That Socrates was a religious man who prayed often is evident enough. But was he a monotheist or a polytheist? He hardly seemed to have felt it worth his while to note such a difference. In practically the same sentence, he speaks of his belief in gods and in God! Thus, in his Apology, he declares: "I do believe that there are gods, and in a sense higher than that in which any of my accusers believe in them. And to you and to God I commit my cause, to be determined by you as is best for you and me."

Socrates does not seem to have elaborated any more details about his belief in God. For instance, what was God's relationship to this world? Did he care about it? Though there is a reference in Xenophon in which he speaks of an intelligence that orders all things, one cannot be too sure that Socrates actually said these things.

1.3.2.3.3. His Philosophy of the World

This is the place to treat of the theory of *Forms* - if, of course, one is convinced that Socrates actually taught this view and was convinced of it. Since I do not think there is enough reason to say so, I prefer to leave to Plato and to him alone the credit (?) of originating the theory of Forms, and treatment of it will be done in the corresponding section.

1.3.2.4. Critical Remarks

1.3.2.4.1. In General

Perhaps more than any particular doctrine or theory, it is the *attitude* and *commitment* of Socrates that entitles him to a place among the "greats" of all time. His sincerity, openness and courage have won him the respect and admiration of succeeding generations. In our times, Gabriel Marcel has rejected the name 'existentialist' and declared himself to be a 'Christian Socratist'. At recent meetings of Amnesty International, Socrates was honoured as the type of those who, even today, are persecuted by the state because of their convictions and beliefs.

1.3.2.4.2. Socrates' views on Education

They offer a welcome alternative to the traditional 'banking system' of education so rightly criticised by men like Paolo Freire who, in his *Pedagogy of the Oppressed*, proposed the 'dialogical model' which has much in common with the maieutic method and the so-called Socratic irony. Socrates' pedagogy gives a very active role to the student and it, at the same time, a very demanding on to the teacher!

1.3.2.4.3. Socrates' Philosophy of Man

We have seen that his "Virtue is knowledge" does not see knowledge from, a narrow intellectualistic stand-point. Be that as it may, it would still seem that Socrates has missed a sad and humiliating aspect of the human experience of all too many of us. For some mysterious reasons – (original sin?) – many of us (if not all!) do evil, in spite of our convictions and best of resolutions. Even the great St. Paul had to confess, "I do not understand my own actions. For I do not do what I want, but I do the very thing that I hate." (Rom 7:15).

1.3.2.4.4. Socrates' Philosophy of God

When Socrates spoke of gods and God in the same breath, he was but making use of the clumsy, as yet not very much developed theological vocabulary of his contemporaries. He does seem to have recognised a distinction of kind - and not just degree - between God and the other deities or presiding spirits in whom he believed, like the other men of his time. In all this, Socrates was but a man of his age and times, though one might perhaps fault him for not 'rising above the limits of his times' in this respect and offer to it a new and valuable insight. But such a remark is not very fair to Socrates and perhaps asks too much from an age whose spirit was different from ours!

1.3.3. Plato (429 – 348 BC)

1.3.3.1. Life

"Plato", it would seem, was a kind of nick-name, given to the son of Ariston and Perictione, on account of his broad forehead or his sturdy physique (*Platos* means breadth, in Greek). His two brothers appear as characters in his dialogues, as also his half- brother from his mother's second marriage after Ariston's death. Little is known about his sister. At any rate, Plato had a very distinguished upbringing in a rather aristocratic family.

The trial and condemnation of his great guru Socrates - Plato had just turned 30 then - came as a great shock to him. He was present for the trial but not for the condemnation. It is quite likely that this shameful event increased his already settled prejudice against democracy. After all, it was the Athenian democratic system that brought about the death of Socrates and this only confirmed Plato's view that the State needed, ideally, a kind of philosopher-statesman at the helm - instead of the rabble - to guide it. In his later years, he felt that he had found such a man in the person of Dionysius II. But Plato was to be sadly disappointed in his dream.

Plato finally brought himself to return to Athens, a city which he could never quite forgive for having killed his great hero and mentor, and founded there (about 388) the *Academy*, so-called because it was situated near the sanctuary of the hero Academus. The Academy has justly been hailed as the first European University and young men came there from Athens and abroad to study subjects ranging from philosophy, maths and the science to the fine arts. We might note in passing that the aim of the Academy was very much the formation of statements and politicians of the better stamp and not time-serving, unscrupulous demagogues. By 367 (in which year Aristotle entered the Academy), Plato's reputation as a philosopher and counsellor to persons in high places had grown so much that he was invited to journey to Syracuse to educate the young Dionysius II, who had just ascended the throne. Dionysius was far from an ideal ruler and Plato soon gave up and returned to Athens. In 361, Dionysius seemed to have turned over a new leaf and earnestly desired his former mentor to resume his duties. Once again Plato's best efforts came to no avail and so he returned, a sadder and a wiser man, to his beloved Academy at Athens where he continued to lecture till his death in c. 348.

1.3.3.2. Sources

If we have a sizeable library of Plato's popular works, his *Dialogues*, we have none of his more scholarly "lecture" material. (We shall see that this is exactly the opposite in the case of Aristotle!) There are many "modem translations" of the better-known *Dialogues*, but the best known and classical collection is the standard one edited by B. Jowett, *The Dialogues of Plato*, in 5 volumes. References to the dialogues are given by citing, first, the title of the Dialogue and then the pagination fixed by Stephanus and marked in the Jowett edition on the inside margins.

There are some excellent books on Plato and his philosophy in the library. Besides the famous manuals - such as Copleston and Hirschberger - we single out for special mention just a few:

C. Field, *The Philosophy of Plato*, London, 2nd edition 1969.

(Most of the essays are on Aristotle, but there are three very good, though technical, articles on Plato's thought. Eminent contributors)

Gregory Vlastes, *Plato's Universe*, Oxford, 1975 (A readable and scholarly study of Greek cosmology, beginning with the Presocratics and culminating with the response of Plato).

Koyré, *Discovering Plato*, New York, 1945 (A good introduction to Plato's thought through some of his major dialogues).

Paul Friedlander, *Plato, an Introduction*, London, 1958 (An excellent, detailed study, translated from the German).

Renford Bambrough, *New Essays on Plato and Aristotle*, London 1965.

In addition to the above, there are some fine books on special aspects of Plato's philosophy, such as N. Gulley's highly recommendable *Plato's Theory of Knowledge*, London, 1962. A glance through the library cards will acquaint you with some of these. In class, further references will be given. There are particular dialogues of Plato which treat more specifically of certain topics. Thus, for instance, if you are interested in Plato's Political Thought - as also his views in Aesthetics, you should read the *Republic* an extremely long dialogue) and some of the better commentaries, such as that of E. Barker. The *Parmenides* takes up the issue of Metaphysics and there is a very good commentary by W.F. Lynch S.J.

1.3.3.3. Plato's Thought

1.3.3.3.1. Plato's Theory of Knowledge

1.3.3.3.1.1 Knowledge as Remembrance

Plato, first of all, argues negatively that knowledge cannot be mere sensation for then even a dog, which has sensation, would have knowledge. His positive theory of knowledge is given in the famous 'myth of the Cave'. There Plato puts forward the theory that knowledge is nothing but a remembering of what we have contemplated before our birth. This theory is supposed to be "confirmed" by the example of the uneducated slave in the ***Meno*** who is led to give correct answers to abstruse questions in Geometry. This is purported to show that he was but bringing to light what was hidden away in the innermost recesses of his mind, birth being accompanied by forgetfulness.

1.3.3.3.1.2. Process of Remembrance

We pass through four basic steps and eventually arrive at perfect knowledge or full remembrance - an explanation which Plato develops by way of the simile of the line, also in the *Republic.* At first our knowledge of things is but vague, shadowy and blurred. Then we gradually pass from this inferior knowledge through our 'imagination' to a clearer, more direct experience of objects. This is the level of firm assent or faith.

Next comes the stage where our faculty of reasoning comes into play as we begin to argue and make comparisons. Finally comes the highest level of knowledge, the realm of pure intellectual activity, where we contemplate the

Ideas and their inter-connections. In all this process, it is love which provides the essential dynamism and impulse in our ascent to the contemplation of the Beautiful. This latter detail is demonstrated in *Symposium.*

1.3.3.3.2. Plato's Philosophy of the World

1.3.3.3.2.1. The Theory of Ideas

The basic inspiration for this celebrated theory was Plato's observation that there are various 'individuals' which share a common form or basic nature. Thus, there are various individual men, horses, plants, minerals. From this he gets the idea - no doubt from his watching artisans at work, following a model or 'type' - that each individual was fashioned after an ideal type or pattern or model which some 'demiurge' or active spirit made us of in fashioning the world around us.

Where later thinkers would give these "forms" a mere ideal existence, Plato conceived of them as really existing somewhere, in another mysterious world "shining with pure light" (Cf ***Phaedo***). Each ideal form is ideal in every sense of the term: that is, it is perfect and all other copies we see of it in the world around us are but poor imitations or "shadows" of it, as he preferred to say. For some time, Plato seemed to hesitate to say that there existed an "ideal form" of everything in this world, including such mundane realities as dirt and mud. Finally, he accepted the logical demands of his theory and admitted that these too had their place in the Ideal World of Forms.

1.3.3.3.2.2. Participation

As he went deeper into this theory, Plato began to remark that the ideas in themselves are not completely unrelated and unconnected. Thus, for instance, the idea of dog would participate (literally 'take a part of' or 'have partly') in the idea of mammal; the idea of sparrow in that of bird. Mammal and bird, in turn, would both participate in the idea of animal. Ultimately all the ideas participate in the Supreme Idea or Form, that of the Good.

1.3.3.3.2.3. A Prejudice against Art

If the world around us is but an imitation - and an inferior one at that - of the real world, the world of ideas, it follows that the arts, such as painting and sculpture are but concerned with imitations of imitations! Not only are they illusory and escapist, for they are twice removed from reality, they are to be avoided as dangerous, for they distract us from our ascent to the Good. For this reason, Plato would exile all artists from his ideal state. Even poets and playwrights fare no better in the ***Republic***, for they trouble the emotions and sentiments of the spectators.

1.3.3.3.3. Plato's Philosophy of Man

1.3.3.3.3.1. Pre-existence of Souls

Before birth the souls of men used to contemplate the pure and perfect forms in the Ideal World. Due to some mysterious fault (here we are back to the age-old myth of a Fall) they are born here, imprisoned in the body (Greek *soma*: Body, *soma*: Prison) and prevented from dearing up to the contemplation of these Ideas. Knowledge is as we have seen, when we are able to triumph over forgetfulness and recall - be it ever so dimly - those forms we had once contemplated.

1.3.3.3.3.2. The Two Horses

Plato noticed the evident fact of conflict within the depths of man. And in the ***Phaedrus,*** he gave his classic comparison-of the charioteer who struggles to control two troublesome steeds who tend to pull in different ways. The charioteer is the rational element in man which struggles to bring about a harmony between the opposing pulls of the spiritual and appetitive elements in man, the two horses. The spiritual element is really a good horse: it is docile and obedient to the reason and would lead it straight up to Good. But the appetitive element is unbridled and unruly and can only be driven by the Whip. It is not difficult to see how an Augustine could be inspired and influenced by Plato, when he looked back upon the experiences of his dissolute youth.

1.3.3.3.3.3. The After Life

If the body is the prison of the soul, then death is the moment of its joyful release. It is the moment when the soul is set free at last from the soma-soma. The immortality of the soul is argued in ***Phaedo*** from the fact that it is, unlike the body, not made up of parts. In the myth of ***Er***, Plato presents his eschatology. He believes in transmigration of souls and finally settles for an ultimate and irrevocable retribution where the good enter a kind of paradise and the recalcitrant are consigned forever to the torments of *Tartarus*.

1.3.3.3.4. Plato's Philosophy of God

1.3.3.3.4.1. A Divine Craftsman, not a Creator

In the ***Timaeus***, Plato takes up the explanation of the generation of the world. Since the world is becoming and that which becomes must necessarily become through the agency of some cause, he argues to the existence of a divine craftsman or demiurge. The demiurge is not a creator, making 'out of nothing. He is the one who gives order and form to all that was hitherto disorder and confusion; this he does after the model of the supreme Form which contains in itself the forms of all things.

1.3.3.3.4.2. The Motive of the Demiurge

What moves the demiurge to fashion the world? Its essential goodness. It wills that all should be as near as possible like unto itself, well ordered and good and perfect. Hence its action.

1.3.3.3.4.3. The Good

Plato speaks of the highest form, the form of all the forms, which is the Form of the Good or the Beautiful. He does not actually call this Form 'God', but he gives to it many of the titles we reserve for God alone, such as the Perfect. It is not easy to clarify the distinction and the relation between the Demiurge, and the Form of the Good, though it is clear that they are not to be identified.

1.3.3.3.5. Some Critical Remarks

1.3.3.3.5.1. Plato's Theory of Knowledge

As for his theory of remembrance, that follows from his particular metaphysics and the theory of forms, does the ***Meno*** experiment really show that all knowledge is remembrance of what we already knew, or does it demonstrate very ably that our mind is made to know the truth, that it is ordered towards the attainment of it and, with proper direction, cannot but attain it?

Plato has well grasped an essential point that many modern thinkers perhaps over-influenced by Kant- have little noticed: that knowledge is a dynamic process, the result of a positive, active striving on our part. Knowledge is not something that merely 'happens to us', something that comes to us passively from the outside, our sole role being to put some order into the passive reception of data. We want to know: the impulse and initiative is ours. But does his remembrance-theory sufficiently bring out the experience of dynamism and striving that is part of the process of knowledge? Do even his 'four steps' take sufficient cognizance of this fact?

1.3.3.3.5.2. Plato's Philosophy of the World

A basic and valid insight - which, no doubt, was the foundation for the Aristotelian theory of act and potency and later elaborations of the notion of participation -a notion sadly undeveloped in Indian thought - led Plato to postulate his 'exaggerated realism'. It would take a realistic metaphysician, such as Aristotle, to show that the sensible real cannot but be individual and concrete and hence the theory of ideal forms actually existing somewhere is self-contradictory.

1.3.3.3.5.3. Plato's Philosophy of Man

The body and the soul: Plato's presentation of the body-soul union as something harmful and negative was going to have far-reaching effects on human thought down the centuries. Through St. Augustine and early Christian spirituality, the body would come to be looked upon as something despicable and loathsome - or, at least, this would be how the common run of Christians would understand Augustine and early spiritual writers. All of which is very bad psychology, to say the least. Even St. Ignatius of Loyola, for all his healthy humanism, was speaking of the 'immortal soul imprisoned in our perishable bodies'. The rehabilitation of the body has not quite-been achieved, in spite of much development in contemporary psychology and ascetical doctrine, so profound has been the wound that Plato has inflicted on it. Once again, we would have to wait for an Aristotle to present the so-called body-soul union as something positive for both 'elements.' Cartesian dichotomism is nothing but a drawing out of this Platonic antagonism to its ultimate conclusions.

The after-life: It would not be out of place, here, to caution the student against identifying the Platonic theory of the immortality of the soul with the Christian dogma of the Resurrection of the body. In the Platonic view, the resurrection of the body is silly and ridiculous: why should the old prison-cell-body be restored to the liberated soul? The Resurrection of the body only makes sense in an incarnational view, where the body is not seen as something merely negative. As for the theory of transmigration, it is essentially a response to the mystery of toil and injustice in the world, but - even if one may not be able to positively prove it to be false - one can show it doesn't provide a very satisfying response to the mystery at all, in fact, it would add to the web of injustice!

1.3.3.3.5.4. Plato's Philosophy of God

Craftsmen and Creators: It should not come to us as too surprising that Plato didn't think of a Creator-God who would make the world 'out of nothing'. Even early Biblical writers were not able to grasp the idea, so removed is it from our human experience. Whatever be the case, this left the problem of explaining from where the primitive "stuff", out of which the demiurge fashioned the world, came. Evidently it would appear independent of him in some way. It is to save the supremacy of God as the originator in the full sense of the term, that many thinkers - notably in India - have given pantheistic and emanationistic theories about the generation of the world.

The Craftsman's Motive: Plato has well brought out the gratuity of the demiurge's activity. He fashions the world out of his own free will, simply as a means to share and communicate his goodness. It is not out of a need. One could remark, however, that if Plato knew how to safe-guard the independence of the demiurge with respect to the world, he wasn't able to show the dependence of the latter on the former!

1.3.3.3.6. General Conclusion

Plato's mystical temperament, which ever sought to soar beyond the sensible realities around us and attain the eternal and everlasting truths of which they can be but imperfect shadows, has always exercised a strong appeal for men of a like temperament, a St. Augustine, a Descartes. Whereas a mere 'down-to-earth' character, as that of Aristotle, would appeal to kindred spirits, such as that of St. Thomas Aquinas and Kant. It is such an observation that has led the American savant Alfred Whitehead to remark that everyone is, at heart, an Aristotelian or a Platonist. Not everyone, of course, knows how to keep the balance and, more often than not, one ends up as either too idealistic, too 'out of touch' with 'the material world' which one tends to despise... or so much enraptured by its beauty as to become imprisoned in it and quite incapable of transcending it.

St. Augustine saw in Platonism and ideal framework to express the Christian evangel. And, what with his dissolute youthful background, he interpreted Christian mysticism in the light of Platonic thinking in such a way as to have a rather negative influence on much of humanistic movements. And Plato, as the mentor and inspirer of St. Augustine, has indirectly caused all this. It is only comparatively recently that a committed Christian can view his body without disgust or shame and can regard the world and its activity as more than the ensnarement of the devil.

Of course, there have been many who were able to rise above this 'popular religion' — else there would have been no saints at all — but, this has long been how many people understood the Christian message. And Plato, as the mentor and inspirer of St. Augustine, has indirectly caused all this. All this is not to say that Plato was, himself, a kind of glorified John Head-in-air. His whole life was a commitment to truth. We have seen how he wished to bring his influence to bear on politicians and leaders. He founded, in effect, the first European University and gave to the Academy the stamp of his own spirit, founding thereby a group of men dedicated to truth and goodness. Though we may hardly be fired with enthusiasm for his *Republic*, it is clear that neither it nor he envisaged a sophist or opportunistic 'get-ahead-at-all-costs' system, bolstered up by the 'might-is-light' thesis. As we have said, his 'other-worldliness' stemmed less from a hatred of this world as from a devotion to the Transcendent and the Absolute.

Plato's greatness can be best seen, perhaps, from the impression he made on his greatest pupil, Aristotle, a man of another character and temperament who hailed him as the first who showed "by word and by deed that he who is virtuous is happy".

Plato is, in reality, one of the makers of the modem mind. Plato's views have had their impact on much of contemporary metaphysics, ethics and politics. As for you and me, little do we realise that when we make distinctions between means and ends or between essence and accidents or talk about arguing in a circle or the law of contradiction - we are only making use of a vocabulary that Plato has worked out and handed down to us.

> "It is and will be the best thing ever said; that the useful is beautiful and the harmful is ugly." – Plato, Republic

1.3.4. Aristotle (384 – 322 BC)

1.3.4.1. Life

Aristotle was born at Stageira in Thrace (hence, he is sometimes referred to as "the Stagyrite") of a rather well-to-do family. His father was court physician of Amyntas II of Macedon. When he was 17 he entered Plato's Academy. That Aristotle had a great admiration for his teacher seems to be beyond doubt, but it is obvious that he had his reservations about some of the latter's views. A remark of his, recorded for us in the Nicomachaen Ethics, sums up well his attitude in this regard: "Plato and Truth are both dear to me," he confesses. "But filial love requires us to honour Truth above all friends."

When Plato died, Aristotle - then about 35 years of age - left Athens. Among other things, he could not get on with Speusippus, Plato's nephew and successor at the Academy. He went to Assos and there he founded a branch of the Academy and married Pythias, the niece and adopted daughter of the local ruler. Here Aristotle began to develop his individual views and sometimes the fire of original thinking led him to speak over critically and even in a petty way of his former teacher.

In 343, Aristotle was invited by Philip of Macedon to become court tutor of his son, the future Alexander the Great. Aristotle did this and found in his pupil a far better subject than Plato had found in Dion. It must even be admitted that Alexander - and court life - did a lot to open Aristotle's narrow and sometimes chauvinistic Greek mind!

In 335 Aristotle returned to Athens, where he founded his own School, the Lyceum (since it was situated near the temple of Appollo Lyceus), which soon eclipsed the Academy. As Aristotle would often walk up and down with his pupils while he lectured or discoursed with, the group also came to be known as the *Peripatetics* (from the Greek verb, *peripatein*: to walk). In 323, Alexander the great died and there was a rise of popular opinion against Macedonian suzerainty. Aristotle, inasmuch as he had been the friend, philosopher and guide of the ruler, was sought after. He fled from Athens (lest, he is reported to have said, the Athenians should sin twice against Philosophy) and lived until his death, 322, on his dead mother's estate in Chalcis. In his will he provided for his two children and second wife (Pythias had died earlier) as well as saw to the comfort and liberation of his slaves.

1.3.4.2. Sources

As we have had occasion to remark earlier, we have quite a corpus of Aristotle's writings, but only his more technical works and nothing of his more popular fare. The classic translation of his treatises is that of J.A. Smith and Sir W.D. Ross (editors: translations made by various scholars), *The Works of Aristotle*, 12 volumes, Oxford, 1908 - 1912. Ross had published also some excellent and detailed commentaries on the main books, such as the *Metaphysics* (in two volumes), the *Physics* and *De Anima* (On the Soul). there are many 'modern language translations' of particular works and among the several accounts of Aristotle's Philosophy, we may single out the following:

D.T. Allen, *The Philosophy of Aristotle*, N.Y., reprint 1957 (good, brief and clear: there is a recent 8th edition, 1970).
Renford Bambrugh, *The Philosophy of Aristotle*, N.Y. 1965 (very good).
Marjorie Greene, *A Portrait of Aristotle*, Chicago, 1963 (excellent).
J.R Randall, *Aristotle*, N.Y., 1960 (presents the philosopher in the idiom of today).
A. E. Taylor, *Aristotle*, N.Y., reprint 1955 (very critical of Aristotle).

1.3.4.3. Aristotle's Thought

1.3.4.3.1. His Theory of Knowledge

1.3.4.3.1.1. Logic

Aristotle is a real pioneer in the field of Logic. Indeed, he elaborated it in such a clear and scientific way, that it is his system that is followed in the main, even today. Kant said of his contribution to this discipline: "since the time of Aristotle, logic has never had to budge a single inch, nor has it been able to advance a single step". Logic, according to Aristotle is the art of right thinking and thereby of attaining truth. As such, it does not have any special object (we would rather say subject matter) as do the other disciplines, but is their instrument or tool (in Greek, *organon*).

1.3.4.3.1.2. Systematisation

Aristotle did a lot of systematisation in Logic. He was one of the first to notice that the mind has a certain basic structure and method and he tried to detail what these were and how it functioned. The ultimate elements of the working of the mind were three: concept, judgment and reasoning. Even today treatises of Logic follow, more or less, this classical subdivision. He defined concept as the "into which the premiss is resolved, i.e., both the predicate and that of which it is predicated." He then went on to reduce the concept to its 10 categories or different types. Thus, for instance, a concept may be predicated of a subject so as to indicate its essence, or quantity, quality, relation, place, time, situation, "habitus", action or passion. He carefully examined what happens when we make judgments, observed that it alone is the source of the true or false. Then he investigated their quality (affirmative and negative), quantity (universal, particular and singular) and modality (factual, necessity, possibility). He also studied the convertibility of judgments. As to reasoning, he reduced the syllogisms to their basic types and exposed the commonest fallacies in reasoning. Finally, he sought to explain how universal premises are formed and how scientific knowledge may be further developed through induction, dialectic (which has a very special meaning for him) and demonstration.

1.3.4.3.1.3. Definitions

One of the major causes of the confusion and dissensions in philosophy is the fact that thinkers do not bother to clarify their terms. Thus, words are often bandied about ambiguously and it is more often than not that conceptual confusion is the bane of philosophical dialogue. This is something very much felt today and has even given rise to a whole school of philosophy! Aristotle seems to have recognised all this, for he not only tried to draw up rules for a good definition, but even gave us some very good examples of this. For example, "The fulfilment of what exists potentially, in so far as it exists potentially, is motion." (*Physics* III, 1). Time is "measurement of movement according to before and after." (*Physics* IV, II).

1.3.4.3.2. His Philosophy of the World

1.3.4.3.2.1. Refutation of Plato's Theory of Ideas

In his ***Metaphysics***, Aristotle advances several arguments against the theory of subsisting ideas of Plato. He shows that such a theory involves no end of contradictions.

Aristotle objected to Plato's view, arguing that one cannot know the type of interaction which is occurring between the two Forms. If the "real or ideal forms" are eternal, pure and unchanging then how do they relate to the material objections or Forms on earth with all their physical imperfections? This participation or imitation link between the real and the imaginary (which Plato claimed existed) is erroneous thinking as no one can/has established such a link – real or otherwise. And even if a link is established it fails to explain all the Forms in the material world. At some point Plato fails to explain how this greater Form was controlled- how can Form control things? Was there energy in "Forms"?

You may look up and examine, for yourself, these arguments which are admittedly difficult to follow but are well worth your while. (Cf. especially ***Metaphysics*** A, 9, M, 9- 10, N).

1.3.4.3.2.2. Substance and Accidents

The ***Metaphysics*** points out, also, an important distinction and has given us two important terms that we have adopted as part and parcel of our everyday speech, while hardly ever noticing their ontological roots. There are various senses in which we say that a thing "is": some things are said to be because they are substances, others are said to be because they are accidents of substances in which they inhere. A substance is that "which is not predicated of a subject, but of which everything is predicated." (*Metaphysics* Z, 3) Or, to put it in another way, it is "that which is primarily and to which all the other categories of being are referred." (*Metaphysics* E, 1) Among the characteristics of substance are "separability" and "thisness". Accidents, on the other hand, are whatever "attaches to something and can truly be asserted, but neither of necessity or usually." (*Metaphysics*, D, 30) We have all heard of 'accidents' and 'substance' with reference to the theory of transubstantiation, which seeks to explain how the bread at the Eucharist is changed to Christ's body yet appears the same. Aquinas' answer: the substance of the bread is changed into the substance of the body of Christ, whereas the 'accidents' of the bread (its colour, shape, taste and so on) remain the same.

1.3.4.3.2.3. The Theory of Act and Potency

This apparently unprepossessing little theory is, in reality, of great consequence. It provides the profoundest metaphysical basis to answer the difficulties raised by Parmenides against movement and multiplicity. Parmenides and others would speak of being and non-being, allowing of no other category and implying that a thing, to exist, must be being pure and simple else it had to be non-being and so, obviously, couldn't exist. In Book of his ***Metaphysics***, Aristotle elaborated his theory which offers a valuable insight and a key to many pseudo-problems in metaphysics.

Basically, the theory is founded on the intuition that a thing can "be" in two ways: it can be able to be such and such (potency) or it can be such and such. Every change implies, first, that the subject of that change had a potency as regards that change. Finally, a change implies the actualisation of the potency in question. Potency, then, is a capacity with regards to actualisation (or act), whereas act (or actualisation) is a perfection or quality of some sort. A potency can be passive - as, for instance, a sound is capable of being heard (i.e., it has a passive potency for being heard). An active potency is a power or capacity to act (e.g. the ear has an active potency for hearing). It should be noticed, however, that even a passive potency implies, in some way, a pre-disposition on the part of the thing concerned: e.g. a sound has a passive potency with regard to being heard, whereas a colour does not. So, the sound is not "merely passive" with regard to being heard: it has a positive disposition towards it, which the colour lacks. The theory of act and potency has many applications in Aristotle's Metaphysics and in his philosophy in general. For instance, a being can be pure act (it has no potencies yet to be realised, it is perfection, actualisation pure and simple). Such a being would be God. At the other end of the spectrum would be pure potency, prime matter (about which more, later). In between come the "mixed acts", the beings of our daily experience. They have some perfections actually realised, but there are also many potencies in them - capacities to acquire or lose perfections. This is the "way out" of the difficulties raised by Parmenides and his school against motion and multiplicity.

The advance that Aristotle made over Parmenides consists in seeing that, although it is true that "nothing can come from nothing," it is not entirely true that "being cannot come from being." One must distinguish being-in-act from being-in-potency. While it is true that from being-in-act, being-in-act cannot come since it would already be. The alternative from which being **can** come is not non-being, but being-in-potency. From being-in- potency there can come being-in-act.

Aristotle discovered the concept of potency by observing accidental changes. He observed, for instance, that a sculptor can make a statue from a block of marble. This is possible only because the block of marble is endowed with a certain property - the possibility and capacity of being transformed. The figure of the statue is in potency in the block of marble. This potency is not nothing, it is not non-being. It is real; not with the reality of being-in-act, but with the reality which corresponds to being-in- potency.

1.3.4.3.2.4. The Four Causes

The study of causes involves yet another application of the theory of act and potency. This study is taken up by Aristotle in the ***Physics***, II. He points out that men only feel satisfied that they have acquired knowledge about a thing when they can understand its "why". He then points out that everything we observe has four principles or causes which influence it. First there are two *intrinsic causes*, so called because they are inadequately distinct from (we could say, though not very accurately, 'part of') their effect. These are the ***material cause*** (that out of which a thing is made, e.g. the wood of a table) and the ***formal cause*** (that which makes a thing to be what it is, e.g., the form of wood makes wood to be table). Then there are the two *extrinsic causes* - adequately distinct from ('not a part of') their effect. These are the ***efficient cause*** (the one who makes or initiates the effect, e.g. the carpenter with regard to the table) and the ***final cause*** (the reason for which the effect is produced, e.g. the carpenter makes a table in order to get money). Aristotle showed, for instance, how the material cause is in potency with regard to the formal cause, as in matter and form.

1.3.4.3.3. His Philosophy of God

1.3.4.3.3.1. Proofs for God's Existence

Aristotle has provided us with classical models of proofs, for God's existence and which, whatever be their merits or demerits, are so well known and so often made use of in apologetics and other textbooks that they are sure to be known to the student. His own favourite argument seems to be from movement to the First Mover, itself unmoved. (Cf ***Physics*** Bk VIII, 6 and also ***Metaphysics***, Bk L, Ch 6-0). He concludes to the fact that the *Unmoved Mover* is but one for, if things can be sufficiently explained by 'one' there is no reason to postulate many! As Aristotle began to go more deeply into this reflection, he gradually seemed to have switched his view that the *First Unmoved Mover* moves the world as efficient cause (he had discussed whether the Mover moved the world by pushing it or pulling it) to the opinion that He acted on it as final cause.

1.3.4.3.3.2. God's Essence

Having established that God exists, it is but natural that we should turn our minds to seeing what we can say about Him: what sort of a being is He like? What qualities does He have? Perhaps the best definition we can have of God is, following Aristotle's terminology, that he is Pure Act. He exists of necessity; he is and cannot not be. As to His "way of life", it must of needs be "the best life". Now since the act of contemplation is, according to Aristotle, what is the most pleasant and the best of all acts, it follows that God is thought: What does God think about? Obviously, the object of His thought cannot be something unworthy of Himself and since he alone is perfect, "therefore, it must be of itself that the divine thought thinks, since it is the most excellent of things, and its thinking is a thinking on thinking." (***Metaphysics***, L, 9). From this last remark, we can conclude that Aristotle's God, though He has some sort of influence on the world, since He attracts it as final cause, is not really provident and can hardly be said to love the world or care for it. Indeed, He seems pretty much wrapped up in Himself!

1.3.4.3.4. His Philosophy of Man

1.3.4.3.3.1. The Soul

We have seen how Plato had a rather dualistic concept of man: he was composed of two, more or less separate and antagonistic parts - his spiritual soul, locked up in his body-prison from which it would be released at the moment of death. At first Aristotle seemed to favour this understanding of the body-soul union in man. Then he gradually began to abandon it, seeing the relation of the two as less antagonistic. He slowly began to see the body as something good for the soul. There are various early texts where he speaks of the body as the instrument of the soul's activity in this world. Finally, he comes to his hylomorphic (Greek, matter =*hulê* and form or shape =*morphê*) conception of the body-soul relationship in man, an application of the same theory that he had for non-living things. The soul is seen as the form of the body.

The body and soul are one single composite of matter and form. But it would now seem that Aristotle has ever-reached himself: he has so well established the unity of the human composite, that the possibility of an after-life, the 'immortality' of the soul, its ability to 'live on' separated from its bodily counterpart at the moment of death, seems to be cast in doubt. Aristotle is uncertain here. He finds himself logically obliged to deny any possible immortality, but casts about for a way out. He seems to have found one in the idea that perhaps some parts of the soul could survive after the decomposition of the body "because they are not the actualities of any body at all." (***De Anima***, II, 2). This type of reasoning, of course, does more credit to his heart than to his head!

1.3.4.3.3.2. Ethics

In his ***Nicomachaean Ethics***, Aristotle exposed what, according to him, is the general ultimate goal of all activity: **the good**. In fact, the good is "that which all things aim." However, in man freedom and decision are involved in his activity. Hence the need for practical wisdom to help him determine just what is his good. Man is not just an individual being, but also a social animal. Hence politics becomes an essential part of the whole enquiry as to what constituted the good of man.

"We are not studying in order to know what virtue is, but to become good, for otherwise there would be no profit in it." *(NE 2.2)*

Aristotle's starting point is that everything humans do is aimed at some good, with some good higher than others. The highest human good that people aim at, he said, is generally referred to as happiness (Gk. *eudaimonia* - sometimes translated as "living well").

1.3.4.3.3.3. Virtues

Aristotle distinguishes two kinds of virtues (1103a1-10): those that pertain to the part of the soul that engages in reasoning (*virtues of mind or intellect*), and those that pertain to the part of the soul that cannot itself reason but is nonetheless capable of following reason (*ethical virtues, moral virtues, virtues of character*). The intellectual virtues include: scientific knowledge (*episteme*), artistic or technical knowledge (*techne*), intuitive reason (*nous*), practical wisdom (*phronesis*), and philosophic wisdom (*sophia*). The moral virtues include: courage, temperance, self-discipline, moderation, modesty, humility, generosity, friendliness, truthfulness, honesty, justice.

The intellectual virtues are those that help us to attain the truth, ultimately the highest of all truths, the Truth - God. However, to reach this sublime goal, we must need to cultivate the moral virtues. These help us in this end insofar as they, by keeping in check our passions enable us to perform right actions. In this context, it is clear how Aristotle came to the conclusion that a moral virtue is "a mean between two vices, that which depends on excess and that which depends on defect." It is not a mere position of mediocrity, but a refinement of attitude. One's attitude in facing death, for instance, can be rashness (vice of excess) or cowardice (vice of defeat) ... or it may be courage (the golden mean)! As regards amusing others, I can be a buffoon (excess), a bore (defect) or I may be capable of ready wit (the mean)!

1.3.4.3.3.4. Art and Literature

In his ***Poetics***, Aristotle answered, in effect, Plato's criticism of tragedy and his desire to outlaw poets from his Republic, on the grounds that they would disturb and weaken the will-power and moral strength of the statesmen and warriors by preying on their emotions. Aristotle made use of the famous theory of *catharsis* to show that through the emotions of pity and fear (aroused by Tragedy), the soul and its passions would be released and purified. This would bring about a certain feeling of pleasure and peace. A chance remark, made in passing, about the importance of preserving dramatic unity was to be taken very seriously by future dramatists. And even until round about Shakespeare's time, playwrights and critics were giving thought to the so-called Aristotelian "law" about the unity of space and time in drama.

1.3.4.3.4. Some Critical Remarks

1.3.4.3.4.1. His Theory of Knowledge

Logic: Modern Symbolic Logic, developed by men such as Wittgenstein and Russell, does not so much supplant or contradict the classical, Aristotelian variety as to complement and enhance it. The use of symbols allows for a working out of the functional implications of Logic more easily, speedily - and with more objectivity!

Aristotle's Systematisation in Logic: He arrived at certain conclusions, concerning the basic structure and functioning of the mind, and these were based on careful, concrete observation of what happens when we think and argue. This existential, down-to-earth method would be, in itself, reason enough to win our approval and admiration for his work. We have, here, a very good example of sincere and dedicated phenomenological observation, so highly rated by Russell and his school.

Definitions: The search for, and attempt to establish clear and careful terminology had already been begun with Socrates and his famous method of irony. Aristotle gave it a more scientific and a profounder dimension. Much of contemporary British and Indian philosophy is concerned with the clarification of conceptual confusion!

1.3.4.3.4.2. His Philosophy of the World

His Moderate Realism: While rightly pointing out the contradictions and inconsistencies in Plato's theory of subsisting forms, Aristotle provided an explanation as to how we obtain our universal ideas and how our knowledge can be valid, even though it involves applying universal, abstract concepts to individual and concrete realities. Nominalism and anti- intellectualism die hard and much of what certain extremist existentials have to say against intellectual activity and knowing, can be responded to by elements taken from Aristotle's moderate realist outlook. (Plato was an exaggerated realist: he held that universal ideas actually exist as such, somewhere; nominalists are the other extreme: they hold that universals exist neither in reality nor in the mind - for them, concepts are mere empty sounds without real content; a moderate realist, as Aristotle, holds that universals exist as such only in the mind, but fundamentally in reality).

Substance and Accidents - Act and Potency: Aristotle's famous theory of act and potency is one of his major contributions to Metaphysics. With it, he not only solves many of the difficulties raised by earlier philosophers, but is able to account in a plausible way, for the basic structure of material and finite reality. He allows, thereby, for a plurality of beings as also for accidental and substantial change. Finally, his theory of intrinsic causes enables him to find a way of explaining the unity of the human composite in a far better way than anyone before him.

1.3.4.3.4.3. His Philosophy of the God

Proofs for God's existence: The classic proofs for God's existence, inspired by Aristotle, and still used - as we have already pointed out - in many a contemporary manual of Apologetics (not to mention some current treatises of Natural Theology), all presuppose the validity of the principle of causality. Such a presupposition can be excused right up till the latter half of the 18th Century. For until then, no one contested this principle - at least, not in a serious enough way. But with the objections of Hume and the critical philosophy of Kant, it became obvious that a much more careful handling of the matter was called for. Such a challenge was ably met by Joseph Marechal SJ and his 5th cahier of ***Le point de depart de la metaphysique*** (1922). It is not that the critical philosophy demolished the "proofs" of Kant, but that they required of them a mere careful and elaborate working out. However, as far as "proofs" for God's existence go, the arguments of Aristotle are still the most accessible for the layman. It would not be out of place, here, to point out that many convinced believers today would agree with Marcel that "proofs" for God's existence only serve to confirm the faith of a believer: they are of no value for an unbeliever. Nobody, it is claimed, ever came to believe in God because of a "proof" of his existence!

God's Essence: Much of what Aristotle deduces about God's nature or essence would square with our convictions. But his intellectualism brought him up short with a God whose perfection was in Thought. He could not yet see Him as Love. And precisely for this reason, he could see no way in which God could interest Himself in anything other than Himself. Thus, we have the cold, "wrapped-up-in-Himself" God of Aristotle - no doubt the type of "God of philosophers" that Pascal would fulminate against several centuries later. Aristotle was not able to see, either, how God could, in any way, be the efficient cause of the world, as creator. The elaboration of this valuable insight would have to await the coming of Christian thinkers, especially Thomas Aquinas.

1.3.4.3.4.4. His Philosophy of the Man

The Soul: Aristotle has certainly given us a more healthy way of viewing the human composite: the body is no mere prison of the soul, it is something good for it. Thanks to the body, the soul can relate itself to this world of matter and senses. However, as we have said, having so well united the two principles in man, Aristotle didn't know how to save the immortality of the soul! Once again, Aquinas would find a way out with the notion of extrinsic dependence which opened a way to the theory of subsisting and non-subsisting forms. Once again, we should point out over here that not a few Christian thinkers are contesting today even the Aristotelian hylomorphic explanation of the unity of the human composite. They find that even such a conception argues too much of a distinction in man!

Ethics: A common criticism of Aristotelian ethics is that it does not open itself sufficiently to eternal life and eternal happiness. It lacks an eschatological perspective, as theologians would say. This is understandable, given his own uncertainties about the after-life. Others also say that his ethics falls short of giving us a demanding enough moral obligation. This too is understandable for he did not see God as creator of human nature, the foundation of the ethical norm. Yet, once again we must point out that many convinced Christian thinkers are challenging the thesis that an ethical system, to be complete as far as moral obligations and motivations are concerned, must needs to have an eschatological dimension. As to the social or political part of his ethics, that seems to respect much more the freedom of the individual and his initiative than the Republic of Plato.

Virtues: The characteristically Aristotelian view that virtues are a golden mean between two vices, one by excess and one by defect, seems to have always won general assent. Time and again, thinkers as widely different in their conclusions, as Spinoza and Pascal, will revive this idea. And much of contemporary psychology and counselling agrees with this approach.

Art and Literature: Aristotle's down to earth view was a fair rejoinder to Plato's other worldliness which would have led him to become a kind of mystical philistine, an enemy of the arts! And if Aristotle's so-called "law" of the three unites (in reality he only spoke of unity of plot and had little to say about unity of time and place) did hamper the work of later playwrights, it is only because they, like later physicists, took him too much as an oracle and didn't experiment and try-out things for themselves, as Aristotle would have wanted them to do. Let us not, then, blame Aristotle for the faults of his would-be disciples. It has been well said that often a man's worst enemies, in effect, are his ever-enthusiastic fans!

1.3.5. General Conclusion

We have already drawn attention to Alfred North Whitehead's oft-quoted remark that everyone is either, by temperament, a Platonist (the mystical, contemplative type) or an Aristotelian (the scientific, active type). If this is an exaggeration then, at any rate, like all exaggerations, it undo scores a solid vein of truth.

Whitehead also went on to say that most of Western thought was but a series of footnotes to them. And there precisely is another problem. Each of these was so universal a genius, taken together they touched upon just about every topic dear to thinking man and they did so such a homely. They stand at the beginning of just about every discipline and no text-book can begin without a reference to Aristotle's or Plato's contribution to that branch of learning. But if they have been an inspiration and a launching-pad for much Western thought and development, they have sometimes had a crippling effect on it. For human they were and human did they remain - and this meant that sometimes they erred. Unfortunately, most people never bothered to investigate and verify their theories, especially when they concerned scientifically observable phenomena. We all know the story of Galileo and his dropping of two different-sized metal balls from the Tower of Pisa to show that, of two objects, the twice as heavy one does not fall twice as fast, as Aristotle taught. Too much of Western thought has for too long imagined that it could add no more than footnotes to them ideas of Aristotle and Plato -- especially to the scientific "guesses" of Aristotle - and so the dawning of the scientific age had to wait so long.

Plato and Aristotle are, of course, old friends for the churchman. For the two most widely respected philosophical systems developed in the Church - the Augustinian and the Thomist - take inspiration from them. If Augustine was to baptise Plato and harness his thought to the expression of the Christian Gospel, Thomas Aquinas would do the same for the Stagirite when he would call quite simply "the philosopher". And that is why most - if not all - Catholic dogma, from Chalcedon to Vatican I has been couched in a Hellenistic (or Greek) idiom and mode of thought. The question raised nowadays is whether the Greek world-view, whether it be the nigh-escapist mysticism of Plato or the overly intellectualistic vision of Aristotle is the best medium of thought and expression to express the good news of Revelation, Incarnation and Redemption. This question was asked, though by no means for the first time and certainly in not the most eloquent and scholarly way, by Leslie Dewart in a controversial book, ***The Future of Belief*** (1967) which provoked a storm of articles and book reviews - not to mention even a scholastic disputation.

Finally, the influence of Aristotle and Plato on the Western "common man" (or the speaker of any European language!) is enormous. For they have both influenced our vocabularies and thereby our way of "looking at the world in the face". This is inevitable, for every language is also a world-view and an attitude. It is good to know this and, for this same reason, it is a very useful thing to know more than one language - preferably one Western and one Oriental. For there is no better way to become aware of our linguistic prejudices than to become aware of the fact that other languages predispose their users to see things differently!

> "Man is a social animal and he who abhors society must be either a god or a beast." (Aristotle)

1.4. The Decline

Expansion and Decadence: The achievements and the conquests of Alexander the Great carried the ideas of Greek philosophy along with them to far-flung corners of the ancient world. Thus, it was, for Hellenistic thought, a period of expansion. But, at the same time, it was also a period of decadence for many of the then Greek systems of thought, though they were able to profit from the political situation to attain a certain notoriety, were scarce able to equal in vigour and originality the insights of a Plato or an Aristotle.

When Alexander died (in 323 B.C.) - lamenting that there were no more worlds for him to conquest, we are told - along with him died the old idea of the Greek city-state. The Empire was born and so the citizen had to work out his sense of "belonging" in a far broader, far wider context. Very soon, even the old distinction between Greek and barbarian would also vanish as Greece itself began to be swallowed up into part of an even large and wider Roman Empire. The individual, then found himself cast adrift in a cosmopolitan society, loosed from his homely moorings to a more or less homogeneous and smaller city-state. He needed, much as we still do today, a philosophy and a world view that would show him how to relate to, how to fit into, this vast society.

Inevitably, the philosophies that characterise this early post-Aristotelian era, would try to respond to these challenges. Thus, ethics begins to pre-dominate and it is more an individual ethics that is developed: a theory that tries to show the individual how to relate to society, tries to tell him what he should do to feel not too "lost" in this gigantic social structure. If Stoicism would give a more or less negative response (rise above all this, be indifferent, detached), Epicureanism would offer a more positive, humanistic way (cultivate friendship, go in for music, the arts). Once again contemporary thinkers contradicted each other. And the foreseeable results obtained. Along came the Sceptics who despaired of the possibility of finding any solution and along came the Eclectics who tried to make a naive hotch-potch answer, culled from ideas (often mutually exclusive) borrowed from just about anyone who had anything to say! The period also saw the emergence of the philosopher-guide, the man who would speak and write with the style and consciousness of a prophet, offering advice to troubled, disoriented souls - something like a spiritual father or a counsellor today. Indeed, much of the writings of Marcus Aurelius or Epicurus and others of their ilk read just like that! From this last remark, it will be easy to understand how and why later post-Aristotelian philosophy took an extremely religious and mystical turn ... which would culminate in the work of the last great Greek thinker whose ideas merit an equal footing with those of Plato and Aristotle: Plotinus!

1.4.1. Stoicism

1.4.1.1. The Name

As is so often the case in the history of Greek Philosophy, a school of thought derives its name from a place with which its origins are associated. "Stoicism", then, is derived from the ***stoa*** or porch where **Zeno of Citium**, the founder, is supposed to have opened a school and lectured. Among the more well-known Stoics are Epictetus, who was a slave, and Marcus Aurelius, the Roman Emperor. Then there was Seneca, the least stern and most understanding of stoics, who was Nero's tutor and adviser ... until he fell into disgrace!

The Stoics did, in fact, hold that emotions like fear or envy (or impassioned sexual attachments, or passionate love of anything whatsoever) either were, or arose from, false judgements and that the sage—a person who had attained moral and intellectual perfection—would not undergo them.

1.4.1.2. Sources

We have a fairly good selection of the writings of some of the major Stoic writers. There are several anthologies as well as some editions of individual authors. It would be a good idea to "browse a bit" in Marcus Aurelius, Epictetus and Seneca in order to get a "feel" of those men whose views had quite an impact on early Christian writers, not excluding the author of the fourth Gospel.

Moses Hadas (editor), *Essential Works of Stoicism*, New York, 1961. (Contains, besides Epictetetus' *The Manual*, Marcus Aurelius' *Meditations* and Seneca's *On Tranquility*, Diogenes Laertius' *Life of Zeno* (founder of the school) and Cleanthes' *Hymn to Zeno*, the anthology includes a pretty good introductory essay).

W.J. Oates (editor), *The Stoic and Epicurean Philosophers*, New York, 1971 (comprises the complete extant works of Epicurus, Epictetus, Lucretius and Marcus Aurelius).

T.V. Smith (editor), *Philosophers Speak for Themselves*, vol II: *From Aristotle to Plotinus*, Chicago, 1960 (Chapter III, "The Cynic-Stoic Tradition", contains an extract from Diogenes Laertius' book on Zeno and the Stoics. Diogenes was not a Stoic; he was of the Cynic school - wherein the stoics find their roots).

Russell Kirk (editor), Marcus Aurelius' *Meditations* and Epictetus' *Enchiridion*, Chicago, 1956 (Good, though brief, introduction by the editor).

Moses Hadas, *The Stoic Philosophy of Seneca*, New York, 1958 (Comprises essays and letters of the philosophers, along with an introduction by the editor).

As regards studies on Stoic philosophy, all the better ones that we have here are in French - with the exception of three chapters (36, 39 and 40) of Copleston, vol. 1.

Beginnings: Stoicism would seem to have a connection with a much earlier movement that went all the way back to Socrates and was supposed to have captured and lived authentically his spirit: Cynicism. Socrates neither despised nor rejected the pleasures of the body or the goods of this life though he could find happiness with little of either. The Cynics did so and often with a great show and much rudeness. The classic type is Diogenes Laertius who lived in a tub, hardly ever had a bath and claimed to be propagating Socrates way of life. They have well been hailed as the first "hippies". The founder of the movement was Antisthenes (445-365) though it was the unconventional and demonstrative Diogenes who won for the group all the publicity and (in) fame that it wanted. Some people held the view that they were dubbed cynics because they lived a regular "dog's life" (Greek *kunos* - dog-like), others, because of their association with the Kynesarges, a gymnasium situated outside of Athens and meant for the use of those who were not of pure Athenian blood. Stoicism added to its cynic origins a metaphysical system and a more or less mystical world-view, so much so that it has often been described as one of the mystery religions of the post-Aristotelian era, rather than a philosophy. Many of the Stoics write in a simple, unadorned style and they offer us much useful practical and psychological advice. However, Pascal was to note that, were one to follow Epictetus' advice, he would probably end up a proud and disdainful person. Marcus Aurellius' views are tinged with a pronounced pessimism.

1.4.1.3. Stoic Philosophy

"Follow Nature": this is the basic stoic principle – "live according to nature". This is the key-note of the stoic ethics and this ethics is closely linked to physics and logic. For physics teaches us exactly what the nature of things are and logic helps us to know whether we are living according to this nature. Happiness, then, comes from living a harmonious life and in this is virtue. Passions are to be avoided, for passions are an excessive tendency and these disturb harmony and lead us away from nature. The main passions are pleasure, sorrow, sensual desire and fear. These are further subdivided and studied with no little psychological expertise! Few Stoics will go so far as **Cleanthes** who held the pleasure is against nature, but all would agree that pleasure may never be made into an end of our action. Freedom consists not in willing things to happen to us as we would like them to, but in willing them to happen as they do happen.

1.4.1.3.1. Stoic Physics

The Stoic philosophy is fundamentally monist. The world is seen as basically one, but constituted by two principles. One of these is passive, matter - a substance without quality; the other is active, Reason (logos) and it works in matter - in effect, this is God! The active principle, Logos or Reason or God, is ever at work in the heart of things, giving them a different tension, which results in the difference of genera and species.

In accord with this ontology, the Stoics, like the Epicureans, make God material. But while the Epicureans think the gods are too busy being blessed and happy to be bothered with the governance of the universe (Epicurus, Letter to Menoeceus 123–4), the Stoic God is immanent throughout the whole of creation and directs its development down to the smallest detail. The world, and its history, is cyclic: that is, there is ever an eternal recurrence. Everything evolves from a primitive fire to the present stage of general multiplicity and complexity. Then comes the final general combustion and everything returns to the state of primitive fire and then the whole cycle starts again.

It is important to realise that the Stoic God does not craft its world in accordance with its plan from the outside, as the demiurge in Plato's *Timaeus* is described as doing. Rather, the history of the universe is determined by God's activity internal to it, shaping it with its differentiated characteristics. The biological conception of God as a kind of living heat or seed from which things grow seems to be fully intended. The further identification of God with *pneuma* or breath may have its origins in medical theories of the Hellenistic period. Since the universe is all one and Reason permeates all things, there is a "universal sympathy" uniting all its parts. Hence the attitude of the wise man who tries to keep himself in union or harmony with the universe - the "follow nature" counsel!

1.4.1.3.2. Stoic Logic

It differs from the Aristotelian variety in the fact that the former busies itself with abstract predicates (e.g. man is a rational animal), whereas the Stoics are more concerned with a "logic of consequence". In other words, their logic was geared to discovering the necessary connections of events in the world. A typical stoic proposition in logic would read something like, "If it is day, then there is light". This follows from the theory of Reason and harmony which prevails in the world. For stoics, concepts are empty words and there are no two individuals which are identical. Hence no "common or universal" concept may be predicated of them.

In general, one may say that theirs is a logic of propositions rather than a logic of terms, like the Aristotelian syllogistic. One of the accounts they offer of validity is that an argument is valid if, through the use of certain ground rules (*themata*), it is possible to reduce it to one of the five indemonstrable forms (Diog. Laert., 36A). These five indemonstrables are the familiar forms:

1. if *p* then *q*; *p*; therefore *q* (modus ponens);
2. if *p* then *q*; not *q*; therefore not-*p* (modus tollens);
3. it is not the case that both *p* and *q*; *p*; therefore not-*q*;
4. either *p* or *q*; *p*; therefore not-*q*;
5. either *p* or *q*; not *p*; therefore *q*

1.4.1.3.3. Ethics

The best way into the thicket of Stoic ethics is through the question of what is good, for all parties agree that possession of what is genuinely good secures a person's happiness. The Stoics claim that whatever is good must benefit its possessor under all circumstances. But there are situations in which it is not to my benefit to be healthy or wealthy. (We may imagine that if I had money, I would spend it on heroin which would not benefit me.) Thus, things like money are simply not good, in spite of how nearly everyone speaks, and the Stoics call them 'indifferents' — i.e., neither good nor bad. They draw a distinction between what is good and things which have value (*axia*). Some indifferent things, like health or wealth, have value and therefore are to be preferred, even if they are not good, because they are *typically* appropriate, fitting or suitable (*oikeion*) for us.

The Stoic doctrine of the natural attachment to what is appropriate (*oikeiôsis*) thus provides a foundation in nature for an objective ordering of preferences, at least on a prima facie basis. Other things being equal, it is objectively preferable to have health rather than sickness. The Stoics call things whose preferability is overridden only in very rare circumstances "things according to nature."

We are finally in a position to understand and evaluate the Stoic view on emotions, since it is a consequence of their views on the soul and the good. It is perhaps more accurate to call it the Stoic view of the passions, though this is a somewhat dated term. The passions or *pathê* are literally 'things which one undergoes' and are to be contrasted with actions or things that one does. Thus, the view that one should be 'apathetic,' in its original Hellenistic sense, is not the view that you shouldn't care about anything, but rather the view that you should not be psychologically subject to anything—manipulated and moved by *it*, rather than yourself being actively and positively in command of your reactions and responses to things as they occur or are in prospect. It connotes a kind of complete self-sufficiency. The Stoics distinguish two primary passions: appetite and fear. These arise in relation to what appears to us to be good or bad. They are associated with two other passions: pleasure and distress. These result when we get or fail to avoid the objects of the first two passions. What distinguishes these states of soul from normal impulses is that they are "excessive impulses which are disobedient to reason" (Arius Didymus, 65A). Part of what this means is that one's fear of dogs may not go away with the rational recognition that this blind, 16-year-old, 3-legged Yorkshire terrier poses no threat to you.

1.4.1.4. Some Critical Remarks

The men of the school cannot but impress us by their strength, their calm and moderation - and all this in the midst of a hedonist society hurrying on to its doom in a blissful orgy. But they seem to lack the human touch and give us the impression that we must become very inhuman in order to follow nature. In character, the Stoics differed widely from each other. There is little in common between the moral fibre of an Epictetus and the easy-going Seneca, counsellor to Nero, who accepted to write a letter to the Senate, trying to justify the Emperor's matricide. Stoic Ethics has had a big impact on early Christian spirituality; though the "indifference" taught by the latter has a different motivation from the "follow nature" of the former. There are still many people today who are quite impressed when they chance upon the writings of a Marcus Aurelius or an Epictetus, for men like those have many a sobering thought to offer people caught up in a consumer society where what you have is more important than what you are and a man's worth is measured in terms of his bank balance. However, for all its moral grandeur, the Stoics do not answer many a tormenting question. For instance, whence come these passions that disturb our harmony and is freedom nothing more than a kind of glorified resignation?

Stoic Physics has been described as kind of "spiritualistic materialism" (?) for its blurs the distinction between matter and spirit, making of God and the soul some sort of fluid working tensions in things. But perhaps we have been guilty of making too much of a distinction between the two, as the vision of a Teilhard seems to indicate. St. John, in writing the introduction to his Gospel, seem to have seized upon the Stoic notion of all-pervading Logos in the world to find a 'link-idea' for presenting Jesus, the Word made flesh, to his contemporaries. However, for the Stoics, God seems little more than a force and far from a person who knows and loves us.

Stoic Logic anticipated the problems of medieval nominalism but, whatever be the insufficiencies of its conditional logic, it certainly has contributed to the development of that part of dialectic.

Stoic Ethics: Even in antiquity the Stoics were ridiculed for their views on the passions. Some critics called them the men of stone. Criticisms of the Stoic theory of the passions in antiquity focused on two issues. The first was whether the passions were, in fact, activities of the rational soul. Note that Platonists consider emotions as a product of an irrational part of the soul.

The other opposition to the Stoic doctrine came from philosophers in the Aristotelian tradition. They, like the Stoics, made judgement a component in emotions. But they argued that the happy life required the *moderation* of the passions, not their complete extinction.

1.4.2. Epicurianism

1.4.2.1. Introduction

The name is derived from that of the founder of the school, **Epicurus** of Samos (341- 270), who had studied under no less a teacher than Democritus himself. We must hasten to add that the present English connotation of "epicure" and "epicurean" (which refer to a person whose sole delights are those of the table and sometimes also of the bed!) does gross injustice to the memory of the kindly, human spirit that was Epicurus. He never taught such an attitude and if his philosophy was a kind of reaction against the stern and inhuman Stoics, he underscored the cultivating of the more refined and humanising pleasures, such as friendship and art and was no mere propagator of cheap and empty hedonism. When he died, after a painful illness, he invited his friends and disciples to continue his care of the poor and the youth. Since he had established his school, in Athens, at a place called "the Garden", his philosophy is sometimes called "The Philosophy of the Garden". Epicurus' greatest disciple and successor was a Roman, the poet and philosopher Lucretius (96 B.C. - 55 B.C.). He did a lot to spread the doctrine of Epicurus abroad. He was convinced that only a god could have taught such a way of wisdom as did his master.

Beginnings: If the Stoic traced their beginning to a movement that went back to Socrates and claimed to have captured and continued his spirit, the Epicureans could casually link their beginnings to another movement that claimed exactly the same thing. This was the Cyrenaic school, founded by Aristippus (c. 435 - 355), one of Socrates disciples. Perhaps one of the signs of Socrates' greatness, his "myriad-minded genius", was the fact that he was able to inspire so many different men of different temperaments, each of which would try to found a school faithful to the master, but in most cases more faithful to the character and interest of themselves, whether they realised it or not! Drawing upon the apparent hedonism counselled by Plato's Socrates of the Protagoras we can detect how one could elaborate a pleasure-centred philosophy, with roots in Socrates, as Aristippus did. Pleasure was the goal to aim at and, if this was impossible, we should at least settle for the absence of pain and we should make use of our intelligence to measure and evaluate our pleasures. Epicurus would build his school on this flimsy foundation and try to prop it up with the atomism of Democritus. It is a sad, sweet philosophy that he teaches, offering an oasis of comradeship in the garden, where a man might find kindred spirits with whom to live in the midst of a vast desert of misery.

And if pleasure is not quite attainable, one could at least hope to escape pain. Such a philosophy is typical of a time of evident decline and decadence.

1.4.2.2. Sources

We have a fair number of copies of the texts of Epicurus and Lucretius in good English translation:

W.J. Oates (editor), *The Stoic and Epicurean Philosophers*, New York, 1957 (Contains the complete extant works of Epicurus and Lucretius)

T. V. Smith, *Philosophers Speak for Themselves*, Vol. II, Chicago, 1960 (2nd ed. Reprint). (There is a chapter on the "Cyrenaic-Epicurean Tradition" which consists of a long extract from Diogones Laertius' writings on Epicurus and the Epicureans).

Herman Shapiro (editor), *Hellenistic Philosophy*, New York, 1965 (contains two complete letters of Epicurus together with generous selections from Lucretius' *On the Nature Things*)

As regards studies on Epicurus, besides the chapters in the standard manuals already referred to, one could look into the excellent little book of Benjamin Farrington, *The Faith of Epicurus*, New York, 1967.

1.4.2.3. Epicurean Philosophy

1.4.2.3.1. Ethics

If the Stoics refused to allow pleasure to become a goal of human life, the Epicureans saw it as the goal of ethical conduct. Epicurus was a man in constant poverty and prey to ill-health. And he noted that "the whole world lives in pain". It is normal, then, that he should direct the thrust of his philosophical vision towards the removal of unhappiness and pain. The first way to do this would be to do away with all unreasoned fear of the gods. This is a chief source of unhappiness. A proper knowledge of the divinity would assure us that the gods never cause trouble to others. Next, one should do away with the fear of death. After all a thing can only harm or hurt us when we have sensation. But when death comes, we have no sensations. Thirdly, we should limit our desires. We should put the health of the body and the peace of our soul in the first place and then we shall see that we need precious little to ensure this. Then we should make use of sufficient foresight and planning to see that our actions and plans do not unnecessarily come to naught. We should honour our social obligations and live justly. Thus, we will be able to keep out of trouble. Finally, Epicurus laid great stress upon friendship as one of the most precious pleasures of human life. He fostered this spirit among his disciples in the Garden. His school was open to women too, unlike, the Academy or the Lyceum, for he did not aim at forming politicians (in those unemancipated days, women had no say in politics). Thus, the Garden besides being a school, also fostered a family spirit which went a long way towards aiding the individual who had been swallowed up in the anonymous structures of cosmopolitanism.

1.4.2.3.2. Logic

This discipline was of interest to Epicurus only insofar as it might help him to attain happiness here on earth. Theoretically, their criterion is sensation. Sensation never is deceptive; the error lies in our judgment (E.g. Man or tree standing in a distance). Several sensations amalgamated in a general picture result in a notion (**prolêpsis**). The notion, however, as regards objective value, is not superior to the sensations from which it arises. From notions arises *opinion*, or *thought* (**doxa, hupolêpsis**), which likewise depends on sensation for its truth. Hence Epicurean Logic limited itself to the discovery of the criteria or canons of truth. So, it is called "canonic". Epicureans list three major canons of truth. In the first place, there are perceptions. Now there are two kinds of perceptions: representative and imaginative. Error arises when we take the latter for the former. However, we are not told much about how to distinguish one from the other. Then there are "previous experiences". They can serve as guide-lines for later opinions and beliefs, for these should always square with the former. Finally, there are feelings. Pleasure or pain are to be the basis for our choosing to take or reject something.

1.4.2.3.3. Physics

Epicurean Physics is nothing but Democritan atomism, which is made even more materialistic, if there is an attempt to make it less mechanistic. An attempt is made to explain the movement of the atoms in the void by postulating a certain "klinamen" (swerve or incline) of oblique inclination of the atoms: this is purported to explain their motion as well as the variety of beings in the universe. The starting point of this argument is the observation that the motions of our bodies respond to our will, and that our will is indeterminate, in that it is "our pleasure" or "our inclination" which brings about the motion. If the motion of the atoms is determinate, there would be no accounting for the indeterminacy of the will. Epicurus introduced this line of reasoning because he was afraid that if an atom always moved by its natural and necessary heaviness, we would have no freedom, since our mind would be moved in such a way that it would be compelled by the motion of atoms.

The atomic constitution of things is universal. Even man's soul is made up of the usual atoms, plus a mysterious subtle one which makes it possible for him to experience sensations.

According to the Stoics, it is the soul which holds the body together; according to the Epicureans, it is the body which shelters the atoms of the soul, so that, when the protection afforded by the body ceases, as it does at the moment of death, the soul atoms are instantly scattered, owing to their extreme lightness. In this way Epicurus, keeping in mind the chief aim of all his physical inquiries, sought to rob death of its terrors by teaching that *there is no future life.*

1.4.2.3.3. Theology

Religion, according to the Epicureans, was of natural growth. *Fear* is the basis of religion. *Ignorance*, too, is a factor in the genesis of the religious instinct. It was owing to ignorance and fear that men attributed natural portents to the intervention of supernatural powers and sought to explain the regularity of the motion of the heavenly bodies by referring it to the agency of Providence. Nevertheless, Epicurus did not wholly abandon belief in the gods. The gods, he said, exist because they have appeared to men and left on the minds of men representative images (**prolêpseis**). They are immortal; they enjoy perfect happiness; formed of the finest atoms, they dwell in the uppermost parts of the universe, in the spaces between the stars. The popular notion, however, that the gods take an interest in human affairs is erroneous, because an interest in the affairs of men would be inconsistent with the perfect happiness which the gods enjoy.

Much of his theological writings consist of attacks on superstitious religious practices. The gods have no control over the earth and do not in any way determine the flow of events. Such an interest would be quite unworthy of them, he asserted. He encouraged, all the same, a certain devotion to the gods, for he felt that celebrating their festivals would help us to share in their peaceful lives - an aspect of the divine life that he greatly admired.

1.4.2.4. Some Critical Remarks

In General: The Epicurean spirit with its stress on cultivation of friendship and restrained pleasures was a welcome respite from the stem and inhuman doctrine of some of the Stoics. But it is a philosophy that could easily degenerate into luxurious living and selfish, escapist sensual pleasure. Or it could be an indulgent quest for the easy way out, the line of least resistance. As Copleston writes, it is not the type of philosophy that would make men heroes!

Ethics: Stoic and Epicureans alike give us some good advice as regards moderation in life. Epicurean ethics is perhaps more realistic than the Stoic variety, for it recognizes that pleasure cannot but be a part of the human quest. But the Epicureans seem to have over- stated the case when they make it the final goal and take pleasure and pain as the ultimate criteria for choosing to accept or reject something. May there not arise a situation where the more human course of action would involve a choice that brings pain? As Maritain so tellingly points out, pleasure is indeed a good, but it is a "good by superaddition". As he explains, one who puts it before moral good is like one who substitutes "the aroma for the roast".

Logic: Epicurean Logic has well brought out the importance of perceptions, previous experiences and feelings. But, as we have said, pleasure and pain may not always be a reliable criterion for choice or rejection of something or a course of action!

Physics: The Epicurean addition of a "klinamen" to the atoms of Democritus didn't explain how this "klinamen" came about and it still left unanswered all the questions of a mechanist system.

Theology: The Epicureans certainly made a valuable contribution to the purification of the idea of the divinity. They helped to lay bare some of the foolish fears and superstitions that had uselessly troubled the lives of their contemporaries. But, on the positive side, they didn't have much to offer. And once again, because of an overly intellectualistic view of things, a school of thought is unable to find a way to link the divinity with this world. As long as one does remain in the realm of thoughts and ideas, it is little possible to see how and why the divinity should be interested in this world. Such an understanding is possible only for one who looks at the issue from the standpoint of love. But then, as Pascal says, the heart has its reasons that the reason cannot understand.

"We must laugh and philosophise at the same time!" – Epicurus

1.4.3. Scepticism

1.4.3.1. Introduction

Scepticism is an attitude of mind rather than a philosophical system, the sceptic tends to a belief that it is impossible to attain truth or, at least, that we must always put our knowledge in question and that our enquiry must forever be ruled by doubt. Few sceptics, if ever, would go so far as to hold dogmatically that there is no truth. Historical sceptics, on closer study, end up by saying that we should be on our guard against hasty assertions and advise a kind of uncommitted, over-cautious approach to knowledge. Such an extreme position is, no doubt, provoked by excesses of the other side: the precipitancy with which some thinkers have proposed all manner of theories as absolute truths and gone to battle over them, instead of being more patient and humble in admitting the limitations and difficulties that bestrew man's path in his pilgrimage to the truth. We have already some examples of the sceptic frame of mind in the Sophists Gorgias and Protagoras, but the most well-known is perhaps **Pyrrho of Elis** (360-275) who lent his name to a specific variety of the product.

Pyrrhonism appears to be more thorough-going in its attitude, inasmuch as it refused to be even sure of its sceptical stance! However, our best first-hand source is Sextus Empiricus, who lived about five centuries later (160-210). Though he did little more than re-present the arguments of his predecessors, he certainly gives the most forceful presentation of the Sceptic position ever known!

1.4.3.2. Sources

As we have said, there is little "first-hand" information about the early sceptics. The following books may be consulted:

T.V. Smith (editor), *Philosophers Speak for Themselves*, vol. II: *From Aristotle to Plotinus*, Chicago, 1956 (2nd edition). (There is a 'chapter on "The Skeptical Culmination", which consists of an interesting extract from Diogenes Laertius: "On Pyrrho and the Skeptics").

Philip Hallie (editor), *Sextus Empiricus: Scepticism*, Middletown, 1964 (selections from the major, writings of Sextus Empiricus, together with introduction and copious commentary)

Herman Shapiro (editor), *Hellenistic Philosophy*, New York, 1965 (Contains selections from Sextus Empiricus and Lucian, a contemporary of Sextus and a satirist).

1.4.3.3. Some Famous Sceptics

As we have explained that Scepticism is more an attitude, rather than a body of systematic philosophy (its avowed enemy), perhaps it would be best to give a chronological presentation of some famous sceptics, according to a convenient historical chart.

1.4.3.3.1. Two Pre-Academic Sceptics

Pyrrho (360-270) inspired a "way of life" which has been taken to be the classic from of Scepticism, so much so that Pyrrhonism is more or less taken to be synonym for it. But we are not sure as to exactly what this "way of life" was. Some interpreters have it that he advocated a kind of neglect of things and even of persons. Others say he merely taught that we should avoid all fanaticism in matters that cannot be proved.

Timon (320-230) was the great disciple of Pyrrho. He taught that we can only know the phenomena or external appearances of things.

1.4.3.3.2. Two Academic Sceptics

Arceilaus (315-240) is famous for having taught that we should try to maintain a suspension of assent (*epiche*) with regard to all truths. However, he added, we should "pay attention" (no more!) to all that may "sound reasonable"!

Carneades (213-139) pointed out the subjective elements in our knowledge and, like the other sceptics, had little love for what he called the "dogmatic stoics". He proposed a doctrine of the "probability" of certain truths, this probability admitting of degrees.

1.4.3.3.3. Two Post-Academic Sceptics

Aenesidomus (C. 200 A.D.) has a great influence in the development of "Sceptic Logic" by proposing his famous list of ten ways (tropoi) of arguing against an assertion.

Sextus Empiricus (c. 200 AD.) was a medical man by profession and applied his sceptic convictions to the practice of his art, ever being on the guard against theorising and speculating and limited himself to mere observation. He gathered together all the main arguments of the sceptics in favour of their stance and advised that, in order to protect ourselves against the temptation to fall into dogmatism, we should always seek to know the other side of a question, a contrary theory to the one that has been presented to us. Thus, there would be less chance of our giving our assent to one exclusive position. This would be a sure way to avoid fanaticism and preserving peace of mind. He attacked the Aristotelian syllogism as basically being a hidden "vicious circle" argument, for the major premise can only be shown to be valid by a complete induction. And the complete induction implies a knowledge of the conclusion - which is what was supposed to be proved! Besides, since man is inapprehensible and he is the sole knower of truth, it follows all the more that truth is inattainable. As for God's existence, it is neither immediately evident nor demonstrable!

1.4.3.4. Critical Remarks

The word scepticism comes from a Greek verb (*skeptomai*) which means to look carefully at. And Sextus Empiricus says, "There are some who think that they have found the truth, such as Aristotle, Epicurus, the Stoics and certain others... But the Sceptics go on searching." Such an attitude, we must confess, is indeed healthy and praiseworthy and understood in this sense, scepticism has rendered great services to philosophy. But scepticism hardly ever stops there. It goes on to assert, more or less dogmatically, that truth does not exist, or is unattainable, or is not the same for everyone. Such views can be shown to be self-contradictory. One might well wonder whether the attempt to hold oneself back from having convictions and commitments actually does give us that peace of mind so beloved of the sceptics. Does it not create what Hegel called the "unhappy consciousness"? And was Sextus right in assuming that the major premiss in a syllogism is obtained some other way (by a total abstraction, for instance). At any rate, the response to the Sceptic's challenges is not to assert that everything is certain or that knowledge is easily attained! We must be cautious and humble. We must recognise our limits and never forget that we remain all our life pilgrims on the path to Truth. But isn't cowardice it to despair and give up in the face of difficulty?

1.4.4. Eclecticism

Eclecticism remains ever the temptation in a pluralist system. It is the attitude of the naive oversimplification, or dishonesty watering down differences that are fundamental and trying to patch up one system from borrowings taken out of irreconcilable theories (*ek-legein* in Greek means to pick and choose). Not that one should not try to reach a harmonious synthesis when possible, Ecumenical movements even in philosophy, are welcome, Eclectics take little care to ensure that the elements of doctrine they have borrowed and adopted to fit together. Of the many ancient eclectics, the best known is probably Cicero, who lived shortly before our era (106-43) and whose Latin orations some of us must have studied.

Eclecticism relinquished the task of constructing a speculative system in the stricter sense of the word, and adopted what may be called a working hypothesis, falling back on common consciousness or uncriticised immediate knowledge as the final test of philosophic truth. The Eclectic tendency penetrated all the schools, everywhere dissolving the spirit of system which, under scholarchs of inferior ability, had already begun to lose its primitive power of cohesion. Accordingly, among the Stoics and Epicureans as well as among the followers of Plato and Aristotle, we find all through the century and a half before Christ as well as during the first three centuries of the Christian era evidences of the Eclectic spirit preparing the way for the more comprehensive syncretic efforts of the school of Alexandria.

Sources: There is a fairly abundant corpus of Cicero's essays, orations and letters. One of the best anthologies is J Warrington (editor), *Cicero's Offices*, London, 1960. This volume contains, besides Cicero's writings on our Duties in life, a translation of his *Laelius* (On Friendship) and *Cato* (On Old Age). There is also an extract from Cicero - "On the Interrelation of the Schools" - in T.V. Smith, *Philosophers Speak for Themselves*, Vol II. On Cicero, there is Anthony Trollope's excellent *The Life of Cicero*, London, 1880 (a classic).

1.4.4.1. Marcus Tullius Cicero

The celebrated Roman orator, studied philosophy in his youth under a great many teachers belonging to different schools and wrote his major philosophical compositions towards the end of his life. He admitted quite frankly that these were mere copies of the writings of others. They did not require much labour, he confessed. He mostly contributed words, of which he had an ample supply!

Theory of Knowledge. All our knowledge rests, in ultimate analysis, on immediate certainty, which is variously called *notiones innatae or*, since immediate knowledge is common to all men, *consensus gentium*. We have, therefore, in Cicero's theory of knowledge, the first explicit expression of the doctrine of *innate ideas*.

Theological Notions. Cicero, in his proof of the existence God, falls back on the *innate idea of God*, the presence of which in the minds of all men is proved by the universality the belief in a Supreme Being. He brings forward also the *teleological argument* in its Stoic form, contending that the Epicurean doctrine of chance is absurd.

Ethics. In this portion of his philosophy Cicero is a follower of the Eclectic Stoics. On the one hand he rejects the Epicurean doctrine that pleasure is the highest good; but when, on the other hand, he adopts the Stoic doctrine of virtue, he is too much of a man of the world not to recognize that the Stoic morality is too exalted or too severe to be applied to everyday life. Accordingly, he modifies the severity of Stoicism by introducing the Platonic and Aristotelian teaching, that honours, wealth, etc., are goods, although subordinate to virtue, which is the chief good.

Cicero seemed to follow the Sceptics in his resolution not to interpose his judgment, to ever be comparing different opinions and never to dogmatise. His ideal seems to be to put common sense and eloquence to the service of the people. He advised the checking of passions, for they are opposed to right reason. Virtue suffices for happiness, but external goods should not be rejected. God exists, as can be shown from the order in the world. Cicero accepted the idea of providence, rejected fate and was also opposed to the views of the Epicureans. The concluding lines of Laelius are worth quoting:

> "There can be no real friendship which is not founded upon virtuous principles, nor any acquisition, virtue alone excepted, preferable to a true friend."

But Cicero didn't want us to stop at individual friendship. He invites us to pass from there to "universal human fellowship."

1.4.4.2. Critical Remarks

The writings of the eclectics make excellent and interesting reading, for they have well-chosen the best ideas of their contemporaries and predecessors. They are, thus, a kind of anthology or encyclopaedia of their age. But their works lack organic unity - which is not surprising for it is sometimes difficult to fit together opinions that are part of contradictory presuppositions!

1.4.5. Jewish – Hellenistic Philosophy

1.4.5.1. The Trend

The spreading of Greek thought and culture all over the Mediterranean world affected the Jewish communities, too. The Jewish religious community of the Essenes (in Palestine) - to which many scholars assimilate John the Baptist - had a doctrine which seems to have been tinged with Pythagorean characteristics. Many Jews tried to synthesis their religion with Greek philosophy and, to this end, attempted an allegoric interpretation of Biblical passages which didn't quite tally with Greek thought. They are forerunners of the Sadducees of the New Testament, a kind of free-thinking, ultra-progressist group and sworn enemies of the strict traditionalists who refused to have anything to do with Gentile speculations, the Pharisees. One of the earliest Jewish Hellenists is Aristobulus who wrote commentaries on Scripture (c. 150 B.C.) and tried to prove, without foundations, that Greek philosophers had really got their ideas from the Bible. But the great luminary of this trend is Philo of Alexandria (c. 20 B.C. - 40 A.D.)

Sources: Philo's views are best expressed in his works *On the Creation of the World*, *The Allegory of the Law* and *That God is Immutable*. We have a 10-volume translation of the writings of Philo, done by F. H. Colson and G Whitaker (Greek text with English translation) plus a further 2 volumes by R. Marcus, London, 1929-62. As for Commentaries and studies, most are in French, but there is the excellent book of E R Goodenough, *An Introduction to Philo Judeas*, Oxford, 1962.

1.4.5.2. Philo Judaeus

Philo Judaeus (i.e. 'the Jew') came from a wealthy and influential Jewish family of Alexandria. A man of vast erudition and extremely versatile, he was a much given to mystical contemplation as he was interested in politics and economic matters. He went as legate of his town to visit the Emperor Caligula in 40 A.D. To his Platonist and Neo- Pythagorean sympathies, he added an assurance of tone which his belief in the revealed word of the Bible gave him. This was a new nuance as far as Greek thought was concerned.

God, for Philo can only be the transcendent God of the Bible, the God of Abraham who becomes the God of all mankind. Man can know God directly through the Bible and indirectly through the created world. Faithful to his Jewish convictions, he insisted 0 n the transcendence and the consequent "unnamability" of God. God is provident, not only inasmuch as he has arranged the general laws of nature, but also by working miracles and wonders in favour of groups or individual persons (the people of Israel, Moses for example). To protect the transcendence of God from the Greek penchant to get him involved with the pettiness of earthly expeditions, he surrounded him with various intermediaries (like the Angels) who would take up the direct handling of this world. There are seven great scales of Reality, God presiding over all in the first place. Next comes the Logos, who is not God for he is not immutable, though he is "the eldest of those that have become". He is God's first instrument in the formation of the world and reminds us of the Hellenist Demiurge. It is not clear whether the Logos is a personal being or not: there are texts which one would use in favour of either view. In the third, fourth, fifth and sixth place are the Powers or Forces, secondary agents of creation who are mainly concerned with man (e.g. the Power of Punishment). In the seventh place there are the Ideas. These are contained in the Logos and serve as models or exemplars for his creative activity.

The World of matter which we perceive around us by our sense is a copy of the ideas on forms that are contained in the Logos, as we have said. Man is a composite of a higher part (the mind) - which makes of him an image of God, and a subsidiary part (the body) which makes him share in the material world. The goal of ethical life seems to be twofold. In this life it consists of dominating the subsidiary part of man by the higher part. Ultimately it involves being reborn into the supra-material world. Philo adds that all this is not possible to man, left to himself alone. A "miraculous elevation of the soul" must be brought about. The Patriarchs and Moses uniquely reveal to us how this can come about. Philo puts the finishing touches to his philosophy, which remains ever faithful to his Jewish convictions, by saying that the best form of government is the one that follows a divinely revealed fixed law.

1.4.5.3. Critical Remarks

It is interesting to have, through the endeavours of Philo, a foretaste as to how the Biblical world-view could try to adapt itself to Hellenistic thought. As we can see, this could be a very fruitful contact indeed. If Philo's working out of his Biblical faith with the help of Greek concepts is sometimes a bit vague and clumsy (for example, the identity of the intermediary Forces - they should be one with God to enable the finite to participate in the divine and they should be distinct from Him in order to keep him free from all contact with the world), yet we have the impression of a man convinced of his religious beliefs and yet trying to give them a sound basis in the ideas of his times.

1.5. The Last Great Flowering: Plotinus (205–270)

1.5.1. The Back-ground: Mystery Religions

Just about the dawn of the Christian era, Greek thought suddenly rejuvenated itself for one final glorious moment, producing its last great system - a breath-taking and complex world-view tinged with mysticism. That the religious aspect should now take on a commanding role in later Greek thought is not too surprising, if we take into consideration the factors involved.

First of all, there had been for quite a long time, a great many "mystery-cults" in the Greek world. All of these claimed to offer to the initiated (Greek: *mustes*; the verb *mysteriazo*, the radical of *musterion*, means to initiate someone into something) truths about the world and the afterlife. The unique and noteworthy element, here, is that they claimed to do this by giving the initiate an experience of these profound inner truths by getting him to participate in the life of the gods or, to put it more clearly, the make him re-live, along with the deity concerned, an experience of struggle or suffering, which would culminate in a kind of re-birth and renewal. It must be pointed out, however, that noble and impressive as all this sounds, most "mystery-rites" involved frenzied sex orgies and wild dancing and drinking. There were special rituals which were necessary to be undergone in order to be considered an initiate and there were various other "festivals" which involved other ceremonies, many of which were crude and sometimes even revolting. Of course, each rival mystery sect kept its ceremonies anti rituals (called *mysteria*) very secret from all non-initiates. It was, paradoxically, the best form of publicity. Pythagoreanism, which borrowed a lot from the Orphic beliefs, was one of the more refined mystery-sects and, unlike many of the others, which were little more than local and provincialistic cliques, it opened itself to everyone.

In addition, there were two other elements involved which were responsible for bringing Greek mysticism and mystery-cults so suddenly into the lime-light, giving them a new popularity. In the first place, there was the direct influence of the oriental religions and their stress on interior life and contemplation. Judaism and early Christian spirituality came in touch with Greek culture, just at a time when people were searching for something deeper and more personal in the sphere of religious experience. All that was needed was a religious and intellectual genius to harness all this into a systematic world-view. Then there was the breakdown of just about every other political and religious structure that had been able, up to the, to provide the meaning and security so necessary to peace of mind. The collapse of the city-state and, indeed, the coming of the Roman Empire, forced the common folk to try and find some new way of "fitting into" and developing a sense of belonging with regard to the huge, anonymous and cosmopolitan society in which they suddenly found themselves. Neither the haughty, disdainful attitude of the Stoics, nor the easy-going solution of the Epicureans, nor even the defeatist resignation of the Sceptics could provide them with a meaningful response. And so, as in so many cases, they looked to the supernatural for hope and new comfort.

And then there came a man, a providential God-send. He was alive to the needs and aspirations of the people. And he had lived in Alexandria, where he had first hand contact with Jewish and Christian thinkers. And he knew his Plato. This man was Plotinus and he knew how to build a harmonious religio-philosophical system out of all this, a system that would be a direct reply to the natural aspiration of so many.

1.5.2. Life

Plotinus was born in Alexandria in Egypt, the great meeting-place of East and West and the melting-pot of many cultures. He was probably an Egyptian by nationality, though he wrote in Greek, the *lingua franca* of the time. He studied at the famous College of Alexandria, under no less a luminary than the renewed Ammonius Saccas, whom many think was a renegade Christian. Our main source for details about Plotinus' life is the writings of his devoted disciple, Porphyry (232-305), who also edited the works of his master. According to Porphyry, Ammonius Saccas' lectures opened Plotinus' youthful and eager mind to the riches of Persian and Indian thought. We can also be sure that the budding young genius pro fitted not a little from Christian and Jewish influences too. After all, there were quite flourishing and active Christian and Jewish communities in the city. At any rate, Plotinus signed up with the Emperor Gordian's troops and took part in the projected Persian campaign. But the death of the Emperor in Mesopotamia put an end to Plotinus' dreams of first-hand contact with Persians and Indians - and very nearly put an end to his life too. He finally managed to get back to Antioch and later, at the age of 40, settled down in Rome.

Now began a very fertile period of intellectual activity. At first Plotinus had conferences only and did not write. Then he set about composing. When he was 59, he had completed 21 theses - less than half of the number he would leave behind him! By now Porphyry had joined him and it seems that for Plotinus too life began at 60. For in the next 6 years - which were all he had left to live - he wrote at least 33 more. When Porphyry set about editing his master's work, after the death of Plotinus, he decided to arrange it in a subject wise classification, rather than in chronological order. He arranged the 54 treaties in 6 topic wise group of nine treatises each and the work of Plotinus has come to be called *Enneads,* from the Greek word for nine.

As regards Plotinus the man, we may note that, according to Porphyry, he was much given to meditation. But this did not isolate him from his fellows. He was of sociable disposition and liked to receive friends. He opened his home to orphans and shared his life with them. He seems to be one of those rare persons who know how to combine contemplation with action.

1.5.3. Sources

Some of the best studies on Plotinus and translations of his *Enneads* are in French, but there have been also some very good English editions too. Since the Enneads are long, we give a brief description of each of the six groups. This may help you to choose your topic of the interest.

I Ennead on Ethics and allied questions
II Ennead on the World
III Ennead on specialised topics cone, the World: e.g. Fate
IV Ennead on the Soul
V Ennead on the Nous or Intellectual Principle of the World
VI Ennead on the Good or the One

Among the better-known English editions of the Ennead are the followings:

Stephen MacKenna (editor), *Plotinus, the Enneads*, 2nd revised edition 1956, with an excellent introduction by Paul Henry SJ (like all good editions of Plotinus' works, contains Porphyry's *Life of Plotinus*).

Turnbull, *The Essence of Plotinus*, New York, 1934 (key extracts taken from the MacKenna translation).

Armstrong, *Plotinus*, London, 1953 (good introduction and some selected texts)

Elmer O'Brien, *The Essential Plotinus*, New York, 1962 (A new, modem translation with selected readings from the Ennead).

T. V. Smith (editor) *Philosophers Speak for Themselves*, Vol. II, Chicago, 2nd ed. 1956 (some very brief selections, taken from the translation of Thomas Taylor).

As regards studies on Plotinus, the following may be noted:

Brehier, *The Philosophy of Plotinus*, trans. J. Thomas, Chicago, 1958 (perhaps the best introductory work in English)

Inge, *The Philosophy of Plotinus*, 2 vols, New Impression, London, 1948 (Gifford Lectures, 1917-1918)

Pistorious, *Plotinus and Neo-Platonism*, Cambridge, 1952.

Rist, *Plotinus: The Road to Reality*, Cambridge, 1967 (A more detailed study of specialised problems)

1.5.4. Plotinus' Vision: Neo-Platonism

Philosophy of Religion: For many people, it would be better to speak of Plotinus' vision as a kind of religion of interiority or a religious wisdom. For it aims at showing us a way to salvation. Yet, this way to salvation implies and presents a detailed picture of reality. Hence, it might be useful - for methodological purposes - to provide the guide-lines for a study of Plotinus' thought in two parts. In the first we shall study the picture of reality that he offers us. We shall call this part "Plotinus' Metaphysics". In the second, we shall consider his mystical pilgrimage to the Real. We shall call this part, "Plotinus' Religious Vision."

1.5.4.1. Plotinus' Metaphysics

1.5.4.1.1. The four grades of Reality

The Real, according to Plotinus, is made up of four grades. Or, to put it more accurately, **the Real** (the One - Monos) communicates Itself by emanation into the Intelligence (Nous), this in turn into the World Soul (Psyche) which, finally emanates Matter, the lowest grade or level of reality.

1.5.4.1.2. Emanation, rather than Creation

In a technical sense, "creation" implies the production of something neither out of some raw material, nor by some kind of overflow of the productive agent. Emanation is the general technical term used to refer to the production of something as the result of a kind of overflow from the productive agent. Perhaps the nearest example of "emanation" from our daily experience, to illustrate the Plotinian understanding of the production of, say, the Nous by the Monos would be our "emanation" of thoughts. As we shall see, Plotinus speaks of fire radiating (or emanating) heat and snow emanating cold.

1.5.4.1.3. The General Principle of Production

"Indeed everything, as existing, necessarily produces of its own substance some further existent dependent on its power and image of its existence. Thus, fire radiates heat and snow radiates cold." *(Ennead* IV, 8, 5) Each grade of reality; then, necessarily radiates or emanates the next one. However, Plotinus immediately tries to rectify this "necessity" aspect, as it seems to weaken the perfection of the Monos. He explains that even if the Monos needs to communicate by necessity, it does not do so in order to seek something which is lacking to it. It "knows not desire - what could it desire?" he asks. This "necessity" with respect to the Monos, then, should be understood more in the sense of "willingness" than as desiring something that is lacking!

1.5.4.1.4. The Productivity of the Monos

"The One ... produces the second substance (i.e., the Nous) without assent or decree or movement of any kind." (V, 1, 6). It communicates itself by a sheer overflowing of its Perfection and this generation does not bring about any change of the Monos. "The eternally perfect is eternally productive, and what is produced is eternal too, although it is inferior." Obviously the Monos, in order to remain unchanging must be eternally productive, if it is to be productive at all. Else there would be an evident change in as it passes from being not-yet-productive to the act of producing and then becomes inert, once again, after having finished its job of producing. As for its present productive activity, that also involves what is technically known as conservation (i.e. keeping in being that which it has produced): "It is because of the One that we can breathe and have our being: it does not bestow its gifts at one moment only to leave us again; its giving is without cessation so long as it remains what it is." (VI, 9,9).

1.5.4.1.5. "Monos" the best name for the first Hypostasis

Plotinus is very careful in his choice of names to give to the first Hypostasis (literally *beneath-standing*, sub-stance) or transcendent source of reality. He prefers to call it "One" rather than "Being" for the latter is a name we give to many other things and Plotinus wants to emphasise the uniqueness of the first hypostasis. At times he will allow himself to speak of it as the Good or the Beautiful (the hand of Plato is evident, here), but that is all. The name "One" is also meant to draw attention to the fact that there is no duality of any kind implied within the One. Thus, he tells us that though the One is aware of itself, this intellectual awareness does not even imply the duality of subject and object.

1.5.4.1.6. Arguments for the Existence of the "One"

Plotinus, drawing inspiration from Plato - especially the "way of ascent" in the Symposium - argues from our experience of limited beauty and goodness to an absolute Beauty and Goodness, other names for the Monos, as we have seen. He also says that the unity which is found in everything indicates that there must be an absolute source of unity. (cf. V, 5 for other arguments)

1.5.4.1.7. The Second Level of Reality, the Nous

We have seen how the Monos emanates eternally the Nous, which is also eternal, though inferior to it. There is a kind of argument for the existence of the Nous, or Intelligence. This is elaborated by a phenomenological observation of how men live. There are those who live by the sensations, the Epicureans. Others manage to live themselves a little above the earth: the Stoics. But there are those who are really godlike: the Platonists, whose sole pleasure is in the truth. The beauty of the soul is its wisdom. "Well, what gives the wisdom that constitutes the beauty of the soul? It is the intelligence." (V, 9, 2)

1.5.4.1.8. The Nature and Role of Nous

"Resembling the Monos thus, Nous produces in the same way, pouring forth a multiple power. Just as that, which was before it, poured fourth its likeness, so what the Nous produces is a likeness of itself." (V, 2) This likeness is, as we shall see, the World Soul (Psyche). The Nous is "a radiation from the Monos, while the Monos remains unchanged, just like the bright light which surrounds the sun, which remains unchanged, though the light springs from it continually." (V, 1, 6) Actually the Intelligence is the real demiurge, for it gives to the World Soul the seminal reasons for its activity, like skill gives to the artist his norms of performance.

1.5.4.1.9. The Third level of Reality, the World Soul

Plotinus was influenced by the view of Plato - which has come down to us in some texts - that the World, as a whole, has a soul. "It is preposterous to make the world soulless, when we, who contain a part of the body of the All, have a soul." (IV, 3, 7) It follows, then, that the World ("the Body of the all") has, itself, a soul! This is borne out from the fact of the basic unity which seems to pervade the undeniable diversity that surrounds us. As we have mentioned earlier, "The soul is word and deed of the Intelligence." (V, 1, 6)

1.5.4.1.10. The Nature and role of the Psyche or World Soul

"From the one Soul proceeds a multiplicity of different souls, as from one and the same genus proceed species of different ranks, some of which are more rational and others (at least in their actual existence) less rational in form." (IV, 8, 3) The World Soul has, thus an inclination to plurality and we can see how more and more of multiplicity steps in as we move away from the perfection of the Monos. The multiplicity of souls takes place, at first, in the pure intelligible realm. But in spite of this, these souls got "tired, you might say, of living with someone else. Each steps down into its own individuality." (IV, 8, 5) To attain and express this individuality the souls must need take on bodies. "Thus ... the Soul enters Body ... A lesser divinity, it is impelled by the stress of its powers and the attraction of governing the next below it." (IV, 8, 5) Thus it is that "every soul has a lower part directed towards the body and a higher part directed towards the intelligible." (IV, 8, 8)

1.5.4.1.11. The Lowest level of the Reality, Matter

Matter is the final level of production. When the soul has generated the sensitive faculty of the animal order and the generative faculty which extends up to the vegetative order, it is no longer productive, "or at least, what it produces is of quite another order; here life ceases; all later production is lifeless." (III, 4, 1) Matter, then, is something very inferior to the Soul: "the thing engendered on the further side can be no image of the Soul, since it is not even alive; it must be utter indetermination." More than that, matter is inherently evil, for evil is nothing but the absence of perfection and this is precisely what matter is: "that which has nothing because it is in want, or rather is want, must necessarily be evil." (II, 4, 16) Still, inasmuch as it is the effect of the soul it has some meaning.

1.5.4.1.12. The Place of Man in this Vision

The Plotinian view of man is little different from that of Plato, as is to be expected. Man shares in three levels of Reality: Intelligence, Soul and Matter. "Physically, we are formed by that inferior soul, given forth (not directly from the Monos but) from the divine beings in the heavens themselves; it is by way of the inferior soul that we are associated with the body (hence this association will not be persistent); for the higher soul which constitutes the We is the principle not of our existence, but of our excellence." (II, 1, 6)

1.5.4.2. Plotinus' Religious Vision

1.5.4.2.1. A Mystical Religion of Interiority

Insofar as Plotinus provides us with a complete and coherent picture of Reality, we may speak of him as a metaphysician. But he didn't stop there. His main intent was to teach a way of salvation. Thus, he is first and foremost a religious teacher. The way of salvation he taught was neither a matter of being initiated into certain secret rites (as in the Mystery Religions) nor in commitment to a historical person (as in Christianity) but in a certain attitude to Reality, itself. Thus, we can see how his Metaphysics and his Religious vision as intimately related and flow into each other, as it were. Reality, as we have seen, admits of grades. And just as there is a general principle of productivity that drives each grade to emanate the next one, so also there is a complementary movement, a movement of return. "Begotten always longs for its begetter and loves it." (V, 1, 6) Now, since each higher grade (the begetter) is already present to the lower (its begotten) each grade must enter more deeply into its profoundest interior to attain its source. As far as man is concerned, this will mean turning his higher, interior faculties towards the various grades of his being. Thus, Plotinian religion is a mysticism of interiority. It is a pretty thorough system with a complete religious vocabulary.

1.5.4.2.2. Conversion and Virtue

"Conversion" or turning towards the Prime Reality is, as we have seen, something spontaneous, for there is a kind of natural longing of begotten for the begetter, a natural "turning towards" its source and, through it, to its Ultimate Source, the Monos. This being so, "virtue" is rather what follows from this conversion, than that which precedes it and initiates it. The concept of virtue, then is not something that belongs to the human realm alone, as conversion, too, occurs at all levels. However, there are certain virtues that are the exclusive prerogative of man alone, virtues linked with his specific condition, as temperance and courage. By virtue, the soul frees itself from the irrational element within, so that its lower part respects the dictates of reason. Some virtues may consist in likeness to good men, such as the civic virtues - e.g., honesty, industriousness and so on. But the higher virtues are more a likeness of God himself - likeness to the model, rather than images of it!

1.5.4.2.3. The Flight of the Lone to the Alone

This phrase of Plotinus ably sums up his particular Way of Ascent, detailing how the "blessed men" detach themselves from all things "here below" and thus, "lone", make their solitary flight to the Monos, or One, the Alone. But just how does one make his way from here below to the intelligible realm, the inner core of the Superior sources of Reality? To begin at the bottom, the man who is used to seek his object of love in bodily, material things, must learn to seek that in bodiless things, in the arts, in sciences and in virtues. A musician will be more inclined to seek and pursue Beauty in itself, rather than in some beautiful thing. A philosopher, too, is more disposed to this sort of thing, but he will need direction. It is dialectic that one must use to attain this end - dialectic, then, is not a branch of Logic, but a kind of initiation into mystical insight "Dialectic is not merely the tool of philosophy. It is not just abstract theories and rules. It works with things as they are about them, the objects themselves." (I, 3)

Dialectic directs us towards full and meaningful contemplation. Now here is another familiar word but, which like other Plotinian religious terms (cf. conversion, virtue), does not quite correspond to our everyday use of this vocabulary. He gives it a very wide meaning and extension. It seems to suggest both immediacy of contact as well as vision. It is an attribute of all things - thus the activity of plants, animals and even the earth are called contemplation. Nor is there any distinction between contemplation and action, as Aristotle and the Stoics suggest, for contemplation is also production. Plotinus goes even a step further than that: he identifies contemplation with things. Thus, Nature is a contemplation, because inasmuch as it is the lowest aspect of the Soul it is the expression of an Intelligence which is in contemplation. In the Intelligence, contemplation is perfect for the subject of contemplation is identical with its object. Plotinus does not say that the Monos is also contemplation. He insists on its superiority to the Intelligence. Thus, its contemplation would be even more perfect than that of the Intelligence, for in it even the duality of knower and known (subject and object of contemplation) has disappeared.

When our contemplation attains that Monos, it takes a very special form, Ecstasy. It is best to let Plotinus speak for himself in this regard.

> As the Monos does not contain any difference, it is always present and we are present to it when we no longer contain difference. The Monos dies not aspire to us, to move round us; we aspire to it, to move round it. Actually we always move round it, but we do not always look. We are like a chorus grouped around a conductor who allows their attention to be distracted by the audience. If, however, they were to turn towards their conductor, they would sing as they should and really with him. We are always around the Monos. If we were not, we would dissolve and cease to exist. Yet our gaze does not remain fixed upon the Monos. When we look at It, we then attain the end of our desires and find rest. Then, it is that, all discord past, we dance an inspired dance around it. (9,8)

> As we turn towards the Monos, we exist to a higher degree, while to withdraw from it is to fall. Our soul is delivered from evil by rising to that place which is free of all evils. There it knows. There it is truly alive. Life not united with the divinity is shadowy and mimicry of authentic life. Life there is the authentic act of the Intelligence which, motionless in its contact with the Monos, gives birth to gods, beauty, justice and virtue. (VI, 9)

> "The man who obtains the vision becomes, as it were, another being." *(ibid)*

> Therefore, it is so very difficult to describe this vision, for how can we represent as different from us what seemed, while we were contemplating it, not other man ourselves, but perfect at-oneness with us? *(Ibid.)*

> When you fall from this vision, you will, by arousing the virtue that is within yourself and by remembering the perfection that you possess, regain your likeness and through virtue rise to the intelligence and thru wisdom to the Monos. Such is the life of the divinity and the divine and blessed men: detachment from all things here below, scorn of all earthly pleasures, the flight of the lone to the Alone. *(ibid)*

1.5.5. Some Critical Remarks

1.5.5.1. Plotinus' Metaphysics

1.5.5.1.1. Emanation

Whereas earlier Greek thinkers - including the men of the Golden Age - were not able to find a way to explain the origin of the cosmos in such a way as to underline the total dependence of the world on its maker, Plotinus was able to do so. There was no Platonic or Aristotelian demiurge giving form and shape to the pre-existing matter (even the Semites could not but see the Maker as one who put order and meaning into primeval confusion). The three levels of reality depend totally and eternally on the Monos - even for their persistence in being. Such are the possibilities of an emanationistic theory of cosmogenesis. But the Plotinus' strength is also his weakness. For if emanation can explain admirably well the dependence of the World on its Maker, totally and forever - it destroys the transcendence of the latter and, with the 'general principle of production' undermines the freedom of the Maker. He is obliged to create or to emanate and, therefore, falls short of that absolute perfection which is supposed to be his characteristic attribute. For were he not to emanate, something would be incomplete in his self-realisation. Plontinian monism (or pantheism) is no crude variety of the same, but it labours with all the difficulties of such a view. All this should not make us shy away from considering the possibility of developing a corrected and purified emanationistic theory of creation. Such an approach is more open to that dynamic conception of the world that seems to be inevitably today and which traditional theories of creation do not seems to be able to bring adequately enough.

1.5.5.1.2. Plotinian "henology"

Since Plotinus prefers to call the Primary Reality the "one" (in Greek 'heno') rather than "being", ontos, or God, theos, his system is more aptly called a 'henology', instead of the usual names, such as ontology or theology. His refusal to give It any other name save that which underscores Its essential Otherness, difference-from-us, unnameability or in-affability, brings out all the advantages of a negative theology (i.e. a theology that insists that we can more easily say what God is **not** than proudly claim to know what he is): it shows our awareness of our limitations when we have to speak of the First Principle. Its also brings out his Simplicity (the fact of being undivided, perfectly one). It cannot be denied that however subtle we make our interpretation of the four "levels" of reality, since each is but an ultimate overflow of the same Monos, its is alleged Oneness does get a bit weakened in process.

1.5.5.1.3. The Plotinian Nous

If Anaxagoras was the first Greek thinker to feel the need to speak of Nous to explain the order amidst all the complexity in the Universe, we have to wait for the Stoics (who preferred to speak of the Logos) to see this insight put to good use. It is Plotinus, though, who really opens a way to full exploitation of this valuable notion. And when St. John calls Jesus the Logos, it is perhaps more a corrected usage of the Neo-Plotinian Nous than to Stoic's Logos, a far less rich concept that we should think of.

1.5.5.1.4. The World Soul

Plotinus, like many a mystically-minded thinkers - be he poet or philosopher - was so alive to, and so struck by, the organic unity of the Universe (a point often overlooked in this age of specialisation), that he felt the need to postulate a common or universal soul to give force and binding to this wonderful harmony. Whether we agree with this assumption of his or not, we cannot but see in it a useful remainder of an observation so little noted today, even by the phenomenological school! He has also well seen what is the characteristic role of matter: to provide for individuality and differentiation through extension.

1.5.5.1.5. The Plotinian Understanding of Man

The Plotinian Man labours under all the Platonic prejudices against matter, prejudices that would go a long way to making him a misfit in the world of matter which, by the way, is the only world we have. Porphyry's biography of his master opens with these telling words: "Plotinus, the philosopher our contemporary, seemed ashamed of being in the body." And that is a pretty good summary of Plotinian anthropology. It is also a neat precis of the main charge we can lay against his ethics! Matter, and that includes the body too, is seen as inherently evil, as something to be, at most, tolerated in life, the world is nothing but a degraded level of reality to be transcended with as much deftness as possible - in short, the revalorisation of the cosmos and the body that only a sound incarnational vision of reality can bring is understandably lacking. And since Christian mystics, when casting about for a vocabulary and a world-view to translate their experiences, found a ready-made system in Plotinian Neo-Platonism, they carried all these prejudices and insufficiencies into their work. And since they wrote at a period that has been taken as more or less normative for future generations, we have all felt the heavy and inhibiting influence of Neo-Platonism on our spirituality and ethics!

1.5.5.2. Plotinus' Religious Vision

1.5.5.2.1. Indian Inspiration?

We have already had occasion to remark that we should not be led astray by Plotinus' apparently familiar religious vocabulary. If "virtue", "conversion", "ecstasy" and so on are terms that we have long been accustomed to in Christian asceticism, we should not hastily assume that Plotinus and we are speaking of the same things each time we make use of the same word. An allied danger is the overzealous conclusion that there is little difference between Plotinus' basic vision and that found in Indian thought - nor is a hasty conclusion that Plotinus was directly inspired by Indian thought in elaborating his system easily established. E Brehier argues in favour of such an influence: Others, as Lacombe and do Gandillac are more guarded in their view. They point out certain affinities but do not wish to maintain a real influence. Lacombe notes Plotinus' silence with regard to Yoga, which, he says, he would have mentioned - especially since he does not hesitate to indicate his sources - had there been any direct influence. The theory and practice of yoga would certainly have come in hand for the Dialectic. Fr. de Marneffe feels that

> we may still think that Plotinus could have assimilated a general idea of Indian Philosophy, such as can be derived by hearsay and popular tradition, but that he would not have known the detail and technicalities of Indian thought, which only the texts and the ability to read then could have transmitted. (p.94)

We have already drawn attention to Porphyry's remark that an interest in Indian thought was one of the reasons why he joined Gordian's ill-fated expedition. So there seems to have been at least a vague knowledge of basic Indian views. Be that as it may, we might also draw attention to some fundamental differences. For instance, never does the Intellect discover itself to be an illusion, nor does it finally lose its identity in the One. There is no room in the thought of Plotinus for the idea that all things other than the One are an illusion or for any change or ultimate disappearance of any of the levels of reality below this One.

1.5.5.2.2. Plotinus and Western Mysticism

The indebtedness of Western mystical writers to Plotinus cannot be denied. But it is more a matter of themes and terms. There still remains two profound differences, even in their vocabulary, which even the most cursory reader of the Enneads would remark: the Christian doctrine of grace, together with allied doctrine of prayer and the doctrine of anguish and mystical "darkness". However, much we try to strain and twist passages in Plotinus, nowhere do we come up with anything suggesting the self-giving on the part of the One. It is quite foreign to Plotinus' thought. As for prayer, it is true that Plotinus does speak of it and in the context of soul's relationship to the Monos. But the closer look at the meaning and full significance of the term once more shows that it is more a similarity of words than of content. Plotinian 'prayer' is, as Fr. Henry observes,

> a tension of the soul, the final leap in the dialectical process; it is not an appeal, not an expectation; it is neither the effect nor the occasion of a movement of grace or inclination on the part of God. (Cf. Introduction to MacKenna's translation of the Enneads, p.1)

1.5.5.2.3. The Plotinian Way of Ascent

Perhaps the best compliment we can pay to Plotinian thought is to note that it was one of the decisive influences in bringing Augustine to Christianity. In the hands of Porphyry, though, Neo-Platonism emerged as a rival to the still nascent Christian faith. He wrote 15 books against the Christians. Thus, the council of Ephesus condemned his works and the Emperors Valentinian III and Theodosius II had them burnt in 448. And since Plotinus had ever been the leading light in Neo-Platonism, there were not wanting a few self-appointed prophets who recognised in him all the traits of the anti-Christ. At any rate, Plotinus' vision, the last great flower of ancient pagan philosophy became, in the thought of St. Augustine, the first stage of Christian Philosophy.

That this was not an unmixed blessing we have already said often enough. It is not fair, of course, to expect that early Christian thinkers should have been able to evolve a more positive attitude to matter and the body, based on the Incarnation, at so early a date. But, if Augustine had not been so heavily influenced by Plotinus, and if the Church had not so heavily influenced by Augustine, we might not have had to wait till the latter half of the twentieth century to develop this perspective.

2. MEDIEVAL PHILOSOPHY

2.1. Introduction

2.1.1. "Medieval"

The word "medieval" or "Middle Period" indicates that the time in question has traditionally been viewed in a prejudiced, disparaging light. It was viewed as mere period of transition, coming in between two great flowerings of Western Culture, a kind of insignificant pigmy standings in the middle of two impressive giants. Nothing really "happened" in Europe, humanly speaking, between Plotinus and Renaissance. And naturally, medieval philosophy shared in the general disesteem that people felt for everything that belonged to the "middle" ages (a little over a thousand years).

Thus, many manuals of Philosophy would do a neat jump from Neo-Platonism to Descartes. We were supposed to believe that, due to the domination of the Church, the human kind had been reduced to a kind of intellectual slavery and could do no more than repeat in unison whatever the Roman Curia was dictating: Men like Francis Beacon and Rene Descartes have done a lot to propagate such a view.

It is only quite recently that everyone has begun to realise that we have given the so-called Middle Ages a very raw deal and that the philosophy of the period is coming to be viewed with a new respect. The continuity in thought and development between the Medieval and Modern period is ever being discovered and underscored. We are now ready to admit that the Western world owes many a debt to the once disparaged thinkers of the age. Indeed, Bacon, Descartes and several other of their ilk are far more dependent on medieval thinkers and medieval thought than they have cared to admit - not only from the point of view of ideas and themes, but even in vocabulary!

Finally-though we cannot say that the authority of the Church - and the Roman and local Curias - was not very often terribly high-handed (a fault which, in all fairness, it must be admitted, even the reform churches and states did also commit), medieval philosophy was not so monolithic and subservient as it is made out to be. Even if medieval thinkers did have the same basic (Christian) vision and look, more or less injunctions of the omnipresent church, and her intelligence agents, they still managed to find quite a margin of freedom and originality. There arose many great, influential and original thinkers in the Middle Ages and they were not all parroting the same things in the same way!

2.1.2. Philosophy

Granted that medieval philosophy is a good deal richer and varied than it has commonly been supposed, it still remains true that the vast majority of medieval philosophers were priests and theologians (and many are canonised saints!), pursuing philosophic studies in the spirit of a theologian or even an apologist. Wouldn't "theology", then, be a better name for what they wrote? After all, their faith in, and commitment to, Christian Revelation was an essential part of their intellectual make-up!

This question can be put in another way (and, indeed, it has!) can one legitimately speak of a "Christian Philosophy"? If one's faith were to enter into the working out of one's thought, then we should cease to speak of philosophy. For philosophy should go by reason and not revelation- the latter is the prerogative of theology. And if one's faith does not play a part in the formulating of one's philosophy, why call it a *Christian* Philosophy? Surely not merely because there is question of Christians who were philosophising. If Christian philosophy is nothing more than philosophy made by Christians, then we should speak of a Christian Mathematics and Christian Chemistry whenever a Christian goes deep into Maths and Chemistry - and so on for every discipline!

When Pope Leo XIII used the phrase in the encyclical *Aeterni Patris* ("Of the Eternal Father") at the turn of the country, he certainly intended to recommend a genuine philosophy, but one consistent with the Christian vision and taking its teachings into accounts. It was in this sense that Jacques Maritain would defend the right of Christian Philosophy to be called a true philosophy. As he said, faith is only an extrinsic criterion for the Christian philosopher. He does not positively (intrinsically) use it to work out his system. But he must check his conclusions each time, to see if they happen to contradict any teaching of the Church. Should they do, he must consider himself mistaken and go back over his arguments. As for the argument of a Christian Mathematics or a Christian Chemistry, one can easily retort that it is not the same thing. Neither Mathematics or Chemistry or any other discipline demands of the thinker that total personal involvement which philosophy does!

The whole debate as re-opened in 1931 by Emile Brehier, the great authority on Plotinus, who concluded that there was no such thing as a Christian Philosophy. This sparked off a lively discussion in which some of France's most eminent Catholic thinkers clashed. Etienne Gilson, for instance, was of the view that not only was there nothing self-contradictory in the idea of a Christian philosophy (for reasons such as those we have already outlined), but that there were, in fact, not just "a" Christian philosophy but several. The debate was, perhaps, providential for it led to much deeper thinking and clarification.

It was pointed out that, etymologically, philosophy was the quest for wisdom, a way of life. Hence it was quite legitimate to speak of a Christian wisdom or quest, a search for a manner of living that was genuinely Christian, even though it appealed to the use of reason. However, under the leadership of Blondel, many Catholic thinkers began to draw attention to the fact that, in order to be truly called a "Christian Philosophy", a system of thought should fulfil some positive requirements. It was not enough that it should not contain any ideas or views that would contradict basic Christian teaching. In addition, it should also contain certain basic, positive orientations and characteristics without which, even if it still did not go against the Christian faith, it could not be called "Christian" in the full sense of the word.

According to the author of *L'Action,* (Maurice Blondel) an authentic Christian philosophy is only one which recognised the limits of human reason, was aware of its own insufficiency in facing the mysteries of life and was therefore in some way open to revelation (at least as a possibility) and even, in a vague way, appealed to it or, at least, expressed a need for it. The refusal to underplay or downgrade the sense of mystery was also taken by Gabriel Marcel to be necessary condition for any system of thought to be qualified as Christian.

2.1.3. The Merit of Medieval Philosophy

Apart from its own intrinsic richness and variety, the thought of Augustine and Thomas, Scotus and Occam and many others has a special lesson for us future priests of India in this latter part of the 20th century. For, whether we endorse their views or not, these men succeeded in a goal that we are far from having realised. They achieved a wonderful "inculturation". They found a pastoral and meaningful (for their times) way of expressing the Christian message in the culture and the philosophy of their times. They made use of Neo-Platonism or Aristotelianism or Stoicism - taking care to correct, purify and modify concepts borrowed from these systems whenever they felt it necessary - and worked out an expression of the Good News in terminology and thought-patterns familiar to their contemporaries. They also made use of the (hierarchic, monarchic) social and political structures then current in formulating all this. This is what we are aiming at in today's India. And it would be useful to see how these men achieved this aim.

Unfortunately, due to historical circumstances, their strength has been responsible for no few problems which are still ours today. Actually, the fault was not theirs but that of their successors. The shock of the Reformation gave to the Church that "siege mentality" of hanging on to and defending (literally to the last comma!) certain formulations of dogmas and the philosophical presuppositions that went along with it. And even when society evolved and underwent radical transformations, such that the language of the people and their thought-patterns were no longer that of the Great Medieval Thinkers, the Church still insisted that the "truths of faith" be taught according to old concepts and thought-patterns, even if no one quite understood them as they had been before ... and even if other, new disciplines and philosophies had grown and developed that might have expressed equally well (and sometimes even better!) the experience of faith. Worse still, there were whole nations and cultures that did not partake of the Western heritage of thought and who had their own rich philosophy and culture (India, Africa ...) who were obliged to teach and celebrate Gospel in a language and style of thought that had nothing at all to do with the people. Let us not forget that the Christian Revelation is expressed (for better or worse) in the language and culture of the Jews, an Oriental people whose mind has much more affinities with Indian thought and philosophy, than with the Greek model. Had Indian Christians been allowed the same liberty as their Western brethren of the Middle Ages, the former would have found — in Śankara and Rāmānuja, to mention just two possibilities — perhaps a far better medium to express the message of Revelation! And had we been allowed to work out our own Indian Liturgy, with the help of the rich symbolism of our people - well, perhaps, we would have seemed less foreign and would not have remained such a "little flock" even though Christianity came to our land long before it came to much of Europe.

Whatever be the case, the challenge that once an Augustine and a Thomas Aquinas had to face centuries back is now ours. Would that the Lord raise up among us men of similar stature who will persevere, like their illustrious predecessors, amid much uncertainty, confusion and persecution to achieve, for our time, that measure of indigenisation or inculturation that they achieved for theirs. And let us hope that, when that day comes, no one makes the same mistake of taking it as "once-and-for-all" normative for all future generations of Indians!

2.1.4. Sources

General Bibliography for this period

Maurice Nedoncelle, *Is There a Christian Philosophy?* (trans by Dom Illtyd Trethowan), London, Faith & Fact Series no. 10, 1960. (A thorough and interesting account of the controversy we have mentioned above. Brief, clear and the to the point).

Philippe Delhaye, *Christian Philosophy in the Middle Ages*, (trans by S.J. Tester), London, Faith & Fact Series No. 12, 1960. (Concise and clear treatment of all major thinkers and trends)

David Knowles, *The Evolution of Medieval Thought*, London, 1962. (Perhaps the best specialised treatment to have come out originally in English; stresses the continuity and development of main currents of thought, showing their roots in Pagan or Christian antiquity)

Gordon Loff, *Medieval Thought: St Augustine to Ockham*, Harmondsworth, 1958 (reprint 1970) (stresses philosophical, rather than political thought; more descriptive, tries to avoid critical comments).

Etienne Gilson, *History of Christian Philosophy in the Middle Ages*, New York, 1955 (A classic; very detailed. Prof. Gilson has written several specialised books and articles on various aspects of medieval thought and on many medieval thinkers. Each of them is a masterpiece of scholarship and readability)

Julius Weinberg, *A Short History of Medieval Philosophy*, Princeton, 1964 (Brief, clear, well-written)

Paul Vignaux, *Philosophy in the Middle Ages*, (trans E.C. Hall), New York, 1959 (Concise, clear treatment by a leading French medieval intellectual historian)

Fredrick Copleston, *A History of Philosophy*, Vol 11: Augustine to Scotus, London, 1950; Vol. III: Ockham to Suaroz, London 1953 (An excellent, detailed treatment combining literary merit with a high intellectual standard, as always)

2.2. St. Augustine (354–430)

2.2.1. Life and Sources

2.2.1.1. His Life

St. Augustine, whose name stands out as that of greatest of the Latin Fathers, both from a literary-and a theological standpoint, and who would dominate Western thought until the thirteen century (and thus would exercise a decisive influence on the formulation of early Christian creeds and spirituality), was born in Tagaste in the African Province of Numidia on 13 November 354, of a pagan father, Patricius and a Christian mother, St. Monica. He was brought up a Christian by his devout mother but his baptism was deferred, according to common custom at the time. He soon mastered Latin, but could make little headway at Greek and a stern application of the of rod in the local school could only got him to acquire a grudging, superficial acquaintance with the language of Homer, whose poems he quite enjoyed, taken as a story.

When he was only 11, he left home for Madaura, where he laid the foundations of his knowledge in Latin literature and rhetoric. The usual problems that come the way of a young student, away from home in the new world of a bustling, beckoning city (with all the implications) soon got the better of him. His easy-going father kept him well supplied with money -- which did not make things easier for the lad's passionate, Southern temperament which was soon coming "of age".

At the age of 16, Augustine arrived at Carthage, the largest city he had ever seen and began higher studies in Rhetoric. His father died that same year, after having embraced the faith of his wife, and Augustine, now well on the way to a life of dissipation and general dissoluteness found in the licentious ways of the great commercial and political centre, much to seduce him. He made a clear break with the moral ideals of Christianity as he had ever known them, took a mistress with whom he lived faithfully for over ten years and who bore him a son Adeodatus, whom he loved sincerely and gave a Christian education. In all fairness, we must point out that Augustine, for all his waywardness, never once neglected his studies and obtained excellent results as a scholar. Indeed, whatever else may have been his private life, Augustine seems to have always been very serious whenever it was a question of knowledge and the pursuit of truth. And we shall note also that he never wooed any system or philosophy that had no connection with Christianity or which, at least, did not claim that! All this will become very clear as we continue our very short biographical sketch of his long and devious pilgrimage to the truth.

Augustine's first halt in this pilgrimage was Manichaeism. It was a reading of Cicero's exhortation to seek after truth that surfaced this passion in him and this third century Christian heresy (an amalgam of Christian and Persian - we would say Parsee - elements) seemed to offer him a better explanation of things than official Christianity and the apparently illogical stories of the Old Testament. Manichaeism provided a simplistic solution to the problem of evil in postulating as do the Parsees today, two ultimate principles - that of light, Ormuzd, and that of darkness, Ahriman. The evil in the world is the work of Ahriman, who is ever in conflict with Ormuzd and trying to overthrow the good he brings about. In man, the soul is the work of Ormuzd whereas the body, the corrupting, dissolute influence, that of Ahriman. It must have also been quite comforting for Augustine to find out that he was not quite to blame for his passionate and sensual outbursts: it was all the doing of Ahriman. It was in 383, just before he left Carthage - where he had lived with his mistress and son, after opening out a school of rhetoric in 374 - that he finally broke with Manichaeism, and this in circumstances that bear eloquent testimony to his intellectual honesty and his sincerity in seeking after truth. Manichaeism, we have seen, solved some of the doubts that had vexed Augustine (regarding the mystery of evil) but not all. His questing, restless mind came up with other problems, this time concerning Manichaeistic doctrine and he waited with eager impatience for the visit of Faustus, a well-respected Manichaean bishop whom he put at once all his questions. It is to the merit of Faustus that the latter, quite frankly, admitted that he knows not how to answer the doubts of his gifted interlocutor. Augustine recorded his esteem and respect for this likeable, honest man, but his adherence to Manichaeism was very much weakened. He left for home, now beguiled by Academic scepticism, hoping to find more serious students in that great capital - and so indeed they were, except that they were not very regular when it came to paying their fees. Finding a post, as professor of rhetoric in Milan, he left the Eternal City the next year and arrived at the place where he would begin a new life in more senses than one.

Slowly, Augustine began to consider Christianity more favourably - due mainly to his having attended the sermons of St. Ambrose in the Cathedral of Milan. He learned how to give an allegorical interpretation to many of the Old Testament passages which had bothered him. He would have had himself inscribed as a catechumen, but the call of the flesh was still a bit too strong: he couldn't bring himself to give up the luxurious and wanton life he had become accustomed to. His mother finally persuaded him to consider marriage to a local 'good girl', hoping - as mothers do, no doubt - that a girl would put some sense and balance into her wayward son's life. Augustine went so far as to agree to separate from his mistress in view of this marriage and it was a very tearful occasion for him and Adeodatus' mother. But, as the girl in question was too young for an immediate wedding and he tired of waiting, Augustine soon found another mistress to keep him company. By now, he had begun to read the Neo-Platonists, especially Plotinus. The net result of these studies only served to open his mind, all the more, to the reasonableness of Christianity. He re-opened his New Testament with renewed interest, especially St. Paul.

Once again there came a terrible internal struggle within him. For he felt drawn to Christianity, but was, at the same time, too enmeshed in a sensual life to give it up without a fight. Matters were not made easier for him by his chance meeting with two men, recent converts of Christianity, who shared with him, quite sincerely, the stories of their search and their new found joy. The decisive moment seems to have been the famous occasion of the "*Tolle, lege*" ("take up and read") wherein he decided, once and for all, to commit himself to the Christian faith that had ever been surreptitiously attracted him. Thus, the intellectual conversion of Augustine to Christianity (his reading of neo- Platonism) was completed by his moral and emotional conversion, that evening in 386.

He then withdrew for a while to Cassiciacum, resigning his professorship (a painful lung ailment forced his early retirement) and there he gave himself up to discussion and reflection with his friends. From then on, he would begin to write his famous apologetic and theological treaties (he had previously written works on - rhetoric and literature) and he carried over his limpid, personal style into those writings. On Holy Saturday 387, Augustine was finally baptised by St. Ambrose. Monica who had come down specially for the occasion, died while waiting for the boat for the return trip. No doubt, it was a great consolation and the crowning of much prayer and sacrifice on the part of Monica to have been able to witness the eventual baptism of her erstwhile pagan husband and "lost" son.

Augustine then returned to Tagaste, where he founded a small monastic community and plunged himself into his studies and writings. He renounced all intention to marry, but didn't seem to have intended ordination. It was not quite according to his will that the Bishop of Hippo ordained him priest in 391, while Augustine was visiting that seaport town not far from Carthage. He was eventually persuaded to establish his community there and combat the Manichaean heresy, where it was at its strongest. More treaties and pamphlets to this effect followed, including several works on exegetical topics. He also began to take part in the controversy against the Donatist sect.

Soon after (395-6), he was appointed auxiliary Bishop of Hippo and he set up another monastic community in his residence. Within a year the Bishop of Hippo died and Augustine succeeded him, a post that he held until his death. Besides embroiling himself in the Donatist controversy, he found time to write several other Biblical commentaries, composed his famous *Confessions* and engaged in epistelary debate with St. Jerome. By 411 Augustine was able to turn his attention to another heresy, since the State had taken upon itself the battle against Donatism, issuing several edicts against the sect. This now heresy was Pelagianism, which seemed to exaggerate man's role in salvation and deny original sin. When opposition against him mounted, Pelagius tried to defend himself by texts taken from Augustine's own work *On Free Will*. To which the Bishop replied promptly with a whole spate of works, pointing out that there was nothing in common between the two opinions. Pelagius was an extremely clever man and an able dialectician, perhaps more so on both accounts than Augustine himself. He seems to have forced Augustine into several questionable positions and it is no small wonder that most Protestant reformers and their theologies - which, as a rule, end to stress man's depravity and his weakness of will - turn to Augustine for inspiration. During this period of anti-Pelagian polemic, Augustine brought to conclusion one of his most famous works, the 15-book treatise *On the Trinity* (417), whose composition had started some 17 years earlier and began work on his celebrated *The City of God*, which would take him some 13 years to complete (426).

In 418, Augustine was able to rest a bit from his anti-Pelagian disputations, which brought about the condemnation of the heresy by Pope, Emperor and Council. But it was not long before he found himself constrained to clash swords with Julian, a local heretical Bishop. Another spate of books and pamphlets followed.

In 426, Augustine was persuaded that his end was not far off. Accordingly, he appointed a successor, or nominated him, rather, and the people acclaimed his choice. He kept on writing, however, the situation of the Empire steadily deteriorating all the while. Among his latter works were writings against the Arian heresy and his last (unfinished) treatise was a reply to a tract directed against him by Julian. Augustine died in 430, on August 28th, while the Vandals were laying siege to the Episcopal city of Hippo.

2.2.1.2. Sources

2.2.1.2.1. Primary Sources

As we have seen, the major part of Augustine's work consists of theological treaties and anti- heretical polemic. As such, they, do not concern us directly in a survey of Western Philosophy. We may single out a few texts, more general, and which touch upon more superlative themes. Such a list would have to include, naturally, his *Confessions* and *The City of God* of which there are a good number of excellent translations. Concerning the former, we may recommend that of Frank Sheed (London, 1943); as regards the latter there is the version of Vernon Bourke (New York, 1958), which includes an excellent introduction by Etienne Gilson. There is also the edition of R.H. Barrow, *Introduction to Augustine's City of God*, London 1950 (comprises main extracts with a running of commentary)

2.2.1.2.2. Secondary Sources

Here are an extremely select bibliography:

Vernon Bourke, *Augustine's Quest of Wisdom*, Milwaukee, 1944 (obviously a very old book, but an extremely good study of the evolution of Augustine's thought, his sincerity and honesty in seeking after the truth; by one of the greatest Augustinian authorities of all time)

Roy Battenhouse, *A Companion to the Study of St Augustine*, New York, 1955.

Mark Clark, *Augustine, Philosopher of Freedom*, New York, 1958 (Tries to exonerate Augustine from the charge of letting himself, in his opposition to Pelagius, diminish human freedom)

Jean Guitton, *The Modernity of St Augustine*, New York, 1959.

Etienne Gilson, *The Christian Philosophy of St. Augustine*, New York, 1960 (Excellent, as are all the books of Prof. Gilson)

Peter Brown, *Augustine of Hippo*, London, 1967.

R A Markus (editor) *Augustine, a series of Critical Essays*, New York, 1972

(Fr Copleston has six chapters - some 50 pages - on Augustine. The title of each chapter and the brief topic-wise summary will help you to choose relevant portion, as depending on your interest).

2.2.2. His Doctrine

2.2.2.1. Philosophy of Knowledge

2.2.2.1.1. The Quest for Truth

Augustine taught - as indeed his whole life exemplified - that knowledge or truth is to be relentlessly sought after, with courage, sincerity and honesty. This is so because that is what gives us happiness, beatitude. Only truth can give man this joy for it is the only object really worthy of his effort, the only goal capable of putting his restless person at rest. Yet Augustine would not go along with some moderns who hold that wisdom consists more in the seeking after Truth than in possessing it. Such was the view of the Academics and Augustine retorted that it is foolish to call a man wise, who does not know the truth. Later, he would see his quest for truth as basically a search for Christ, *the Truth* and avowed that it was the attraction of divine beauty which had lured him on, though he was unaware of it at the time. The famous phrase from the

Confessions should be read in this context: "Our hearts were made for you, O Lord, and oh, how weary they are, till they rest in you!" (L, 1)

2.2.2.1.2. Truth is attainable

We have already said that Augustine held that man attains happiness through wisdom and that man attains wisdom by attaining knowledge, i.e. he comes to Truth by attaining truths. He provided the classic refutation of Scepticism in his *Against the Academicians* with his famous *"si fallor sum"* argument (from where, obviously enough, Descartes got his *cogito).* Even a sceptic is bound to admit that he is certain of some truths - his own existence being one of these. After all, "even if I am in error, I exist". If you did not exist, you could not be deceived! (cf. his *On Free Will,* 2,3,7). And whether one were sleeping or dreaming or quite mad, it would still remain true that he existed! Apart from this, there are also mathematical truths of which we are certain. No one really wishes to say that seven plus three ought to make ten; he knows that they do make ten! Then the doubter is certain that he doubts! Finally, as regards the Sceptics' charge of the senses giving wrong information, he has a very sensible observation. The apparent contradiction arising from the fact of one person claiming that a certain bowl of water is hot, while another says it is cold is solved were one to assert that to him, the water **felt** cold while the other maintained that, to him, it **seemed** hot. No one could refute or challenge that!

2.2.2.1.3. Theory of Illuminations

That we can attain certainty never posed a real problem for St. Augustine; it was evident enough to him that we do so, inevitably and unconsciously. The problem that bothered him was more precisely the following: how does it come about that our minds finite, changing and fallible are able to attain necessary and eternal truths, truths which rule and govern the mind and transcend it? The answer to this question is to be found in his theory of divine illuminationism. We could not perceive and apprehend these immutable truths unless our minds were illuminated by God, the "intelligible light" in whom and by whom and through whom all those things which are luminous to the intellect. The origins of this theory are, of course, Platonic and go back to the passage in the *Republic,* where Plato compares, the Idea of the Good to the sun, the idea of the Good radiating the subordinate intelligible objects of ideas. In his treatise on *The Trinity,* he draws his simile to the full, making it very clear that, just as we require "corporeal light" to see corporal things - without in the process actually seeing this light - so too our intellect, the "spiritual eye" needs this "spiritual light" to see those spiritual and immutable truths, but does not see this light, in effect. The elements of necessity and eternity in the necessary and eternal truths (e.g. 3+7 are 10; the whole is greater than the part) are made visible to our mind by the activity of God.

2.2.2.2. Philosophy of God

2.2.2.2.1. Proof of God from Eternal Truths

The fact of the existence of these eternal truths provides St Augustine with his famous proof for God's existence from thought, that is from within, whereas Aquinas and the Scholastics, as a rule, prefer to start "from without" i.e. from the outside world. The starting point of the proof, then is these necessary and eternal truths 'which thou canst not call thine, or mine, but which (are) present to all and give themselves to all alike." *(On Free Will* 2, 12, 13). Such truths are superior to the mind, inasmuch as the mind finds itself constrained to accept them. It can neither modify nor reject them. Indeed, it finds that they existed before they were discovered by it. The mind varies in its understanding and apprehension of truth, grasping it now more clearly, now less so. Whereas these truths come from a Truth that ever remains the same. Now such eternal and unchanging truths must be founded in the Ground of all Truth itself, just as our human imaginations reflect our own changing, imperfect mind. In brief, if there is an intelligible sphere of absolute truths, this cannot be conceived without a Ground of truth, "the Truth, in whom, and by whom, and through whom those things are true which are true in every respect." *(Soliloquios* 1, 1,3)

Augustine has other "proofs" for God, beginning *ab extra,* but this one is so characteristic of him and his philosophy, that we have singled it out.

> the order and unity of Nature proclaims the unity of the Creator, just as the goodness of creatures, their positive reality, reveals the goodness of God and the order and stability of the universe manifest the wisdom of God. On the other hand, God, as the self-existent, eternal and immutable Being, is infinite, and, as infinite, incomprehensible. God is His own Perfection, is 'simple', so that His wisdom and knowledge, His goodness and power, therefore, transcends space in virtue of His spirituality and infinity and simplicity, as He transcends time in virtue of His eternity...[1]

2.2.2.2.2. Exemplarism

Plato had spoken of Ideas or Perfect Forms of all existing things which would exist, themselves, in some place "shinning with light" and which were the archetypes or models or exemplars from which individual existents were made. Augustine would put the eternal ideas *rationes* (reasons) in God's mind. He saw in Himself, for all eternity, as possible reflections of Himself in so many ways, the things he would create. He knew them before creation as they are in Him, as Exemplar, but He made them as they exist, i.e. as external and finite reflections of His divine essence. However, he would not have us imagine that

1 Frederick Copleston, S.J A History of Philosophy (Garden City. NY: Doubleday & Company Image Books, 1962 and later years). Vol.2, Part I, p.87.

this plurality of divine ideas introduce some sort of multiplicity in God and weaken His unity, nor do they involve any kind of change. They are "certain archetype forms or stable and unchangeable reasons of things, which were not themselves formed but are contained in the divine mind eternally and are always the same. They neither pass away nor arise, but whatever passes away or arises is formed according to them". *(On the Ideas,* 2)

2.2.2.3. Philosophy of the World

2.2.2.3.1. Free Creation out of Nothing

We have seen none of the Greek thinkers were able to conceive of free creation in the full sense of the word. God was no creator: at the most, he was a kind of artisan, giving form and order to some already existing shapeless and chaotic primitive matter. Plotinus tried to improve on this by suggesting an alternative understanding of cosmogenesis, which would underscore, more perfectly, the total dependence of the world on God - not only for its beginning, but also for its conservation. His theory of emanation did this - but at what expense! First, the world came to be, somehow or the other identified with God and secondly, the production of the world was not a free act but a necessity. He tried, it is true, to save the independence of God by saying that insofar as it was an internal necessity and not by a force from without, the divine autonomy was not diminished. Augustine, inspired by his Christian faith, taught that God created the world out of nothing - neither out of some pre-existing primitive stuff, nor as an overflow of his own nature - and did so in complete freedom, being necessitated neither by an external force nor some inner psychological or moral compulsion. All things owed - and still owe - their being to Him. Thus, Augustine showed how we could maintain the utter supremacy of God and the total dependence of the World on him. (Cf. *On Free Will* 3, 15, 42) He seems to have felt that he could find support from Plato and later Neo-Platonists for this view. This is contestable but, be that as it may, he certainly taught free creation in the fullest and clearest sense of the term.

2.2.2.3.2. A Theory of Evolution?

Augustine proposed an original and interesting understanding of creation which was rejected straight away by St. Thomas but which sounds very modern to us, nowadays. He suggested that when God created things, he didn't create them as finished products. Instead he created *rational seminales* (literally, seed-reasons), the germs of the things which were to develop in the course of time. Even man - at least, as far as his body was concerned - was created in the *rationes seminales,* "invisibly, potentially, casually in the way that things are made which are to be but have not yet been made." *(On the literal interpretation of Genesis,* 6, 5,8). Thus, the *rationes seminales* or germinal potentialities, as Copleston translates, are the germs of things; they are invisible powers, created by God in the beginning and left to slowly develop into the objects of various species. Actually, the idea was not so very original: the inspiration had obviously come from Plotinus and even then the term *rationes seminales* goes back to the Stoics. Let us note that the Augustinian *ratio seminalis* does not fall within the realm of sense-experience. It is invisible and has only an inchoate form, and has an active orientation to develop itself into its perfect form, though this development could be aided or hindered by external circumstances. What moved Augustine to think up and propose such a theory, which he did little to work out? Nothing more than a problem of exegesis! The book of *Ecclesiaticus (18:1)* declared that God "created all things together", whereas, according to Genesis fishes and birds appeared on the "fifth day" of creation, and cattle and other beast of the earth on the "sixth". How does one harmonise these two assertions? Obviously but holding that God created the *rationes seminales* of things together, but that the various species attained their full development at different times.

2.2.2.4. Philosophy of Man

2.2.2.4.1. Body and Soul

Man is seen by Augustine, after the biblical view, as the peak of material creation. The Platonic view of man still has its repercussions in him for, if he does not quite see the body as the immortal soul's prison, he will call it the soul's "instrument". He defines man as "a rational soul using a mortal and earthly body." *(Commentary on St. John,* 19, 5, 15) As a spiritual entity, the soul is superior to the body, and it is the province of the soul to rule the body. Advanced this may be - inasmuch as the body-soul relation is soon, at least in some way, as positive and useful - but that man is a psycho-physical organism is not held by the great African doctor.

2.2.2.4.2. Traducianism

Augustine wished to underline the absolute supra-materiality of the soul, the fact that it is, in every way, superior to the body. Hence, it could not develop out of the unfolding *rationes seminales.* But he was not quite sure as to just how and when it came into existence, though he was quite sure that this would be though a special act of God. For some time, he was inclined to accept the Platonic theory of pre-existing souls, but refused to go along with the view that it was locked up in the body-prison as the result of some fault committed in its pre-earthly condition. Such a view would seem to go against the teaching of Genesis about the Fall of our first parents. This story seemed to imply, for Augustine, that children, in some way, receive from their parents, not only their bodies but also their souls - for how else to explain the transmission of original sin, except through some genetic process? Thus, he proposed that the soul of a child is somehow "handed on" (traducianism) by the parents, God having created all souls in Adam. This theory seems to imply a somewhat materialistic view of the soul, no matter how one tries to refine it - for it implies that the soul is divisible and having parts is the characteristic of matter! Of course, Augustine never had the least intention of saying anything like that, but it is difficult to see how one is to avoid such a logical conclusion. Traducianism was condemned by Pope Aanastasius II in 498 and rejected again among various errors of the Armenians condemned by Benedict XII in 1341.

2.2.2.4.3. The Final Goal of Man

Augustine's ethics, in common with the typical Greek view, is eudaimonistic in character, i.e., it proposes as ultimate goal for human activity, happiness. However, for Augustine, this happiness is to be found only in God. Neither the Epicurean ideal - which places the supreme good of man in fulfilment of his body - nor the Stoic ideal - which finds peace and calm in virtuous resignation and "universal sympathy" (according to which, each part of the world has a sympathetic relation with every other) - can bring man the happiness he seeks.

> "It is not the virtue of thy soul that maketh thee happy, but he who hath given thee the virtue, who hath inspired thee to will, and hath given thee the power to be." -- (*Sermons*. 150,8,9).

2.2.2.4.4. Freedom and Grace

Augustinian ethics is, then, an ethics of love: it is by his will that man reaches out towards God and finally takes possession of and enjoys Him. Indeed, all man's striving - as Augustine discovered in his case - was nothing but an unconscious seeking for Him who alone can put our restless hearts at peace. This love is a dynamic love for it gives force and direction to our actions: *pondus meum, amor meus: illo feror, quocumque feror.*" (My love is my weight; where it goes I go.) Love is a gravitation toward that which is loved. However, man's will is free and thus, able to turn his will away from the immutable good and attach himself to mutable goods. Since he has no direct vision of God, man can - and does - turn his attention to perishable goods and cling to them in place of God. Now "this turning away and this turning to are not forced but voluntary actions.' *(Letters,* 140,21,14) All men are guilty when they turn away from God and His law to seek after perishable goods for they know the "rules of justice", having read them "in the book of that light which is called Truth." *(On the Trinity,* 14, 15,21) In other words, just as there is a kind of divine illumination which enables man to perceive eternal speculative truths, there is also an illumination which helps him to perceive eternal moral or practical truths. God's help, grace, is required for man to be able to attain God by reaching out to Him by fulfilling His Law. "When man tries to live justly by his own strength without the help of the liberating grace of God, he is then conquered by sins: but in free will he has it in his power to believe in the Liberator and to receive grace."

2.2.2.4.5. Evil

A reflection on Plotinus provided Augustine with his refutation of Manichaeism and a kind of definition of evil which would be picked up and developed by the Scholastics. As Plotinus had pointed out, evil is not, in itself, a being: it is a privation, an absence of a due perfection, a kind of non-being. As such, it needs no creator, for a creator makes **being** and so evil does not require somebody to create it! Thus, Augustine was able to do away with the Manichaean idea of a 'bad principle' who would create evil. Nor should we, as an alternative have to say that the good principle, the Creator - God, made evil. Evil is nothing positive in itself and so is not created or made, as such.

2.2.2.4.6. The Two Cities

Augustine goes on to project the struggle between good and evil which takes place within the heart of man, due to his free-will, to society at large. The whole human race can be divided, then, into two camps, at war with each other. There are those who love God more than themselves and there are those who love themselves more than God. And the history of man comes about-by the reaction and struggle that goes on between these two camps. Augustine prefers to call them two cities, respectively, the City of Jerusalem, and the City of Babylon. "Let each one question himself as to what we loveth; and he shall find of which (city) he is citizen." *(Commentary on the Psalms,* 64, 2) Though there are many texts that indicate that Augustine had identified the Catholic Church with the City of-Jerusalem and the State - especially the pagan State - with the City of Babylon, he does not make such an overly simplistic distinction. He explains that an Emperor, a civic or military official could, in reality, belong to the City of Jerusalem if "he has his heart above," whereas a member of the Church could be as much belonging to the City of Babylon if his heart is below, filled with self-love. "Let us not therefore despair of the citizens of the kingdom of heaven when we see them engaged in the affairs of Babylon (i.e., temporal administration of the State), doing something terrestrial in a terrestrial republic; nor again let us forthwith congratulate all men whom we see engaged in ecclesiastical matters, for even the sons of pestilence sit sometimes in the seat of Moses ... But there will come a time of winnowing when they will be separated, the one from the other with the greatest care." *(Comm. on the Psalms,* 51, 6)

2.2.2.4.7. The Church-State Relationship

A society, according to Augustine, is "a multitude of rational creatures associated in a common agreement as to the things which it loves." *(The City of God* 19, 24) It follows, then, that if the things it loves are good, a society will be a good society and if the things it loves are bad, it will be a bad society. That the State, certainly the pagan State, is bad, seems quite clear to Augustine. Pagan Rome did not give God His due place and worship; more than that, she tried to prevent Christians from doing so. The Pagan State in the eyes of Augustine, is not founded on justice, but on force. As such, it cannot make of men good citizens. Only the Christian State can, for it is only Christianity can make men good. A State, left to itself, can only be informed by love of this world. It can however be informed by higher principles, principles which it can derive from Christianity. It is the role of the Church, then, to inform the State with its celestial principles of conduct; such is its mission as leaven of the earth. The Church, as the only perfect society on earth, is superior to the State. The Church must give to the State its principles and is in no way inferior to it. It is not even on an equal par with it.

2.2.3. Some Critical Remarks

2.2.3.1. Augustine's Philosophy of Knowledge

2.2.3.1.1. The Quest for Truth

Augustine's intellectual honesty and his willingness to take risks in order to come to the truth, the story of his long and devious pilgrimage cannot but impress. We may even be reminded of Gandhiji's oft-quoted statement to the effect that denial of God we have known, but no denial of truth and so for him Truth is God. Augustine's language of seeking and striving after the Truth, the description of the anguish and risk that characterise this pilgrimage, have won him a wide popularity among many an existentialist writer. There are even some who would call him the first of their school. Yet, one cannot overlook a certain fanaticism in his views when he so identifies Wisdom with Christianity and all too easily seems to consign everyone who knows it not to the exterior darkness.

2.2.3.1.2. An Answer to the Sceptics

Augustine's *si fallor, sum,* and his other reflections that bring to light the number of truths that the sceptic has overlooked in his thesis, have provided the basis for all future responses to this objection and, at the same time, presented the starting-point for a positive epistemology. Descartes was far more indebted to him than he cared to admit and had he taken better note of Augustine's observations about sense-knowledge, he would have been all the richer for it.

2.2.3.1.3. Illuminationism

Illuminationism is a plausible theory. It explains the facts, contains no contradictions and cannot be disproved - like any good theory. Still, Augustine, with a convert's excessive zeal, has sought once again to bring in God to explain something which could equally well have been accounted for without having to postulate a special divine intervention. The Aristotelian theory of abstraction explains equally well all the facts and contains no inherent contradictions. Why not accept preferably a theory which does not have to call for supernatural explanations to account for everyday things when such can be found? The principle of subsidiarity has a universal application!

2.2.3.2. Augustine's Philosophy of God

2.2.3.2.1. Proof of God from Eternal Truths

Our response to this clever and original "proof" would be along the same lines as our reaction to Augustine's theory of illuminationism. There are other theories which explain the origin of those truths plausibly enough - as the Aristotelian- Thomist theory of abstraction - and which do not necessarily lead us to recognise the hand of a Divine Being in all this. Marechal would later, starting from Kant's initial insights, develop a more detailed and carefully worked out analysis of the act of direct judgement (which, as such, is not a purely *ab intra* approach) and discover, at the end of a long road, not so much the Ground of all Truth, as the Ground of all Being.

2.2.3.2.2. Exemplarism

Augustine was the first of a long line of Christian thinkers who would put Plato's Ideal Forms into God's mind, where they would serve as the Exemplars of creation. Augustine, however, never felt obliged to assume from this that God created things as finished products, direct copies of these Ideas. He was able to think out a much more dynamic understanding of creation (cf. the *rationes seminales).*

2.2.3.2.3. Free Creation

Augustine was the first to see how to explain the divine origin of the world in a way that would impair neither the transcendence of God nor the vital dependence of the world on him. Previous thinkers had managed to save the transcendence of God by postulating some kind of demiurge working on previously existent matter, his sole contribution being putting order and shape into chaos. Or, they proposed some kind of emanation which, though it brought out the total dependence of creation on God, did so at the cost of his transcendence and freedom of action. Augustine, with his characteristic sharpness of vision and creative insight, saw a way out of the impasse. Other Christian thinkers would but perfect and develop his original intuition.

2.2.3.2.4. Evolutionism

A minor problem in exegesis led Augustine to make another creative breakthrough in cosmogenesis. His dynamic theory of the *rationes seminales,* though it owed a lot to Stoic thought, is once again eloquent testimony to his rich and creative approach to intellectual challenges. But this idea was never really worked out by him or integrated into his entire vision, so we cannot blame too strongly the people who came after him and ignored this intuition as, probably, an all too human lapse into the eccentricity that we may allow to one whose mind is so fertile and imaginative. It was only rather recently when evolutionism came under fire that some of its champions capitalised on the unexpected discovery that they had an ally in the great and orthodox African doctor of the patristic period, Augustine! Be that as it may, we should not exaggerate the place of this theory in Augustine's thought. After all, it was little more than a passing reference and, in fact, is a very much mitigated theory of evolution, although it did anticipate Darwin by almost 1500 years! And it is a far cry from Teilhard's all-inclusive vision.

2.2.3.3. Augustine's Philosophy of Man

2.2.3.3.1. Body and Soul

Augustine's conception of man is, more than Plato's with regard to his attitude to the body. But is the promotion of the body from the soul's prison to its instrument so much progress, after all? Man remains essentially a soul. The body is a useful appendage that he has: that's all! There is little to explain how the "ghost in the machine" works and how the organic unity of the composite is achieved. And then there are several texts that make it obvious that he too was, like Plotinus, very much ashamed of having a body. The fact that he considers that married couples sin venially when they perform the conjugal act for what he calls "carnal reasons" and without explicitly desiring that it be ordained to the production of offspring, shows a very narrow understanding of the role of the body in personal growth. Psychologically, such a view is understandable: a convert has a tendency to let the pendulum swing to the other extreme. The markedly rigid and stern attitude of some Protestant sects with regard to the body and simple pleasures derives, to a great extent, from Augustine (whose influence can be discerned behind almost every Protestant reformer, by the way). And we are very much aware of the effects of such a view on Catholic spirituality, too!

2.2.3.3.2. Traducianism

St. Augustine has played a leading part in the thinking that led to the formulation of the dogma of original sin, as laid down by the Council of Trent. That he had a very impersonal and legalistic view of the matter is evident from the theory of traducianism which he advocated to explain its transmission. The "stain" of original sin was something passed on mechanically from parent to child along with various other genes. Did he not realise that "sin" involves a personal decision and can't be related to the level of chromosomes? How was it that he could, without being filled with revolt, speak of a loving God who would visit upon succeeding generations the guilt of some mysterious crime of an untraceable ancestor? And to the extent of excluding un- baptised babies from heaven, since they died without having the "stain" of original sin removed from them? Perhaps he did feel somewhat shocked at God's punishing them for a guilt that was not personally theirs and that is why he held that tiny little babies (even before birth!) could commit sin. In this way he felt, no doubt, that God would look less unjust and petty, since the poor little things could be branded wicked sinners. Happily, few theologians would go along with his theory of Limbo and the dogma of original sin and its transmission is being given a much more personal (and biblical) interpretation!

2.2.3.3.3. Man's End

If Augustine wanted to strike a decisive blow at the hedonism and materialism of his times - a characteristic of all societies that are marked with a sense of decay (the "barbarian hordes" were knocking at the doors of every outpost of the once proud Roman Empire) - he rather overdid the job. "Let Thales depart with his water, Anaximenes with the air, the Stoics with their fire, Epicurus with his atoms." *(The City of God,* VIII, 5) All these were materialists. Plato alone was not. Aristotle was inferior to Plato, though far above the rest. To throw out everyone else in the name of materialism, was to exclude all those whose views might be a healthy corrective to the extremes of a certain interpretation of Platonism. According to Augustine, then, every atheist's views are suspect and it is difficult to see him as other than insincere and evil, which was the unofficial view in Church circles till very recently, anyway.

2.2.3.3.4. Freedom and Grace

Not a few writers have tried to make a point in favour of St. Augustine as a philosopher of freedom (cf. our bibliography). But the wily Pelagius forced Augustine into so many awkward statements that it would seem that one has to deny freedom to make room for God's grace. Which is what many early Lutheran theologians did, following their leader who claimed to take his cues from Augustine. When Jansenism - a more recent form of the typically pessimistic and morbid ethics wedded to an awesome picture of mankind as a heap of sinners in the grasp of an angry God who saves a few elect souls and consigns the majority to hell - grew up in 17 and 18c. France, once again, it found inspiration in Augustine's anti-Pelagian writings.

2.2.3.3.5. Evil

Once again, this time, in his reflection on the nature of evil, Augustine came up with a valuable and interesting insight. His definition of evil as a privation of a perfection, as a relative non-being, was something that later thinkers would come back to, time and again. Not only St. Thomas Aquinas would make use of this insight, but even a modern like Leibniz, who devoted such a great portion of his thought to wrestling with this issue, expressed indebtedness to Augustine.

2.2.3.3.6. The Two Cities

Shortly after the Council, when a lot of thought was being given to dialogue with the World, many Christian thinkers - such as Michael Novak and Harvey Cox - pointed out that the Church had developed a "siege mentality" that stemmed from the "Two Cities" approach of Augustine. Augustine had encouraged the Church to take a very negative attitude to the "world" (as if it were something apart from her) and to see it mainly as something to battle against. It was not long before those thinkers observed, the Church felt herself outnumbered and withdrew to the sanctuary, occasionally issuing forth Jeremiads and calls to unity. She hardly ever tried to really "dialogue" with the "world". And even when, during the Council, she tried to change this attitude, there were not a few who felt she was betraying her identity and role. If Augustine did not make a simplistic "Church=City-of -God" and "The-rest=City-of- the-Devil" distinction (as we have shown in the notes), he certainly made it easy for such an interpretation to develop out of his writings. And one might well question his hasty generalisation about "pagan States" as being inherently incapable of building up a just society.

2.2.3.3.7. Church-State Relationships

Augustine's view of this thorny question is typically theocratic - and this remained the Catholic view for a very long time. Indeed, many a Bishop (and Pope) made good use of this understanding to advance his imperialistic ambitions which had little do with his Christian and responsibility. The reformers, having rejected Church authority and finding that they needed some other force to control the "liberated" peasantry, transferred to the State all the authority the Church had claimed - plus some more (cf. the notes on Luther and Calvin, later). The furore that the preparation, voting and reception of the document on *Religious Freedom (Dignitatis Humanae)* stirred up at Vatican II is a good indication as to how Augustine's paternalistic understanding of the problem still has its mark on the Church today.

2.2.4. General Conclusion

2.2.4.1. A Man alive to his Times

The early Church stood in great need of an outstanding thinker to help her understand and express the experience of faith. And Augustine, who had known first-hand some of the best thinkers and philosophies of his time, was a veritable God-send. His gift for writing, his deeply sensitive soul and his rich mind, at once synthetic and creative, he put to good use for a Cause to which he committed himself completely. He was very much alive to his times and its problems and never hesitated to throw himself into the thick of the fray. The struggles he had had to face as a youth gave him a deep insight into the upheavals and uncertainties of his time. Coupled to all this was the fact that he was, first and foremost, a mystic and a saint. In all this, Augustine was a great and providential blessing for the infant Church.

2.2.4.2. A Mixed Blessing

We have suggested that he was not an unmixed blessing, but that is scarcely his fault! In our glimpse of his life, we have brought out carefully how so many of his writings have a polemic slant. This was necessary, at the time, but polemic writings always constitute a danger as Hans Kung so ably points out. They concentrate on reacting to and refuting an extreme view. Hence, they develop and underline only one aspect of an idea. For instance, Augustine was obliged, in his anti-pelagian works, to stress the role of grace and said little about man's free will. A polemic work is, naturally, biased and one-sided. There is a danger, then, in trying to build a system out of the views assembled in polemic writings. Augustine may never have tried to do that, but that is just what his disciples did and the official Church relied too heavily upon "Augustinianism" in the formulation of her doctrine on grace and sin. It is not so much that something was wrong with what was said in all this: it was a question of a tremendous lot being left unsaid and unsaid for too long a time. It is very easy to conclude that Augustine had a morbid and negative vision of man and his possibilities when, in reality, he was only trying to show, against Pelagius, that man needs grace (however he defined it!) in order to be saved. He wanted to bring out the fact that salvation is a free gift of God's love, not something we merit by our achievements. But the controversy with his clever opponent forced him to appear to say much more than that. And so, for many other disputes that were part of his writing activity!

> Late have I loved Thee,
> O Beauty so ancient and so new;
> late have I loved Thee!
> For behold Thou wert within me, and I outside;
> and I sought Thee outside!
> (Augustine, *Confessions)*

2.3. The Formation of Scholasticism (7c–12c)

2.3.1. Introductory

2.3.1.1. “Scholasticism”

“Scholasticism” is a term which generally designates the dominant doctrinal movement in the western or Latin Middle Ages. The origin of the word denotes that a “Scholastic” was, originally, a master teaching in a school. During the long period that spans the seventh and twelfth centuries, the Christian West developed an ensemble of doctrines which interpreted the universe in the light of reason and in a manner coherent with the basic biblical vision (at least, as it was currently understood). This is not unusual, since the only schools at the time were monastic (annexed to the Benedictines abbeys) or episcopal (established at the cathedrals) and the masters who taught there were, as a rule, monks or priests. At first these “schools” were public, but as the civil arm began to come of age and take up the education of the people, the monastic “schools” came to be reserved to the monks. The episcopal schools, on the other hand, became more numerous and powerful till, in the XI and XII centuries they were having quite an important influence on European thought and culture.

2.3.1.2. One or Many Scholasticisms?

The use of the term “Scholasticism” should not make us think that there grew up one single system: there were many scholastic authors, whose views differed very widely and each of the major teachers acquired quite a devoted and staunch following. Yet, there was still a certain basic unity behind all this evident diversity that might justify grouping them all under a single common name. First, they made use of the same method and language. At the time, all learned men and philosophers, be they Churchmen or not, spoke Latin - the international language of thinkers and this made for ready and easy interchange and discussion. As regards the method, it shunned all pretence of oratory and preferred the direct method, favoured by the deductive approach and the unadorned syllogism. Second, it looked for inspiration to Greco-Roman philosophy, though it did not merely repeat what Plato and Aristotle had said, but sought to re- think their views and, in effect, was pretty original in all this. Finally, it was consciously subservient to Christian Faith. It was called the "hand-maid of theology" *(ancilla theologiae)* and was proud to be so. At first, when the demarcation between philosophy ("reason") and theology ("faith") was not so precise, as for instance at the time of St. Augustine, there was much intermingling of Scholastic Philosophy and Scholastic Theology. Due to the distinction made and developed by St. Thomas Aquinas, it became more evident that we had two obviously separate disciplines.

2.3.1.3. Scholasticism Today

When the word is used today, it usually means one of the systems of "Christian Philosophy" officially approved and encouraged by the Church and whose roots go back to the Middle Ages and which is taught in seminaries to candidates for the Catholic priesthood. Papal documents have, as a rule, favoured Thomism (the Scholastic synthesis of Thomas Aquinas) or Neo- Thomism (its updated variety as developed by mainly French speaking Catholic intellectuals, priests and laymen, of our century - e.g. Cardinal Mercier, Joseph Marechal SJ, Jacques Maritain, Etienne Gilson). But there are other Scholastic systems such as Augustinianism and Scotism (from the Franciscan John Duns Scotus, 1266-1308).

2.3.1.4. Precursors of Scholasticism

The barbaric invasions, that devastated the already decadent Roman civilisation towards the end of Augustine's life and continued till way into the sixth century had so upset Western society that it took almost yet another century to re-establish enough equilibrium to be able to come back to sound philosophical and cultural development. Non-Christian thinkers, such as the Arabs and Jews, who had kept in touch with the West, played as much a formative role in all this as some Christian intellectuals. The Muslims were perhaps the most influential. Their warriors (and merchants) penetrated almost all of Europe and their philosophers furnished the future Scholastics with their first full-fledged translations and commentaries on the works of Aristotle. That is how it came about that this era would be more marked by Aristotelianism.

2.3.2. Sources

As regards the bibliography of this period, there are several manuals that treat, in a general way (and very comprehensively) of the contribution of Islamic and Jewish thinkers to the formation of medieval thought in Christian Europe. In addition, we have some of the ore important works of these men (the Arabian philosophers are mostly in French translation, though).

As regards the Islamic philosophers mentioned, the following may be noted as being books worth reading. There are others - you can consult the library cards under Avicenna, Alghazali and Averroes, if you are interested.

M. Goichon, *The Philosophy of Avicenna and its Influence on Medieval Europe*, (trans. M.S. Khan), Delhi 1969.

Soheil M. Afran, *Avicenna, His Life and Works*, London 1958.

Montgomery Watt, *Muslim Intellectual: A Study of Al-Ghazali*, Edinburgh, 1963 (A sympathetic and interesting study of the theologian and mystic whom many of his co-religionists consider "the greatest Muslim after Mohammed" which also treats of the general and allied question of the role and intellectual in a scientifically - minded pragmatic world)

There are two extremely thorough as scholarly accounts of Jewish Philosophy which deserve special mention.

Julius Guttram, *Philosophies of Judaism*, (trans by David Silvermen) New York, 1963 (A classic; spans from Biblical Times to Franz Rosezweig - obviously includes a study of Maimonides)

Zvi Cahn, *The Philosophy of Judaism*, New York, 1962.

We also have several editions of Maimonides' *The Guide of the Perplexed*. The best is probably that of the University of Chicago Press, 1964. The translation by Shlorne Pines and includes copious notes and an introduction. There is also a kind of bonus introductory essay by Leo Strams.

We have the works of Boethius and the Pseudo-Dionysius (in Latin!). Of these there is a good edition of Boethius' *On the Consolation of Philosophy*, which is worth consulting. It is an abridged copy and is ably presented by 1. Buchanan (New York 1964).

2.3.3. Three Muslims...

The Syrians - Nestorian Christians or Edessa - were the first to translate a considerable number of Greek philosophical works into their tongue (c. 450); these translations concerned mainly the works of Aristotle, but not a few commentaries were also included. When the Caliphs of Baghdad summoned Syrian scholars to their Court; one of these, Henain Ben Isaac, translated the Syriac Aristotle into Arabic. Thus it was a second-version - the translation of a translation - that the first Arabic scholars had of Aristotle and it was this second-hand translation that would provide the basis for a further translation that would hand on to the West! At any rate, as with the Scholastics, there was a great divergence in views among the Islamic philosophers, but some basic characteristics give them a kind of unity. They were all unbended in their respect and admiration for Aristotle. They all unconsciously misrepresented and deformed his views - this was due partly to the inaccurate second-hand translations that served them as their source- material, together with the admitted ambiguities in Aristotle himself. Apart from this, they were very much influenced by several Neo-Platonic writings and interpretations of the Stagyrite then current. Finally, like the Christians would attempt later, they too tried to make their philosophy subservient to, and in harmony with, Scripture - in this case, the Koran. The first great thinkers in this line were the encyclopaedists Alkindi (died 873) and Alfarabi (died 950). They set a trend for future Arab thinkers by seeing in philosophy a means to correct and purify their religious faith or errors. Thus, in the long run, they give the priority to philosophy, not Scripture.

2.3.3.1. Avicenna

His real name was Iban Sina and he was born in 980 at Bokhara in Persia. A precocious genius, he mastered the sciences - especially medicine - and devoured all of Aristotle at an early age. He began writing at the age of 21 and then on but deepened his basic vision through his works. He served under various Sultans and, on account of his busy life, had to do most of his writing at night. He died in 1036, leaving behind him as may philosophical treatises as works on medicine.

As a general principle, Avicenna held that truth is One and so there could be no real contradictions in philosophy. As a consequence, he sought to harmonise Plato and Aristotle, being assured that there could be no real differences between their points of view. Besides, the revelations of the Koran could hardly be at variance with philosophy either. In working out all these harmonies, he came up with his theory of hierarchy of beings and of causes.

As to the hierarchy of beings, he divided the universe into three orders. The lowest order is that of the terrestrial world, whose summit is the human soul. Next comes the celestial world at whose apex is the "first cause". Then comes God who presides over all as supreme.

In explaining the make-up of the terrestrial world, Avicenna is a faithful Aristotelian. Act and potency, matter and form, the four causes and the ten predicaments - all the Stagyrite's metaphysical and logical equipment he presses into use. As to the human intellect, he offers some original thinking, separating it into the active and passive intellect (as Aristotle had done, but making of the distinction a real separation). Within the passive intellect, he distinguishes as many as five levels of potency, each of which demands the influence of an Active Intellect to be brought to act. He held that this Active Intellect is quite separate from the human intellect, that it belongs to the celestial sphere and is man's link with it. In it are the ideas and through it man is able to think. Through his intelligence, then, man is able to detach himself from the body and break through to the celestial world. As to the human soul, Avicenna held that it had an identity of its own and was not to be identified with the Active Intellect. It is spiritual and immortal. In itself, it is simple, indivisible and a complete spiritual substance, (as Plato taught). With reference to its body, the soul is its form, as Aristotle taught. Thus, though very vaguely and clumsily, he reconciled Aristotle and Plato on the soul and saved its personal immortality and refuted transmigration, all as the Koran taught. As to the Celestial World, Avicenna found inspiration in explaining it, as much in Aristotle's metaphysics as in Ptolemy's astronomy. The heavens consist of a series of crystal spheres into whose transparent forms are fixed the various planets and stars, the turning of these spheres explaining the movement of the heavenly bodies across the sky. The revolution of the spheres is accounted for by the fact that each one is provided with an intelligence that sets them in motion. Since Aristotle's God could not be considered as doing things like creating and taking care of the universe (since this would mar his perfection and transcendence) and since Islam would admit of no other God to account for the origin of the universe, but a very perfect intellect who would be uniquely occupied in contemplating God. This intelligence is the "first cause", summit of the celestial world. This intelligence is active at three levels: it knows and contemplates God, it knows itself as possible and it knows itself as having been created. Consequent upon this, it produces three things; the first celestial sphere, which it animates; the soul of this celestial sphere and finally a second, Intelligence, distinct and separate from itself. This latter, it turns, has three similar activities and corresponding productions and creates, finally, a third separated Intelligence. This process goes on until we come to the Active Intellect which moves the last celestial sphere - that of the moon - which immediately surrounds the earth. The Active Intellect, the last of the separate intelligence is creative and produces human souls and terrestrial bodies.

With respect to God, he is viewed in the Aristotelian fashion as pure actuality, first mover and necessary being, where existence is called for by the fact of contingent beings in the world.

2.3.3.2. Algazel

If Avicenna exemplifies the alleged Aristotelian temperament, then Algazel (1058-1111) illustrates the Platonic, mystical cast of mind. He was born in Tus, in Persia, and though he studies law and philosophy under excellent teachers, his mystico-religious character set him against such "worldly" disciplines. After a brief and brilliant career as a teacher at Bagdad, he gave himself up to prayer and contemplation. He served in various mosques, made the pilgrimage to Mecca, taught a little more and died at his native Tus.

With this background we should not be surprised to learn that his major work the *Ihya or Revivification of Religious Sciences* is still the peak of orthodox Islam and that his main philosophical work is called *The Destruction of Philosophers* and is directed against Avicenna and his school. He is a kind of mystical sceptist, holding that the only way to harmonise faith and reason is to hold that the latter cannot attain truth by itself and that man can only do so by opening himself to mystic illumination. For Algazel, the sole valid "proof' of truth was the authority of the Koran. Since he saw Avicenna's theses on the eternity and necessity of creation as an undermining of the sovereignty of God, he attacked such views saying that they involve ridiculous contradictions. He also taught a type of occasionalism - i.e. he held that creatures don't really act as agents in the full sense of the word: they are more occasions for God to act through them. He saw God as acting in almost complete disregard of the merits and wishes of creatures, in a very arbitrary manner and was instrumental in giving to Islam much of its spirit of fatalism and predestinationalism.

2.3.3.3. Averroes

The violence of Algazel's anti-philosophical polemic, coupled with the force of his person and reputation, effectively put an end to all philosophical activity in Eastern Arabia, for quite some time. Thus, the next great Islamic thinker was a man who grew up in Cordoba, in occupied Spain, Ibn Roschd or Averroes (1126-1198). At the beginning of his career, Ibn Roschd quite enjoyed the favour of the Spanish caliphs, but his disrespectful views of the Koran earned him the disfavour of a later ruler. He was accordingly sent into exile where he died.

He resembles Avicenna in many ways and was even a physician like him. His major work was *The Destruction of the Destruction,* purporting to be a refutation of Algazel.

Averroes wrote some important commentaries on Aristotle, which were pretty influential among Scholastics. These were not unmixed with the usual Neo-Platonist accretions common to Arabian thinkers. But he added some elements uniquely his own, elements which concern some obscure aspects of Aristotle.

He argues for the necessary eternity of creation plus the fact that the concentric spheres, together with their indwelling intelligence owe nothing to God as to their origin. They coexist with him and are co-eternal with him. But they are neither created by him nor emanated from him.

More faithful to Aristotle than the Koran, he denies all providence. God knows himself perfectly and this knowledge is enough for him. He knows naught of the world, nor needs to (cf. God as 'Thinking about Thought'- in Aristotle). Natural laws, not providence, govern the world.

Avicenna has postulated a separate Active Intellect. Averroes would have it that the Passive Intellect is equally separate. At least in its superior form, it is perfectly spiritual and one and the same for all men. The lower soul, source of man's vegetative and sensitive life is many and in union with matter!

Finally, he proposed an unusual - to say the least - manner of reconciling reason with faith by his theory of the three orders. Such a theory was necessary, since many of his ideas were in flagrant contradiction with the Koran. According to him then, there are three distinct orders of truth which are quite impervious to each other. Thus, the Koran, though it is addressed to all men, can be interpreted according to the three orders as follows. In the vulgar level, that meant for the common people, there is the obvious or literal sense. This is the area of faith and by way of proof oratory is used. Then there is the mystical order: this is for the theologian. Mystical interpretations are to be aimed at and proofs are to be based on probables. Finally, there is the area of science. This is for the philosopher and here the true meaning is to be discovered by the help of scientific demonstration. In the event of conflict, science must prevail and faith is to be given an allegorical interpretation.

Those three meanings are not always harmonisable. One should not worry about this. Averroes holds, each one should be happy with the level or order of truth which is proportionate to him. Thus, all heresies and difficulties are resolved.

2.3.3.4. Some Critical Remarks

One cannot but be disappointed by the two extreme attitudes taken by the Islamic thinkers. If Algazel was anti-intellectual and fideist, Averroes would be violently rationalist and anti-faith. The attempt to harmonise to apparently conflicting views cannot be achieved by a sheer denial of one of those. That is a too easy way out. Most regrettable is Averroes' theory of the three orders of truth. Such a view encourages all manner of dishonesty and superficial eclecticism. Avicenna has a much more balanced approach and argues for the unity of Truth. But his system is as fragile and ambiguous as it is attractive and leaves much unsaid.

2.3.4. …One Jew…

Aristotle's work revived Jewish intellectual activity, dormant since Philo. Thus, the Stagyrite had an impact on all three religions that grew out of the Old Testament. The first really great Jewish thinker, whose writings were to play an important part on the formation of Scholasticism was Avicebren (Salomon Ibn Gabriel) who lived about 1021-1070 in Spain. His *Fons Vitae,* which was widely discussed by the XIII c. Scholastics advocate Aristotle's hylemorphism plus an emanationistic explanation of the origin of the world, obviously enough influenced by Plotinus and the other Neo-Platonists. Jewish rationalism was given an even greater development by Maimonides in the XII c. and his work was even more influential in the making of the Scholastic mind.

2.2.4.1. Moses Maimonides

"Rabbi Moses", as St. Thomas called him, was born at Cordoba in Spain into a family of fervent Jews in 1135 and died in 1204 in Cairo, having had to flee

Moorish Spain, which was no longer a hospitable place neither for Jews nor for philosophers (which made him a marked man on two counts). What with the persecutions that they had to face from Muslim and Christian alike plus their rationalistic difficulties with the Bible, many of his coreligionists were losing their faith and it was to restore this faith that Maimonides dedicated himself with much success. To this end he composed several treatises, particularly his *Guide to the Perplexed,* a veritable *Summa* of Jewish theology which, since it was addressed to mature theologians, was much less didactic than Thomas Aquinas corresponding work. Like his Muslim counterparts, Maimonides held that there was a necessary harmony between faith and philosophy - i.e., between the revelations transmitted through Moses and wisdom as developed by Aristotle. In case of conflict, reason seems to have the primary since it was the duty to explain, though it cannot contradict, revelation. In any case, contradictions are to be resolved by allegorical interpretations of the Bible. For we must hold fast to what is given us by sense-perception or can be strictly demonstrated by the intellect. Many Jews felt that he was going a bit too far in his attempts to rationalise their faith and some French Jews even tried to get the Inquisition to quash his "heresies"!

Maimonides assembles proofs for God's existence, taken from Aristotle and from Avicenna. He invites us to reflect on the attributes or names we ascribe to God, in many ways reminding us of the *De divinis nominibus* of the Pseudo-Dionysius. In the first place, he points out that we must not take literally the anthropomorphic descriptions of God given in the Old Testament, as for instance, "jealous" and "angry". He went a step further in this to add that we know rather what God is not, than what he is. He is of the view that we can assert nothing of God's real Nature. To call him "Wise" or "Life" would mean no more than to say he is the cause of these perfection in creatures. Other titles or names, such as eternal, merely express that God does not possess some perfection as do creatures; for instance, "eternal" merely means that there is absence of time in God (though this is present in creatures). We shall see how Thomas Aquinas would disagree with Maimonides and say that when we say God is Life or Wisdom, we actually say something about his very Nature. Finally, Maimonides said we could attribute to God only titles that concern his action on the world - such as Creator, Provident and so on - since they designate him as unknowable cause of the world under various aspects. Like Aristotle, he will say that God is Pure Thought, perfectly knowing Himself.

The Rabbi also taught a kind of restricted immortality, reserved only to philosophers and saints. He accepted Avicenna's theory of degrees and concluded that spirituality is only proper to the two higher levels of intelligence. Since only the philosopher and the saint attain this level of intelligence, only they can know life after death. This immortality is, however, impersonal: it involves the ultimate absorption of the intelligence concerned into the Active

Intellect. He added that there would be, eventually, a special resurrection of all other men (the non-saints and non- philosophers!) but said that this was an article of faith.

In the sphere of morality, he attempted to make use of Aristotelian logic to account for the many prescriptions put forward by Moses. He tried to give a kind of rational explanation to justify the great number of prescriptions of the Mosaic Law.

2.3.4.2. Some Critical Remarks

Moses Maimonides made a far better job of reconciling faith and reason than had either Avicerron or the Muslims. Aquinas was perhaps not as alert to the greatness of the Jew's insights as he should have been, but that is understandable given his intellectualism. Not that the Rabbi, himself, was able to break away from that intellectualism that characterises Aristotle and Greek thought in general. For instance, he too defined God as Pure Thought, perfectly knowing himself (rather than as Love). But then even Thonnard finds this a "beautiful view".

2.3.5.... And Two Christians

Apart from Muslim and Jewish philosophers, all of whom championed Aristotle in the attempt to reconcile philosophy with their faith, there were also a few Christians who prepared the way for the full blossoming of Scholasticism in the centuries just after the fall of the Roman Empire. We signal out just two: the pseudo-Dionysius in the East and Boethius in the West.

2.3.5.1. The Pseudo-Dionysius

In the fifth century, there appeared a number of works on mystical theology, purporting to have been written by a certain "Dionysius the Presbyter, to his fellow-presbyter Timothy", as the exordium to one of the works had it. It was assumed that this was none other than Dionysius the Areopagite, St. Paul's Athenian convert (cf. Act 17:34). Naturally, a lot of weight was attached to the corpus and the writings were referred to in many a doctrinal controversy and enjoyed considerable esteem in the East where as late as the eight century we find St. John Damascene appealing to them. It soon became obvious that they dated from a much later period in history and were an attempt to reconcile Christianity with a rather developed version of Neo-Platonism. It is not possible to identify the actual author, though various names have been proposed. Hence, by common consent, he is referred to as the Pseudo-Dionysius. The most famous of all these works is the treatise *On the Divine Names.* The others are *The Celestial Hierarchy, On Mystical Theology* and *The Ecclesiastical Hierarchy.*

2.3.5.1.1. His Thought

With regard to the giving of names or attributes of God, the Pseudo-Dionysius provided the classic method of the three ways. There is first the positive way or the way of affirmation *(via affirmationis)* which consists of affirming of God all perfections found in creatures which are compatible with his spiritual Nature, such as goodness or wisdom. Some creaturely perfections which involve materiality, such as height and extension, are obviously incompatible with the spiritual nature of God and so cannot be affirmed of him according to this way. Next, we must make use of the negative way, the *via nagationis,* according to which we exclude from God all the imperfections that are involved in creatures. Thus, he is not Life in the sense of our vegetative and sensitive life (which involve certain imperfections tied up with matter). Finally, we must also use the way of eminences, the *via eminentiae,* whereby we add that the God does not merely possess life or wisdom in a superior degree than we, but the it is of a qualitatively superior kind. Thus, we should say that he is super-essential Life or super-essential Wisdom. Careful attention to all this would show that ultimately the Pseudo-Dionysius emphasises what is known as a negative theology, that is, he holds that we can more easily say what God is not, rather than what he is. Finally, we told that when we apply to God terms such as "rock" or "shield" (which involve, as we can see, material perfections) they are being applied to him only metaphorically or in the sense that he is the cause of these things (the *via causation is).*

When he speaks of the Trinity or the origin of the world, the author is on less sure ground. He was a bit too influenced by Neo-Platonism and though his basic vision is perfectly orthodox, his language is clumsy. For instance, he differentiates the Father, Son and Holy Spirit very carefully from each other and, in his attempt to bring out the ultimate and essential unity that is at the heart of the Trinity, he almost talks as if there were a separate fourth originating principle, the Platonistic *Monos* from which these emanate or of which they are manifestations. Creatures are overflowings of God's Goodness, but in such a way that there is a distinction between God and the world, a real distinction. Finally, God is at once the origin and the goal of things, attracting all things back to him. His goodness overflows and descends into creatures and then return to himself. In effect, a deification is offered to all creatures and is achieved in man through grace, love and ecstasy. The language is often ambiguous but the overall intent of the author is evident: he has no other desire but to be an orthodox mystical teacher and we should try to find an interpretation of the ambiguities that agree with this general purpose.

2.3.5.1.2. Some Critical Remarks

The Pseudo-Dionysius, whoever he was, sincerely meant to harmonise Neo-Platonism with his faith. He sought to express Christian theology and especially Christian mysticism in a Neo-Platonic framework and scheme. He was a bit clumsy, at times, in the process. But one can hardly assert that when a clash occurred, he wanted the Neo-Platonism to prevail over the Christianity. Still, one can safely remark, with Copleston, that it is little likely that this author would have had such an influence on Christian medieval thinkers had they not really believed that he was the celebrated Pauline convert.

2.3.5.2. Boethius

Boethius (480-525) was a Christian who, after having studied at Athens, found favour with the Ostrogoth ruler, Theodoric, and was appointed by him consul from 510 to 522. Wishing to set up an intellectual and cultural oasis in the court of the barbarian king, Boethius translated the *Isagoge* of Porphyry and several other works of Aristotle and these translations would be later on much used by the early Scholastics. He also added some of his own original works, mainly on logical questions, plus a little theology. Unhappily he incurred the displeasure of Theodoric and was imprisoned and finally executed on a charge of high treason. While in prison he wrote what came to be his most popular work, *On the Consolation of Philosophy.* He represents Philosophy as a comely woman who visits him in his sorry cell and gives him comfort and happiness. It is not too difficult, then, to understand why this slender work, fragmentary and of little originality, was to play an important role in the formation of Scholasticism.

2.3.5.2.1. His Works

The works of Boethius were responsible for circulating a large number of ideas from Aristotle and, to a lesser extent, St. Augustine. Right up until the thirteenth century, Aristotle was known to the Western Christian thinkers mainly though Boethius. When the famous controversy about universal ideas began, practically all the participants took Boethius' translation of Aristotle and Porphyry as their starting-point. But Boethius was also important for having given to the Scholastics some famous definitions which would become part and parcel of their varied systems. For instance, beatitude is "the perfect possession of all goods"; eternity is "the total, simultaneous and perfect possession of unending life". Both these definitions are from his *Consolation.* Another definition which would be taken up and perfected by St. Thomas and other writers was that of the person, defined as "an individual substance of a rational nature".

2.3.5.2.2. Some Critical Remarks

The testimony of a man's death or his composure at the hour of crisis is sometimes more powerful than that of his whole life. Though Boethius' life and writings, in themselves, merited the interest in philosophy that, they provoked, it is certain that the context in which he wrote his last work and the serene courage with which he could meet his cruel death had itself a part to play in the importance he assumed in the history of medieval thought.

2.3.6. General Conclusion to this Formative Period

Thanks to the persevering efforts of several clever - and brave - men of various faiths, philosophic activity at the time of the barbarian invasion did not come to an end altogether. More than that, such men not only passed on the torch of learning, but by the testimony of their lives and their own original contributions, would speak of lively debate and be instrumental in the growth of the Golden Age of Western Christian Philosophy.

But one has to wait for the Emperor Charlemagne (742-814) and his decrees on education before the intellectual movement that had begun earlier could be revived. Still, philosophy did not quite come into its own until the XII century when it was given its own place on the Scholastic program, along with the liberal arts and with theology.

2.4. Scotus Eriugena (c 810–c 870)

2.4.1. His Life

John Scotus Eriugena was born about 810 and studied in an Irish monastery. "Eriugena" means "from Erin" (Ireland) and since Ireland was also called Scotia Major and the Irish Scoti, the Eriugena is obviously a pleonasm. In 850 we find him in France, at the Court of Charles the Bald (840-877), where he had been invited to translate the works of the Pseudo-Dionysius, which had been presented to the French court about 100 years earlier by a Byzantine emissary, Denis (Dionysius) being considered one of the major patrons of Paris. However, no one at the court could understand Greek and the fact that John Scotus could assume this work testifies to the fact that he was a cut above the normal, average intellectual of his time, lay or clerical. Though there is no evidence to say that he was a priest, we can see once again the prestige he enjoyed from the fact that Hinomar, Bishop of Rheims, conscripted him to intervene in the debate he was having with Gottschalk, a Saxon monk who affirmed that there were two predestinations: that of the good to eternal salvation and that of the evil to hell. The result was the publication of his On Predestination, a work that pleased neither side and brought himself under suspicion of heresy. In about 862 John Scotus began composing the work that it justly his title to fame, the five books of The Division of Nature, written in the then customary dialogue form and ready by 866. This book, too, has been the occasion of much controversy. Though the author seems to have been orthodox enough in his private and public life, there are ambiguities that one can quite easily exploit. In fact, a good number of suspect heretics tried to shield themselves with appeals to his writings - which in itself is indication that John Scotus neither wished to be heretical in any way, nor was he seem as so by his immediate contemporaries. Be that as it may, Pope Honorius III condemned the work in 1125. It had already been listed among the forbidden writings by an earlier Council at Sons.

2.4.2. His Thought

John Scotus elaborated a very interesting theory to explain how the organisation of truths of faith by the reason, as he held, is based on the idea of a hierarchy in the order of knowledge. God has put into man's heart, in giving him reasons, an innate desire to know the truth. The revelation he has given us through Jesus is meant to help us in this advance towards the truth. This revelation, far from being something imposed on us from without, comes not only to inspire man's mind to action but lead him and guide him towards perfection. He illustrates it by the words of Jesus to the Samaritan woman: "Give me to drink." (Jo 4:7) The Lord makes her, already moving towards him, act herself before providing her with the water that gives eternal life. So, it is with the relation between revelation and reason. And, since revelation is expressed in the Scriptures, it is by critical acquittance with, and study of, these that our minds attain the truth. Philosophy and religion are thus interchangeable: the former is the application of our mind and reason to the study of the Scriptures, whereas the latter in none other than the submission of all our faculties to revelation. Thus, he declares in his *On Predestination* "true philosophy is the same as true religion".

2.4.2.1. Authority

John Scotus admitted authority along with reason and the Scriptures as means to truth. But he had no hesitation in putting it in a very low place indeed, far inferior to the others. He is much less inclined to bow the knee before Augustine, Gregory of Nyssa and so on as unthinkingly as his contemporaries. He expresses the greatest admiration for them, but admits their authority only when their thought conforms to the demands of reason. What God says, and only what he says, is un-contestable authority. What later interpreters say is another matter. This is borne out, he says, by the fact that they frequently contradict one another!

2.4.2.2. "Nature"

Right at the beginning of his Division of Nature, John Scotus explains what he means by "Nature". In effect, it means the sum total of all reality and denotes as much God and the supernatural sphere as the natural world of experience. He then says that this "Nature" is divided into four species: (i) Nature which creates and is not created (*natura creans non creata.*) (ii) Nature which is created and creates (*natura creans creata.*) (iii) Nature which is created and does not create (*natura creata non creans*), and (iv) Nature which neither creates nor is created (*natura neo creans neo creata*). Such an assertion seems, at first value, to embody a kind of pantheistic monism. But he himself will say in Bk 2 that he intends in no way to imply that creatures are a part of God or that God is a genus of which creatures are a species. He retains the fourfold division of "Nature" and says that all he means is that God and creatures could be looked upon as forming together a kind of totality. However, much in his rather careless vocabulary seem to imply - whether he realised it or not - a kind of panthiesm.

2.4.2.2.1. *Natura creans non creata*

This is, very obviously, God. He is the cause of all things while, in himself, is uncaused. He is the first cause and brought everything else into being from a state of non-being (ex nihilo). This is perfectly orthodox. He will say, later on, that God may be said to be created in creatures, to be made in the things he makes, to begin to be in the things that begin to be. In the light of his other remarks (cf. the preceding paragraph), in the light of the whole thrust of his thought and, in the light of his emphatic formula *natura creans non creata*, it should be clear that the he was not teaching a kind of anticipatory Hegelianism, but was merely saying (ambiguously enough!) that creatures are a kind of manifestation of God, that he "appears" in creatures, that creatures are a theophany.

2.4.2.2.2. *Natura creata creans*

This second division of Nature refers to the now familiar 'ideas' or exemplary forms which exist in the Word of God: they are the divine ideas, prototypes of all created essences. The only problem here is how these divine ideas can be created! For Scotus, the eternal generation of the Word, God's Son, would involve also the eternal constitution of the archetypal ideas or exemplary causes in the Word. The emergence of these archetypes is logically anterior to the eternal procession of the Word, but insofar as they are part of this procession, they may be said to be "created'. John Scotus adds that there is, in reality, no plurality of exemplary ideas in the Word. As causes existing in the Word they are one and not really distinct, though in their effects, which are an ordered plurality, they are multiple.

2.4.2.2.3. *Natura creata non creans*

This is nature in the narrow sense, creatures, all of which were created by God out of nothing. John Scotus, faithful to his Neo-Platonism, calls them "participations", explaining that they participate in the primordial causes, the divine ideas, as the latter participate directly in God. He uses an emanation terminology to explain the participation, speaking of the overflow of a river and other such examples. But it is clear that these are but metaphors, since he keeps insisting that there was a regular creation ex nihilo (out of nothingness), whereas any emanation is a making *ex aliquo* (from something).

2.4.2.2.4. *Natura neo creata neo creans*

This is God, as the term and end of all things. This stage is that of the return to God, the corresponding movement to the procession from God. "For the end of the whole movement is its beginning, since it is terminated by no other end that by its principle, from which its movement begins and to which it constantly desires to return, that it may attain rest therein." There is, then, a cosmic process which affects all matter. Once again, faithful to his neo-Platonistic prejudices - and following equally St. Gregory of Nyssa - John Scotus will add that all mutable and unspiritualised matter will finally perish in this movement. Finally, he incorporates into this cosmic process of the return of creation to God, the Christian theme of redemption. Man is led back to God by the incarnate Word of God who has assumed human nature, entered personally into this movement and takes mankind back to the Father with him. He thus emphasises the solidarity of mankind both in Adam's fall and in Christ's resurrection.

2.4.2.3. On Man

It will not be too out of place to collect together here all of what John Scotus says of man in the fourth book of the Division of Nature. He remarks that one could call man an animal inasmuch as he shares in vegetative a sensitive activities with other animals. But he is no mere animal, for he has the faculty of reason which lifts him above them all. However, he would not hold - as some later Scholastics (rather inconsistently) would - that man has two souls, an animal and a rational one. He has but one in which are also included the inferior animal and vegetative faculties. He also points out that man is the microcosm of creation, since he sums up in himself the material world and the spiritual, sharing in the powers of plants, animals and angels. Here too, he draws attention to what will become a favourite theme in later medievals.

2.4.3. Some Critical Remarks

Hirschberger, viewing the achievement of Eriugena, avers that "we can discern that a new springtime hovers in air and we may expect that it will bring forth abundant fruit." Actually, it might even be mere correct to say that, when we contemplate John Scotus' breath-taking and original (and bold!) vision, we could justly feel that this spring has already come! In the words of Copleston, his system "stands out like a lofty rock in the midst of a plain." John Scotus Eriugena was not only a philosopher and theologian, he was a mystic. And all mystics lay themselves open to the charge of pantheism and unorthodoxy from the part of doddering nit-pickers who appoint themselves watch-dogs of orthodoxy and little understand the language of love. St. Paul's famous *anakephleaiosisesthai* in Ephesians (to single out only one text) is as vulnerable to such accusations. "For amateur heretic-hunters, Eriugena is an easy target:

one can score a hit first shot. But then one has to admit sheepishly that in shooting at Eriugena one has been shooting at Pseudo-Dionysius, St. Maximus the Confessor, St. Gregory of Nysa, St. Gregory Nazianzen, St. Ambrose or St. Augustine" (Etienne Gilson).

2.5. The Controversy about Universals

2.5.1. Introductory

2.5.1.1. Universals

This term comes from three Latin words (*unum* versus *alia* - *universalia*) which means, literally, one standing before many. And such is what are our ideas and words (philosophically, it would be more precise to say, concepts). The concept "man" is applied to several individuals: I say Peter is a man and John is a man and so on. The meaning of the concept is ever one and the same, but I apply it (make it stand for) different individuals that cannot be identified simply (Peter is certainly not John). A little reflection will make it clear that there is no little problem at issue here - one which, if inadequately or incorrectly solved, would have repercussions in a good many other fields.

2.5.1.2. The Problem

One may approach the problem by asking the question in this way: "What is there in Peter and in John and all other individuals in that species, which corresponds to the concept "man" in my head and justifies my calling them by that common name?" At first sight, there would appear to be no real justification for doing so. After all, Peter is not John. If I call them both "man", this seems to apply they are the same thing. Yet it is clear that they are not. Besides, the concept is, in itself abstract and applicable to many (formally universal). Yet, Peter, John and so on are concrete and individual (not applicable to many). There seems to be precious little ground to identify these individuals with a common concept. Anyway, this way of posing the question ("What, if anything, in extra-mental reality corresponds to the universal concepts in the mind?") may be called the **ontological** approach and was how the medievals approached the matter. Or, we may prefer to formulate the question with the accent on **how** we form our concepts: this is the **psychological** aspect and is probably the form under which moderns would tackle the issue.

2.5.1.3. Relevance

At first sight, this may appear a rather academic problem, a theoretical question rather than a down-to-earth practical one. But, as G. K. Chestertan one wittily remarked, Nothing is more practical than a sound theory. For one thing, refusal or inability to treat this question would throw all our human knowledge into question, beginning with scientific laws. A physicist, for instance, investigates the properties of electrons or studies the behaviour of a ray of light when passed through a prism. He would not be satisfied in making a statement about the particular electron(s) he has worked on or on the particular light ray(s) he has been observing. He will speak about electrons or light rays in general. In other words, he makes his conclusions in the form of abstract and universal terms. And if there is nothing in extra-mental reality to correspond to his "universals", then he is talking about nothing at all! The only conclusion to all this would be rank, negative scepticism!

In fact, there are not a few trends in present-day thinking that are due to a revival of unanswered (if not forgotten) questions and answers about universals. Much of contemporary phenomenology and existentialism is a kind of neo-nominalism. Indeed, the whole of the present prejudice against the intellect - which dates from Descartes, really - stems from the same difficulty!

Still, after all this has been said, we might well ask ourselves if this was the most relevant question that medievals could have bothered themselves at that time of unrest and rampant social injustice that very soon was going to produce the rending of the Church, a schism whose effects we still feel today and whose results might have been avoided had those great thinkers focussed the earliest scholastic controversy on a more crying and urgent matter!

Anyway, it was reflection on this topic that stirred up philosophical interest and ferment in the eleventh and twelfth centuries and set the scholastic movement on the road to doctrinal progress through precision of concepts. It would be unfair, of course, to say that the problem of the universals was the only matter taken up at the time. There was also the remarkable synthesis of St. Anselm. But universals will occupy the front of the stage in most of Europe.

2.5.1.4. Origins

It all began with Porphyry, fervent disciple and editor of the works of Plotinus. He was also a translator of Aristotle, as you will remember. In his *Isagoge* (Greek for Introduction) to Aristotle's writings on Logic, he raised a question to which he did not venture to offer an answer: these genera and species which Aristotle speaks about (e.g. animal and rational respectively) - do they really subsist outside of the mind or are they mere concepts? And, should they exist, would they be material or immaterial? Boethius, in his translation and commentary on the *Isagoge* suggested a possible response. He remarked that abstraction could explain the formation of these concepts and that, therefore, these ideas would be true even though the thing conceived does not exist in reality in an abstract or "universal" way. In other words, Boethius showed how a convinced Aristotelian could find, in the works of the master, material for tackling this ticklish question.

2.5.1.5. Two Schools

First attempts to answer these questions ignored the insights of Boethius and proposed a naive realist answer. Abelard would refer to this school as the *antiqua doctrina.* Others set themselves against this over-simplified view. These, the *moderni,* forced the traditionalists to re-think and clarify their opinion.

2.5.2. The Realist Response - Metaphysical Aspect

The realists held, in general, that there existed some sort of extra-mental reality that corresponded exactly to the universal idea in the mind. Thus, corresponding to the idea "man" in the mind, there subsisted in reality something that existed in the same way as it did in the mind. Since the concept "man" is always numerically one, it would follow that there was some subsistent extra-mental reality called man that was also numerically one. Either there exists in reality only one human substance and the different men of our experience are only accidentally distinct, or each man is some kind of inferior participation of the one perfect, ideal "man" who exists somewhere or the other. Such a view could (and, in fact, did) lead to monism, for it is only a logical step to reduce all beings to one really subsistent being. As we shall see, many a thinker was lured into this extravagant dangerous way of thinking because of his desire to explain how original sin was transmitted.

2.5.2.1. Odo of Tournai

He died in 1113 and is also known as Odo of Cambrai since he later became Bishop of that place. Influenced by Augustine, he conceived original sin as some kind of positive infection of the soul. Thus, he was faced with an embarrassing dilemma. Either he held that God, at the birth of a child, creates a new human soul (and with it its positive infection, original sin) and thus would God be responsible for something evil, or he would have to say that God did not create the soul of the child.

He found a way out of this impasse in the writings of Remigius of Auxerre (c. 841-908) who had taught that all "individuals" of a species make up, in reality, one single substance and that they differ from each other only accidentally. This was convenient enough for Odo. Thus, he held that when a child is born God only creates a new accident of the tainted human substance.

2.5.2.2. William of Champeaux

Almost all that we know of William of Champeaux (1070-1120) is thanks to Abelard, who attended his lectures at Paris. Though he had initially studied under the "nominalist" Roscelin, who belongs to the other school, he soon developed views totally opposed to his erstwhile teacher. Like Odo, he too ended his days as a Bishop in 1113 he was appointed to the Sve of Chalon-sur-Marne, He is famous for his theories of identity and indifference.

According to his theory of identity, William of Champeaux held, much like his fellow- Bishop Odo, that each nature - humanity for instance - is numerically one and totally present in each individual. Individuals are only distinguishable from each other through their accidents. Abelard wasted no time in pointing out the absurd consequences of this view. For instance, if we accept the theory of identity, we must admit that a single man, Socrates for instance, though actually at Athens is also at Rome at one and the same time, since there too is to be found the human nature which he totally possesses. And "if Socrates is whipped, then every human substance is whipped." Such evident absurdities obliged William to abandon his former identity- theory and replace it with a theory of indifference.

According to the indifference-theory, two members of the same species are the same thing, not essentially *(essentialliter)* but indifferently *(indifferenter)*. What does this mean? Evidence from fragments of William of Champeaux writings seem to indicate that this meant that he had actually abandoned his former ultra-realism altogether and come round to a characteristically Thomist moderated realism. He explains that we must clearly distinguish between being one (the area of "indifferent") and being similar (the area of 'essentially'). Thus, for instance, Peter and Paul are both mortal, rational and so on. In other words, they are men "indifferently". But their humanity (their human substance) is not the same (i.e. they do not possess the same numerical essence or nature). It seems clear enough that this is, in reality, a complete retraction of the original stance. However, it leaves several ambiguities and unanswered questions. These will be taken up by a group of thinkers who make up the famous School of Charters.

Gilbert de la Porrec (1076-1154) had studied under Bernard of Chartres and taught, later, at the same school. He became Bishop of Poitiers in 1142. He was quite clear in his view that each man had his own human nature or humanity and there was no question of monism or pantheism with him. The "native forms" of things are quite distinct from the Divine Ideas of which they are but copies and multiplied with individuals. All this is moderate realism, yet, because of certain peculiar view about the inner constitution of the individual - which brought him into difficulty with the celebrated Council at Rheims - he may be classified among the ultra-realists. He distinguished between the individualised essence or substance of an actual man, say, in which his particular accidents inhere and the "native form" which is common to all of the same species - common in the sense that they are alike inasmuch as they are copies of the one and the same Divine Idea in God.

He even added that by "abstraction" we can discover the similar elements in numerically distinct members of the same species. Yet he seemed to make a real distinction between the individualised form and the native form of the same thing. For instance, he would make a distinction between Socrates and humanity (i.e. between Socrates and the humanity of Socrates. The only difficulty about all this is that such a theory, if applied to the Trinity (and he did apply it there, too) appears to undermine the unity of God. For it would involve making a real distinction to the point of separation between God and Divinity, Father and Fatherhood and so on. Thus, he had to retract his allegedly heretical view at the Council of Rheims in 1148.

2.5.2.3. Incorrigible Pantheists

We have seen how ultra-realism, unless radically modified, inevitably lands on in pantheism. All the ultra-realists we have studied so far wished to avoid such a conclusion at all costs. And so, they strained and twisted their theories, in an attempt to be loyal to their faith and remain orthodox Christians. But there were others who preferred to be loyal to logic rather and drew the ultimate conclusions out of their premisses.

Amalric of Bone (who died towards the end of the 12th C.) appealed to the doctrine of Eriugena to justify his blatant pantheism - and thereby brought about the condemnation of *The Division of Nature,* whatever its author might have meant by his original ideas. According to Thomas Aquinas, he taught that God is the form of all things and it appears that he even went so far as to teach that the persons of the Trinity are creatures, that all three became incarnate and that every human being is as much God as Christ was. It is difficult to believe that a man who ended his days as a professor of Theology at Paris actually taught these things, but so we are told on good authority. Perhaps it was more his disciples who developed the ambiguous views of their master into such strange theses. At any rate, his views were condemned in 1210 along with those of Eriugena (after his death), he being obliged to retract his doctrines.

David of Dinant, a Belgian found at the court of Pope Innocent III around 1205, identified God, not with the form of things (as Amalric had done), but with prime matter, in the sense of the potentiality of things. It is difficult to pass judgment on his authentic views for his writings were destroyed after his condemnation in 1210. All we know of him comes to us from reports or quotations in St. Albert, St. Thomas or Nicholas of Cusa. According to St. Thomas, David divided reality into three classes: bodies, souls and eternal substances and added that ultimately there is only one substance, God. David tried to justify his pantheism by dialectic - a dialectic turn that would have repercussions on the famous theory of universals and that is why he is included here. This is his argument. If two substances can be said to differ from each other, this can only be by reason of some difference in them. However, to speak of a difference implies that there also be something in common. In other words, substances that differ from each other must be composites (sine they are made up of an element of similarity plus an element of difference). But neither God nor prime matter are composite. Therefore, they can't be differentiated. Since you can't differentiate them, they are the same. St. Thomas retorted with a precision, Composite things, he pointed out, may be said to differ from one another by virtue of some difference. But simple things are another question. Strictly speaking we cannot speak of them as being different *(differre)*, but as being diverse *(diversa esse)*. In other words, as Copleston sums up, David of Dinant was "playing with terms (and) choosing, to express the diversity of God and matter, a term which implies composition in God and matter." It is also pretty evident that Aquinas gave so much importance to his refutation of David's view, not because he feared the latter's influence (which was nothing to speak of, anyway), but because his peculiar understanding of prime matter might lead the authorities to think that Aristotelianism would necessarily load to pantheism. Hence his trouble to show, by way of extensive quotes from the *Metaphysics,* that only an unfair and distorted interpretation of the Stagyrite could come to such conclusions.

David of Dinant's views were accordingly condemned in 1210 and the magisterium, thereby, checked the excesses of the ultra-realist viewpoint and paved the way for the realist reaction.

2.5.3. The Anti-Realist Response: Psychological Aspect

The realists maintained that there was an exact correspondence of thought and extra-mental reality. The opponents of this naive view held another extreme position. According to them, only individuals exist. In one way or the other, they argue that each member of a species is unique and there is no correspondence between extramental reality and the concept, which latter is a mere 'empty word', a kind of short-hand formula to evoke the thing and which, in no way, really seizes some element of its essence.

2.5.3.1. Roscelin

This Canon of Cornpiegne Cathedral was born about 1050 and died in 1120 after having had, as his pupils, such illustrious men as William of Champeaux and Abelard. The only document we have from his is a letter to Abelard. The rest of his writings are lost and so we have to try to reconstruct his doctrine from the testimony of others, mainly Abelard.

He appears to have been one of the first to attack ultra-realism and point out that universals, inasmuch as they are general and abstract, cannot exist, as such, in reality. The famous description of a universal as a mere word *(flatus vocis* = mere emission of sound*)* is his, if we believe St. Anselm.

It seems clear enough that Roscelin denied that there was a "universal in things". But does his *flatus vocis* mean to imply that there is no real universal even in the mind? He affirmed the universal "in speech" - namely that we use words universally. But is there a concept, universal and abstract, representing the things in the mind? Roscelin was not clear about this at all. The one thing we can be sure of was that he was an avowed anti-realist. But we are not certain whether he was a mere nominalist (denying that universals existed except "in speech") or a conceptualist (admitting that there are universals "in the mind", i.e. in concepts, but not in reality, i.e. "in the thing").

Roscelin carried his anti-realism a bit too far when he applied it to the doctrine of the Trinity and concluded that the three divine persons were, in reality, three separate beings and that their unity consisted in the fact that they possessed the same power, wisdom and will. This heresy of Tritheism was condemned in 1092.

2.5.3.2. Peter Abelard

Born at Le Pallet, near Nantes, in 1079, into a military family (he came to be known as "the knight of Philosophy"), he studied under Roscelin and the ultra-realist William or Champeaux whom he worsted in debate. It was his decisive work that gave a death-blow to ultra- realism. After the celebrated affair with Heloise (immortalised by many a romantic poet) he had to retire from teaching theology at Paris to the abbey of St. Denis. He was another eminent thinker to get in trouble with Church authority: his views on the Trinity were condemned in 1121. Twenty years later he was once again accused of heresy by St. Bernard and condemned at the Council of Sens. His appeal to the Pope, Innocent II, only led to a further condemnation and a prohibition to lecture. In disgrace, he retired to Cluny and died there in 1142. As de Wulf remarks, "in theology as in philosophy, the present tendency of historians is rather to rehabilitate Abelard."

Abelard was a man skilled in repartee and merciless with his adversaries. He had no hesitation in attacking and ridiculing the views of his former teachers. We have already seen how he pursued William of Charnpeaux, his former teacher, till the latter all but retracted his original ultra-realism. Then, as if the matter had not been sufficiently complex already, Abelard introduced a new distinction into the debate: *vox* and *sermo*. *Vox* is the word viewed as a physical entity in itself, a sound, a thing. In this sense a *vox* cannot be predicated of any object (you cannot predicate one thing of another thing). But there is also the *sermo,* the word inasmuch as it represents a certain logical content and hence can be predicated of things. This would show that one is not quite justified in calling Abelard a nominalist. He is, at least, a conceptualist - though could argue that he may not have come near to elaborating anything like the traditional scholastic "moderate realism".

He very nearly did, though. In fact, we might even be able to make out a case in his favour to the effect that it was he who provided later Scholastics with the basic ingredients for their moderate realism.

For he points out that universal concepts are formed by abstraction and that through these concepts we conceive what is objectively in the thing, though we do not conceive it as it is in the thing (we have, here, the basic distinction between the *id quod* and the *modus quo).*

2.6. St. Anselm (1033–1109)

2.6.1. His Life

St. Anselm was born at Aosta in Piedmont (northern Italy) and his early life, as much as his latter days, was marked by unhappy relationships with authority. At the age of 20, he left home after his mother's death as he was not able to get on very well with his father. He went to France and, not long after, entered the Benedictine order, eventually succeeding his compatriot and mater, Lanfranc, as prior of the Abbey of Bee and once again as Archbishop of Canterbury. As Archbishop, he boldly resisted the demands of the royal authority who wished to encroach upon religious appointment. He was exiled to the Continent and was able to return only after the death of his opponent king William Rufus. His return was short-lived for he soon clashed with William's successor and had to leave England once again. After three years of a Roman exile, peace was restored - this time definitively and he was able to come home and pass the rest of his years in peace with the king.

2.6.2. Bibliography

The most famous of St. Anselm's philosophical and theological writings are the *Proslogium*, the *Monologium* and the *Cur Deus Homo*, the last of which has been hailed by a contemporary writer as "one of the most penetrating and thoughtful works in the history of Christian speculation." We have a very convenient edition of all three under the covers of the same book, translated by S. Deane, St. Anselm, Illinois, 1951. There is a longish introduction plus "reprints of the opinions of leading philosophers and writers on the ontological argument. Naturally Gaunilon's *On Behalf of the Fool* and Anselm's reply are also included.

Then there is the recent work of Charles Hartshorne, *Anselm's Discovery: A Re- examination of the Ontological Argument for God's Existence*, Illinois, 1965. In this stimulating book, the author calls for a more careful consideration of "the challenge that Anselm issued to his contemporaries", convinced that "there is not shorter way to the understanding of essential metaphysical issues" than by such a study. He introduces the term actuality into the traditional essence - existence discussion. Whatever one thinks of the author's re-examination of the argument, it is not likely that he will regret having gone through the volume.

2.6.3. His Thought

2.6.3.1. Faith and Reason

In the *Proslogium* is to be found his famous *Credo, ut intelligam (I believe so that I may understand)* statement which expresses his basic Augustinianism and which merits being quoted in its full context: "I do not attempt, O Lord, to penetrate Thy profundity, for I deem my intellect in no way sufficient thereunto, but I desire to understand in some degree Thy truth, which my heart believes and loves. For I do not seek to understand, in order that I may believe; but I believe, that I may understand. For I believe this too, that unless I believed, I should not understand." It should be obvious that the reason is not supposed to be used, after Anselm's approach, to strip away all mystery from faith (as if it could), but only to plumb them as far as possible, drawing out - so far as human reason can - all its implications. Thus, in his *Cur Deus Homo,* he remarked that it would be negligence for a believer not to try and understand what he believed in.

2.6.3.2. "Necessary Reasons"

The Anselmian motto *Credo, ut intelligam* should not make us believe that he confined his work to seeking to understand revealed doctrine. He also applied himself, with the same zeal and spirit, to the study of truths like the existence of God which are indeed believed in, but can be attained by human reasoning. Indeed, quite apart from his insights as a dogmatic theologian, Anselm so much laid the foundations for a systematic approach to metaphysics and the philosophy of God, that he is hailed as one of the pioneers in the field of natural theology. Like Augustine, Anselm never made a clear distinction between philosophy and theology and this led to at least one curious and interesting development in his thought. Thomas Aquinas would ever hold that reason can never demonstrate truths that have been revealed to us by faith - such as the Trinity. Anselm did not hesitate to try and find "necessary reasons" to substantiate such revealed doctrine. Thus, he would go one step further than Aquinas who would admit the value of reason in such spheres only to show that no contradictions were involved and to refute objections to the effect that doctrines, such as that of the Trinity, implied belief in utter nonsense.

2.6.3.3. Anselm's Theory of Truth

Another evidence of Anselm's Augustinian inspiration is with reference to his concept of truth. He does present a very Aristotelian vision of truth when he speaks of it with reference to judgment, defining the latter as a statement which affirms that something does or does not exist. As a consequence, the thing would be the cause of truth which resides in the judgment should there be a correspondence between judgment and reality. But, as a whole, he prefers to speak of God as the cause of truth - in which case he is clearly treading in the footsteps of Augustine. According to this way of thinking, truth is "the rightness of the essence" of a thing, that is, the fact that it corresponds with the exemplar in the mind of God. Thus "the truth of things is their rectitude," he says and goes on to define it as "rectitude perceptible by mind alone." In other words, soon as we perceive, through reason, that God exists, we will discover their rectitude in conforming to the exemplary idea of them in the divine mind.

2.6.3.4. The Ontological Argument

This famous argument for God's existence, put forward by Anselm, is his unique and quite original contribution of philosophy. It reveals, once again, his Augustinian outlook (the *ab intra* approach) and has probably caused more ink to be spilled on account of it (for and against) than any other "proof' for God's existence. It was labelled the "ontological proof" by Kant several hundreds of years later and the name has stuck.

The proof attempts to reveal to the atheist his illogicality. He tries to show to him that he is foolish to deny God's existence, for the very fact that he is able to form the concept of God (whose existence he denies) obliges him to accept that he exists.

He quotes **Psalm 14.1** which remarks that "the fool says in his heart there is no God" and then proceeds to show how foolish such a position is. The fool has a concept of God he knows what is meant by the term God, for the very fact that he denies that such a being exists implies that he has some grasp of the meaning of this word. What does the word mean, anyway? Everyone would agree - atheist and believer alike - that by the word "God" is meant "a being than which nothing greater can be conceived." The "fool" (atheist) only goes on to deny that such a being exists. But, re-joins Anselm (and here is the crux of the argument), that being than which nothing greater can be conceived, must exist, else it would not be that than which nothing greater can be conceived. After all existence is greater than non-existence. Therefore, in order to fulfil the definition of "that than which nothing greater can exist", God must exist. The foolishness of the atheist is thus revealed for he is making use of a word that implies necessary existence, claims to understand the meaning of this word and yet denies that the corresponding reality exists!

2.6.3.5. Caunile's Objection and Anselm's Reply

Caunile (or Gaunilon), a monk of Marrnoutier, felt that the atheist had been given a raw deal by Anselm and so, convinced Catholic though he was himself, he wrote a short work *On Behalf of the Fool.* He pointed out - and rightly - that there is no parity, here. The idea of God is the idea of an all perfect being. Now if existence is a perfection it is necessarily contained in the idea of God. The idea of perfectly beautiful island does not include existence. Thus, the concept of a perfect being, of an all-perfect being, necessarily implies its existence. Therefore, an analysis of that concept, and that concept alone, obliged us to conclude to the existence of the being concerned.

2.6.4. Some Critical Remarks

2.6.4.1. Faith, Reason and Necessary Reasons

Vatican I, in 1870, condemned the view that "all dogmas of faith can be understood and demonstrated from natural principles by reason, if properly trained." In so doing, the Council but confirmed a long-standing tradition against extreme rationalism. We have seen how Anselm spoke of demonstrating the Trinity of Divine Persons "by necessary reasons" and of showing, in the same way, how it is impossible for man to be saved without Christ. Of course, we cannot censure Anselm for holding views which would be declared heretical after he died. But, can we call him a "rationalist"? Not if we take rationalism in the usual sense of the condemnation which refers to the denial or revelation and faith, for it is evident that Anselm was very far from such a position. But, to quote Copleston again, "if by rationalism one includes also the attitude of mind which leads to the attempt to prove mysteries, not because the mysteries are not accepted by faith or would be rejected if one could not prove them, but because one desires to understand all that one believes", then we might be justified in qualifying Anselm's attitude would never have led him to deny the Trinity or the Salvation of all men by Christ if he were unable to find "necessary reasons" to support these. Catholic thinkers would never subscribe to Anselm's attitude after the distinction of the two separate provinces of thought, theology and philosophy, by Aquinas.

2.6.4.2. Anselm's Theory of Truth

The Augustinian conception of truth, with its concomitant exemplarism, was retained by Aquinas as ontological truth. The latter, however, gave more place in his thought to epistemological truth, conformity of intellect and object. Anselm neither denies nor ignored this latter understanding of truth, as we have seen. It is just that his Augustinianism led him to place more emphasis on that truth which is rested in God's mind rather than in man's.

2.6.4.3. The "Ontological" Argument

Though the famous *a priori* (some prefer to call it *a simultaneo)* argument for God's existence was revived, time and again, by various modern authors - notably Descartes and Leibniz - it is quite probably Kant who provided the clearest critique of its reasoning. He showed that "existence" is not an essential perfection. It belongs to a totally different order and so cannot be included in the concept of anything, let alone the concept of an all perfect being. Hence the conception of an all-perfect being must necessarily admit all essential perfections as pertaining to it. But existence is not one of these and so it does not have to be granted to the concept, along with all other essential properties! Hartshorne, like Donceel in his *Natural Theology,* have both shown that Anselm, though his argumentation may be invalid, has certainly put his finger on a very important and key issue in metaphysics. It would be worth your while, in this connection, to read Donceel Chapter 1 (at least pp. 15-19). There, he shows how Marechal, beginning where Anselm had left off, hit upon a very rich and remarkable discovery, thanks to his following a lead of Kant!

2.7. The Synthesis of St. Thomas Aquinas (1225–1274)

2.7.1. His Life

St. Thomas Aquinas, otherwise known as the "angelic doctor" *(doctor angelieus,* on account of the lucidity of his style and his brilliant intellectual vision - he is also called the 'prince of scholastics', 'founder-father of scholasticism' etc.) was born in about 1225 to a wealthy Italian family at Roccasecca, near Naples. His father was a count and his mother was related to the Emperor Frederick II. Though his future relationships with his family and elder brothers were rather stormy, we may assume his parents did love him, even if they placed him - at the tender age of five - in the nearby Benedictine Abbey of Monte Cassino. As we shall see, they hoped that the little oblate would grow into a rank of ecclesiastic standing. Little did they realise how high that standing would be, though it was not quite the type of rank they had had in mind. Little Tom stayed nine years in the Abbey until 1239, when his mother's imperial relative expelled the monks from their mountain retreat and the fourteen-year-old lad returned to the bosom of his family ... for a short while.

Thomas of Aquino left home again, this time for the newly-founded University of Naples where he soon felt attracted by the life and ministry of the Dominicans there and entered the Order in 1244, against the 'wishes of his parents who saw little chance for ecclesiastical honours for their son in that particular Order. Accordingly, they had him ambushed by his elder brothers while he was travelling to Bologna with the Dominican General who was, no doubt, hoping to get him safely away from his violent-tempered and powerful family. Thomas was carried off and confined for a year by his family who tried, by all manner of inducements, to wean him away from the Order of Preachers. But Thomas could be as determined and stubborn as the rest of the family and they had to let him go in 1245. He immediately made his way to Paris where he met and studied under his fellow-Dominican master, Albert the Great, with whom he went later to Cologne and founded there the new Dominican house of studies.

In 1252 he returned to Paris and taught there as a Bachelor of Arts until 1255. In 1256 he acquired the licentiate but the shameful controversy between diocesans and religious broke out, which was not at all helped by the fact that students began deserting the lecture halls of the other teachers, diocesans who had been teaching for a much longer time than the mendicants to attend those of Thomas. Classes at the faculty of theology in Paris were disrupted and the diocesan teacher went on strike it was only when the ring leader had been "kicked upstairs" to the Papal court and Aquinas started a regular session of disputations to prove the capacity of the regulars to teach, that everything returned to normal. The matter of these solemn discussions was later edited and published by Thomas as his *Disputed Questions.* In 1257, Pope Alexander IV forbade all further harassment of the regulars, punished the guilty ring-leaders and Thomas was able to give his first lecture as a Doctor and became an official teaching master. All this while, he kept on writing his commentaries on the Bible and on the works of other thinkers.

There followed a long enough sojourn at the Papal court (1260-1268) where, as professor of theology, he had to travel quite bit all over Italy with three pontiffs. Here he came in contact with the Hellenist, William of Moerbeke, whom Urban IV got him to meet, after lifting the earlier papal ban on Aristotle. From this fruitful encounter and enriching friendship date Thomas' great philosophical commentaries on Aristotle.

Thomas' two great works saw the final light of day about this time. First his *Summa Contra Gentiles* (English translation: *On the Truth of the Catholic Faith),* begun in Paris in 1259, was completed in 1264. This four-book treaties seeks to provide an integrated and coordinated theology, natural and revealed and is a systematic apology of the Catholic faith as against the attacks of Jews and Moors. The following year, he began working on his masterpiece with which he would ever be busy, dying before he could complete it: *The Summa Theologica.*

In January 1269 the Dominican Order, going back on its established custom, sent Thomas back to Paris for a second term as a teaching master in theology. This only shows the authority that the comparatively young thinker had acquired in the heat of the intellectual controversies of the time. But no sooner has he settled down than Thomas found himself, once again, the centre of opposition. This time the diocesans were joined by the Augustinians and the Averroists in their attack on the young upstart!

Averroism is a word that Thomas coined to denote a kind of extreme and radical Aristotelianism advocated in Paris between 1260 and 1265 under the guidance of Siger of Brabant, a Belgian canon. As for the Augustinian Neo-Platonists, it is not difficult to find that they viewed anything that smacked of

Aristotle as heresy. “Averroism” was finally condemned by the Bishop of Paris in 1270, but the Augustinian opposition died hard. Several letters were sent to the Dominican General, asking for the recall of Thomas to Paris when he had been sent to Naples to found a house of studies there, his superiors wishing, no doubt, to remove the source of trouble from Paris.

At Naples, Thomas’ life centred a period of quiet study and comparative seclusion. This tranquil retreat was disturbed when he was summoned to attend the Council of Lyons by Gregory X. On his way home he fell ill and died, in 1274, at the Cistercian monastery of Fossa Nuova. He had kept steadily at his work and when death came, he was still busy with his commentary on the *Canticle of Canticles*.

However, the death of Thomas was but a signal for the Averroists to marshal themselves for a final and decisive attack on their rival and opponent. But they were so vocal that they only succeeded in getting John XXI order an enquiry into their own orthodoxy. The Bishop of Paris, Stephen Tempier, had his faculty of theology list some 219 condemnable propositions of Averroism. The anti-Aristotelians did a thorough job and saw to it that not a few of Thomas’ own theses were included in the list. Bishop Tempier than condemned all the doctrines concerned and excommunicated everybody involved. The worthy Bishop would have gone even further in his condemnations, but luckily for Thomas there were many cardinals in the papal court who were favourable to him.

The net result of the whole affair was the destruction of all attempts to revive and propagate “Latin Averroism” in thirteenth century France. Siger of Brabant, its leading light was summoned to appear before the Grand Inquisitor of France. He, understandably, fled, betaking himself to Italy, where he met a violent death at the hands of a crazed *cleir* of his. The anti- Aristotelian tide was powerful enough to rally the Augustinian traditional sits who gave birth to a kind of eclectic neo-Augustinianism, of the type especially championed by Duns Scotus.

None of this, however was able to deter the Dominicans from adopting Thomism as the official philosophy of the Order, ignoring the condemnations that they had been directed against Thomas. In 1319 when Pope John XXII eventually raised Thomas Aquinas to the altars there was - for obvious reasons - a hasty and embarrassed removal of the condemnation of the saint’s writings.

In the light of the foregoing, it is quite possible that we forget that Thomas was not just a philosopher. He was a theologian, a mystic and a poet, as his composition of hymns for the feast of Corpus Christi show so well. It has rightly been said that he knew to “wed metaphysics to devotion” as even a cursory perusal of the *Adoro Te Devote* and the above-mentioned works will show. Thus, we can understand how it is that, a few months before his death, he ceased working on academic and speculative questions and remarked that all he had hitherto written of was mere trash compared to the more direct and certain vision that had slowly become his.

> It is not originality, but the boldness and compactness of structure which distinguish Thomas from the rest of the Scholastics. In regard to universality, he was surpassed by Albert; in regard to ardour and to logical subtlety he was outdistanced by Scotus - St. Thomas excelled them all in the art of didactic style and as master and classist of a synthesis of luminous clarity. (Etienne Gilson)

> The Church still rests convinced, officially at any rate, that dogmatic theology can know no better method to "penetrate the mysteries of salvation" than "under the tutelage of St. Thomas." (Vatican II, *Decree on Priestly Formation, Optatam Totius,* No 16)

2.7.2. Bibliography

2.7.2.1. Primary Source

For obvious reasons, I am not listing the Latin texts of Aquinas' writings that we have here. Instead, I'm singling out the better English translations of the more well-known books of St. Thomas.

St. Thomas Aquinas, *Summa Theologiae* (60 volumes), Latin texts with a now English with extensive notes, introductions, appendices and glossaries, prepared by the Father if the English-speaking Provinces of the Dominican Order; London, 1963 (Is now the definitive source-book of the Summa, extremely well done and thorough. The introduction and notes to each topic are to be specially recommended)

_______, *On the Truth of the Catholic Church* (4 vols.), A new English translation of the Summa Contra Gentiles with introduction and notes by the Fathers of Baden College; New York, 1956 (A very good edition, though one might have preferred a better title!)

_______, *Truth* (3 vols), translation of De Veritate, with introduction by the Fathers of West Baden College, Chicago, 1954.

_______, *The Soul*, translation of De Anima by John Rowen, New York, 1951.

Anton Pegis (editor), *Basic Writings of St. Thomas*, (2 vols), New York, 1945 (Readable and dear translation of key passages from ST and SCG; volume I: God and the Order of Creation; volume II: Man and the Conduct of Life)

2.7.2.2. Secondary Source

We cannot but begin this list of secondary sources by referring you once again to the introductions to the topics in the English edition of the Summa listed above. In addition, here is an (extremely select) bibliography of secondary sources on Thomas Aquinas and his thought:

Bourke, Vernon: *Aquinas' Search for Wisdom*, Milwaukee, 1965

Copleston, Frederick, SJ: *Aquinas*, Harmondsworth, 1955.
Chenu, N.D., OP: *Towards Understanding St. Thomas*, trans. Landray and Hughes, Chicago, 1964
D' Arey, Martin, SJ: *St. Thomas Aquinas*, London, 1963
Pieper, Josef: *Introduction to Sf. Thomas Aquinas*, trans. Richard and Clara Ward, London, 1962.
Weisheipl, James, OP: *Friar Thomas d'Aquino: his life, thought and works*, Oxford, 1975.

2.7.3. His Thought

2.7.3.1. Philosophy of Knowledge

2.7.3.1.1. Distinction between philosophy and theology

That St. Thomas, unlike St Augustine before him, made a clear-cut distinction between those two disciplines is clear enough; we have already had occasion to point this out. Philosophy and other 'human sciences" rely simply on "the natural light of reason". Of course, God's general *concursus* is ever involved (just as it is for any creaturely activity), but the "supernatural light of faith" does not come into the picture and the conclusions one reaches are the fruit of human reasoning alone. The philosopher must work out his conclusions by the light of human reason alone. It follows, then, that the principal difference between theology and philosophy lies in the fact that the theologian receives his principles as revealed and considers the objects with which he deals as revealed or as deducible from what is revealed, whereas the philosopher apprehends his principles by reason alone and considers the objects with which he deals, not as revealed but as apprehensible and apprehended by the natural light of reason.

2.7.3.1.2. The Process of Knowledge

In the first place, let it be clearly underlined that for St. Thomas sensation is the act of the total human composite, body and soul and not (as St Augustine would have it) an act of the soul using the body. Next, there are no innate or in-born ideas to be found in man: all his ideas come to him, ultimately, through the senses, though he may develop and reason about them until he reaches conclusions that go beyond the immediate evidence of his senses. This we shall see, is a valid operation for it involves using his intellect to draw out the supra-sensible implications of his sense-experience, based on, as it were, tell-tale sensible traces of those.

Sensation, however, gives us knowledge of particulars, not of universals. Animals have sensation and they only know particular men and, say, specific bones or a saucer of milk. They cannot apprehend universal concept of man or bone or milk as such. It's all a question of particular experience and concrete memory-pictures of particular experience of past. Each act of sensation yields a phantasm or image (the sensible species) in the imagination and this presents the material object as perceived by the senses. Man, however, does not stop there as do brutes. In and through this particular, material sense impression he apprehends the universal and the abstract. How does he do this? After all, even though sensation is an activity of the total human composite, the spirit cannot be immediately acted upon by what is material; the intellectual activity, proper to the spiritual soul cannot be sent in motion by a material phantasm!

Obviously, the intellect has to actively, in some way, render the above-mentioned species intelligible. St Thomas uses the phrase "active intellect", borrowed from Aristotle to designate the intellect from the point of view of this function. The "active intellect" is not a part of intellect, much less a second intellect in man. It is nothing but man's intellect viewed under its function of rendering the sensible species intelligible. St Thomas says that it *illumines* the phantasm and abstracts from this particular sensible species the universal 'intelligible species'. Aquinas' use of the word "illumination" to describe the characteristic activity of the active intellect should not lead us to think that he was postulating some special help from God to bring this about (as in Augustinian theory of illumination). He means that the active intellect "abstracts" the universal element in itself, producing the *impressed species* on the passive intellect (i.e. the intellect viewed under its aspect of receiving the species: thus, there is no question of the spiritual intellect being passive with respect to the material and particular phantasm). To abstract means to isolate intellectually, to consider one aspect of a thing, leaving out (ignoring, not denying) other aspects. Since the active intellect, as such, is purely active, it cannot "impress" the universal on itself; this it does on the passive intellect and the reaction to this impression is the concept in the full sense of the word.

Aquinas accepts the proposition that any knowledge that is to count as real knowledge must be universal, but he rejects Plato's view that knowledge derives from a contemplation of ideas that exist latently and innately in the mind. Aquinas insists that the soul, which includes the intellect, would have no use for the body if, as Plato held, all knowledge was derived from the mind alone. Not only does Aquinas thereby affirm the necessity of the body and reject the notion that the body is an impediment to our acquisition of truth, he also rejects the doctrine of innate ideas. In other words, he contradicts Plato in asserting that *"there is nothing in the mind that was not first in the senses"*. At the same time, though, he says that the mind contributes to the acquisition of knowledge by forming "phantasms," that is, mental images, that are ultimately derived from sense experience and by forming universal ideas and principles. Thus, sense experience provides the passive component of knowledge and the mind provides the active component of knowledge.

Finally, it must be added, that when we affirm a universal concept of a particular thing, we are performing a valid enough operation for we merely affirm the *id quod* of the concept as being objective (i.e. its meaning: when we apply the concept "man" to Pope Paul VI, we are affirming that he a rational animal). We do not, in any way, mean to say that there is any identity as regards the *modus quo* (i.e. the mode by which the concept and the object, respectively exist: the one is abstract and universal whereas the other is concrete and particular).

2.7.3.2. Philosophy of God

2.7.3.2.1. Needs of Proofs for God's Existence

There were many illustrious thinkers, mystics and saints who had held, before Thomas, that the knowledge of God's existence is naturally innate in man (e.g. St. John Damascene). Aquinas will say that this is, at most, confused and vague. St. Thomas did not live in a world where large-scale and systematic atheism was common, but he felt it necessary to establish proofs for God's existence (he, significantly enough, referred to them as "ways") in so far as this was not a self-evident truth *(propositio per se nota),* at least, not immediately, from our point of view. As a matter of fact, after raising the question "is there a God?", Aquinas' first reply is 'it seems that there is no God." (S.T. Ia, 2, 3). In other words, the force of evidence is rather against God's existence than for it! However, we must admit that the reasons adduced by Thomas are characteristically abstract and speculative and have nothing to do with those which we would spontaneously cite today. (e.g. the fact of evil, psychological objections).

2.7.3.2.2. The "Five Ways"

Accordingly, St. Thomas proceeds to delineate "the five ways in which we can prove that there is God." (S.T. Ia 2, 3: op. Cit. P. 13) Each of these "ways" starts out with some phenomenon taken from "the observable world" and then, by way of some particular application of the principle of causality (e.g. "anything in process of change is being changed by something else"; "a series of causes must ... stop somewhere" etc), establishes a necessary connection between this fact and the existence of a being "to which everyone gives the name 'God'".

1. The first way (he calls it the "most obvious" way) is based on change in general.
2. Then, passing from the element of passivity observed in all inferior causes (whatever is changed, is changed by another), he takes up a consideration of their activity and thereby comes to the first cause.
3. Thirdly, there is the fact of contingency, implicit in our observation of things that are forever "springing up and dying away".
4. Fourthly there is the proof the "gradation observed in things" whose Platonic roots are evident enough.

5. Finally there is the proof from finality, "based on the guidelines of nature claim for originality can be made out on Aquinas' behalf as regards these arguments.

Aristotle, Maimonides and Avicenna, to name but a few, had all made use of them before the angelic doctor. The latter's contribution was to assemble them together systematically, polish them up a bit and then present them in a very clear and lucid way. So much so that anyone who would attempt to present proofs for God's existence, usually but quotes St. Thomas' version of the 'five ways" and adds his commentary.

2.7.3.2.3. God's Nature

Having established that God does exist, St Thomas now busies himself with the question of *what* God is. And first he says that we cannot know God's essence (what He is). We can only know his existence (that he is). But this statement of agnosticism is not his last word on the subject. Like the pseudo-Dionysius, he accepts the negative way as a valid method for understanding God. Thus, he invites us to deny of him any predicate that would involve imperfections, such as body. Yet, he adds - and this is an improvement over the pseudo-Dionysius - as we deny of God all these predicates, we slowly begin to get a clear idea of that which belongs to him alone. Furthermore, when we deny a predicate of God, we do not really mean to say that he lacks all perfections expressed in that predicate; only that he infinitely exceeds that limited perfection in its richness. Finally, St Thomas will say that the most appropriate name for God is "he who is", the name he was supposed to have given to Moses at the burning bush (Ex 3: 14). In other words, in God there is a distinction between essence and existence: his very essence is to be! (Cf. S.T. la, 13, 11) Needless to say, all these attributes of God and the various names that they give rise to, are not really distinct from one another. They only express the different angles or aspects, according to which we are viewing God who is perfectly one.

2.7.3.3. Philosophy of the World

2.7.3.3.1. Creation out of nothing

As Augustine before him, Aquinas shows that the only way in which finite and contingent beings could proceed from God would be through creation. This creation would entail being made out of nothing, *ex nihilo.* Here, too, Aquinas adds a precision. Making "out of nothing" is not to be taken to mean that "nothing" was some kind of material out of which God fashioned the world; it merely means that, at first, there was nothing and then there was something. Saying that God made the world "out of nothing" could also be taken to mean that it was not made "out of something". Furthermore, precises Thomas, creation is a particular prerogative of God alone. It cannot be attributed to, or shared by him with, any creature. Creation involves bridging the infinite gulf between non-being and being. Now a creature, precisely because it is finite, cannot bridge this gulf. People, like Peter Lombard, who taught that God could communicate his power of creation, in the full sense of the word, to a creature, do not realise how this involves a contradiction. God creates, not out of any necessity or because he was lacking in something, but as the result of a completely free choice and solely in order to give and diffuse his goodness. In short, he created in order to give, not to get.

2.7.3.3.2. Creation in Time?

Most of us cannot help thinking that creation necessarily implies having a beginning in time. An "eternal creation" is normally taken for granted as a contradiction in terms and, conversely, many think that if we could somehow prove that the world is eternal, then we have struck a blow at God as the perfect being whom all things depend. Aquinas saw no difficulty in the concept of an eternal creation. After all, God is eternal. Hence, he could have created from eternity. He maintained that one could not adduce any philosophical proofs to argue that the world had a beginning in time. Nor, for that matter, could one prove philosophically that there was an eternal creation. However, Thomas believed that revelation teaches us that the world was actually created in time. Such was his interpretation of the *Genesis* story. Yet, he was adamant in saying that it was *possible* for God to create the world in eternity and he rejected the reasoning of St Bonaventure, for one, who tried to show that an eternal creation was quite impossible.

2.7.3.3.3. Analogy

This topic might have, with equal logic, been treated along with Aquinas' philosophy of God, that is, with reference to giving names to God. But I feel that it might be pedagogically better to treat it here, in the section on Aquinas' philosophy of the world. This is because the Thomistic use of the analogy of being, which justifies applying this term, in the full sense of the word, to finite beings, has an important lesson for us in India.

Some of the words which we apply to many things have a univocal sense, i.e. they mean precisely the same in each case. Thus, when I say Paul VI is a man and Morarji Desai is a man, the meaning of "man" in each case is the same, Paul VI, as much as Morarji Desai, is man. There is no question of gradation, of more or less, here. Obviously, we cannot apply the same word "being" univocally to God and creatures though. The former is necessary, uncaused and infinite and the latter are contingent, caused and finite. Hence, they are not both being in exactly the same sense of the word. This, Indian thinkers since Śaṅkara and Rāmānuja, rightly emphasised. Does this mean, then, that, if we were to apply the word "being" to God and creatures, it would be in a purely equivocal sense, that is, there would be nothing in common except the mere label, the meaning in each case being entirely and completely different (as, for instance, when I speak of the "bark" of a tree and the "bark" of a dog). There is, indeed, as St Thomas took such pains to show, a kind of half-way house between the two extremes of univocity and equivocity, neither of which could be used to predicate "being" of God and creatures. This is the way of analogy.

We predicate "being" of creatures and of God in so far as the former had a real relation to the latter, they depend on him. He is the creator, infinite and self-existent. Hence, he merits the word primarily. Creatures, since they are finite and dependent on God, from whom they receive their derived existence, can be called **being** only secondarily. Thus, we may call both God and creatures 'being", but while so doing, we are perfectly aware that a creature is a different kind of being from the divine being, since it is a received, derived, dependent, finite being. That is why St Thomas will define being in a way that admits of analogy: being is, for him, that which "exists in its own way". God is being because he exists in his own way (which is uncaused, infinite etc.). A creature is a being for it, too, exists in its own way (caused, finite, etc as its case is). This definition if being does not require that, in order to be called "being", a thing should be a perfect being or able to exist by itself. It is open to every possibility of existing "in its own way".

Thus, we can call God "being" and also call creatures "being" without having to use these words in an equivocal sense (in which case we would have to write off creatures as some kind of *māya* or *non-being)* or in a univocal sense (in which case we would have to fall into pantheism).

2.7.3.3.4. The Problem of Evil

Aquinas, following Augustine, defined evil as a privation, i.e. the lack of a **due** perfection in something. Evil, then, is not a positive entity and so is not creatable. Hence, there is no necessity to seek creator for it, either in God (who is all good and so wouldn't create what is evil) or in some evil principles, as the Manichaeans had done. Not that Aquinas (or even Augustine, for that matter) wished to say that evil is an illusion, does not exist. What is meant that evil does not exist as something positive on its own: it is just the absence of something that is supposed to be in a creature, e.g. blindness. Aquinas goes on to say that evil cannot be positively willed, as such, by even a human will. For the object of the will is always the good, real or apparent. Even the most vicious sinner is but seeking an apparent good, something that he sees as good for him and it is this "species of good" that urges him to act. Aquinas made a distinction between **physical evil** (privation of some due perfection in a creature, e.g. blindness in man, inability to fly like an eagle) and **moral evil** (privation of due order in a will - i.e. sin). As for physical evil, one might go so far as to say that God not only permits it, but even wills it. Of course, he does not will it for its own sake. But he willed a universe, which could not but finite and therefore the possibility of physical defects and suffering is inevitable. Yet, St Thomas adds, all is not lost for God still can - and does! - draw good out of the evil; it is God, not evil, that ultimately gains the day. As for moral evil or sin, that arises from man's freedom - which is a good without which man could not give to God any love, or gain any merit. Still, precisely because it is a true genuine freedom, man can - and often does! - choose against loving God by sinning. God, then, merely permitted sin in making man free and this for a greater good: that man might be free and love and serve God of his own choice.

2.7.3.4. Philosophy of Man

2.7.3.4.1. The Human Composite

We have already pointed out that for Aquinas sensation was an activity of the total human composite and not an act of the soul, using the body as its instrument, as Augustine would say. It follows, then, that the Platonic understanding of the body-soul relation was quite unacceptable to St Thomas. The union of body and soul is not something unnatural, a kind of punishment due to some fault in a previous state. The soul of man has no innate ideas: it needs a body in order to have sensation and to think. The union of soul and body is not to the detriment of the soul but to its good. Furthermore, (and here, especially, did St Thomas differ from the general run of his predecessors and contemporaries), there is only **one substantial form** in man and this is his human soul which confers on him his bodylines (which includes his vegetative and sensitive functions) together with his rationality.

The soul is indeed capable of existence apart from the body death. This capacity is because the actualities of understanding and willing are not the actualities of any bodily organ, but of the human animal as such distinguished by the rational form. However, Aquinas merely concludes from this that the soul is a subsistent after the death of the body. A subsistent is something capable of existing on its own, not in another. But that capacity to exist on its own is not distinctive of a substance. A chair subsists. But on Aquinas' account, it is not a substance. A hand that has been detached from a living body is also a subsistent. (*Summa Theologiae* Ia75.2 ad1) It is not properly speaking a human hand any longer, because it cannot do the sorts of things that human hands do. Whatever it is, it can exist apart from the substance of which it was formerly a part.

A substance, on the other hand, is something that is both subsistent and complete in a nature—a nature being an intrinsic principle of movement and change in the subject. A detached human hand, while subsistent, is not a substance because it is not complete in a nature. A human hand is defined functionally as part of a human substance. A detached human hand is the remains of a human hand properly speaking, and is only called human analogously. So, it is subsistent but not a substance. Similarly, a human soul is a constitutive element of the nature of a human substance. It is the formal principle of a human substance. It is what is specified when we say what the substances is. But it is incomplete. What it is for it to be is to be the formal part of some substance. In that sense it is a principle of a substance, 'principle' being a technical term that refers back to the first entry in Aristotle's philosophical lexicon in the *Metaphysics*, and Aquinas commentary on it, as well as Aquinas *On the Principles of Nature*. As the principle of a nature, its nature is to be the formal element of a complete substance. Consequently, it is not a substance in its own right, even if it is capable of subsisting apart from the living body. It is because it is naturally incomplete as subsisting apart from the body that Aquinas sees this state as unnatural for it, and an intimation of, but not an argument for, the resurrection of the body.

However, that a principle of a substance should be capable of subsistence while not itself being a substance is no surprise for Aquinas in this account of substance. The body that remains after death is itself subsistent at least for a time. But it is not a substance. It is the material remains of a substance. And so, the soul can be called 'substance' by analogy, insofar as it is the formal principle of a substance. In English it might be better to call it "substantial" rather than "substance."

But all this brings us face to face with a problem similar to the one Aristotle had to deal with, and he not too effectively, it must be said. The theory of the substantial union of the human composite ensures man's unity; but doesn't it overdo it, somewhat ... to the extent that his personal immortality becomes impaired? Aquinas got out of this difficulty by making his famous distinction between intrinsic and extrinsic dependence. The (purely sensitive) soul of an animal is totally dependent on the body for all its operations. Hence when the body, on which it totally, intrinsically depends, perishes or corrupts, the sensitive soul of the animal cannot but corrupt too. But man has a rational soul which does not always depend on the body for all its actions. It has a subsistent form and so is only extrinsically dependent on matter. Hence, when the body corrupts, the soul is not affected.

2.7.3.4.2. Ethics

St Thomas Aquinas followed in general the basic ethical theory of Aristotle. However, early in the discussion, he introduces an important distinction between human acts *(actiones humanae)* and acts of man (*actiones hominis)*. The former proceed directly from man's free will and have the good (real or apparent) as their object, whereas the latter are inadvertent, unconscious.

Only the former come within the proper sphere of ethics. Like Aristotle, also, Aquinas held that happiness is the ultimate end of the human agent: this is his good. Again, with Aristotle, Aquinas will hold that this happiness is not to be found in riches or any created good, but only in God. Where Aristotle would seem to include the contemplation of the highest objects as comprising man's happiness (assuredly a very intellectualistic understanding of the matter), Aquinas would emphasise that this is true only when it comes to talking about the very imperfect happiness we can attain in this life. Actually, even in this life, we are to attain this happiness in knowing God. Admittedly, we can only know him in a very imperfect and analogical way. In the next life can we know God as he is in himself and in a way that can, alone, perfectly satisfy man.

2.7.4. Some Critical Remarks

2.7.4.1. His Philosophy of Knowledge

2.7.4.1.1. The Distinction between Philosophy and Theology

The wheel has now come full circle! However useful Aquinas distinction might have been from the point of view of a certain pedagogy, and however useful it might have been from a Hellenistic perspective, we are too aware of the deficiencies of a "pure-reason" "pure-faith" approach and now are seeking a more integrated vision of reality which, if it would not be exactly as St Anselm expressed in his famous "credo ut intelligam", would make for a more integrated vision of reality which, if it would make for more "holistic" (to use a fashionable word) response, as well as capture the spirit of our great Indian thinkers. In the West, a philosopher is not expected to be a holy man. In the East, it is part and parcel of his personal make-up. Philosophising is not just a kind of intellectual refinement: it involves the flowering of all that is most human and personal in the visionary. Besides, a rigid attitude to the two disciplines inevitably leads to a let of repetition, not to mention confusion and dissatisfaction when a topic, such as the question of evil is treated 'only philosophically" and the student is told to wait some three or four years until the "rational response" to the issue will be completed with a "faith response" which will be taken up somewhere in theology. Finally, one can well ask if the intellectualistic vision of Hellenistic philosophy will prepare one best for the more personalistic vision of the Semitic and Biblical mentality and outlook.

2.7.4.1.2. Aquinas on Knowledge

St Thomas has certainly built a very masterly syntheses as regards epistemological theory out of the basic observations of Aristotle. He developed and perfected all that he had found in 'the Philosopher" and added his own keen insights. Indeed, many a contemporary critic has held that Aquinas' main relevance, today, is in the area of theories of knowledge. He offers a sound and common-sense approach to the complex problem of human knowledge and shows us how to respond to the age-old objections of nominalism and neo-nominalism (the latter voiced by not a few existentialists and phenomenologists of our time). There is perhaps only one area in this connection which he left totally unexplored and that is the sphere of language. He never paid attention to what Wittgenstein and other would call "language games". Yet it is true that "religious language" and "scientific language" (to give but two examples) need be carefully observed and analysed from the point of view of the very special "rules" that they consciously or unconsciously use, the sentiments they arouse in us as we speak them and so on. All this should be taken into consideration in the theory of language and of knowledge. This is the great contribution of contemporary British philosophy.

2.7.4.2. His Philosophy of God

2.7.4.2.1. Do we need to prove God's Existence?

Many Catholic thinkers today would agree with Marcel that "proofs" for God's existence have only a confirmatory value for one who already believes. It is pretty certain that no atheist was converted due to a proof for God's existence. That is because, as Frank Sheed so tellingly put it, God is not a proposition to be proved, but a person to be experienced. A proof is directed at the head but faith is the response of a total human person. At best, a proof for God's existence would win from one the admission that belief in God is reasonable, that the search for God is not the search for an elusive will-o-the-wisp of whose existence we haven't any 'invitation to believe' even. It might even elicit a remark as fine as, "Sounds like someone worth meeting." But, in the last analysis, it boils down to experiencing God. Most believers know how to set about proving God's existence. How many of us can help others to encounter him? And yet that's what the Liturgy - and all of Christian life - is about! Yet, because God has chosen to be, in Pascal's well-known phrase, "a hidden God", proofs, perhaps, have their place in this world. But they can never be expected to "convert atheists" or replace experience!

2.7.4.2.2. The '"Five Ways"

All these "ways", as we have shown, are ultimately based on an application of the principle of causality in its transcendent sense. Now Hume - and Kant after him, even more conclusively - had shown that the traditional treatment of this famous "principle" leaves much to be desired. Kant, himself, had the greatest respect for the fifth proof from finality. Yet, he showed that, at most it can but prove the existence of some finite demiurge and, in any case, is reducible to an unjustified usage of the principle of causality. We had to wait for the first half of our century and the brilliant work of the Belgian Jesuit, Joseph Marechal, before an adequate response to Kant could be made. Unfortunately for Marechal, he was living at a time of strict censorship and the modernism scare had not quite died down. And so, we were able to profit little from the insights of this humble and original thinker who fell into disrepute because he opened himself to the charge of being labelled a Kantian.

2.7.4.2.3. On God's Nature

Nowadays, we would be more inclined to endorse a more negative theology. We are less inclined to make all sorts of statements about God's essence and nature, as if we could claim to be authorities on the subject. It is true that Thomas was well aware of the silly pretentiousness that any theodicy could fall into in this regard and he made a conscious effort to avoid it. Yet, there are times when we, men of today, are not a little shocked at the apparent bland way in which he speaks of divine psychology and so on, as if he had a special insight into all that. In any case, much of St. Thomas' observations in this line stem from his Aristotelian outlook which was somewhat intellectualistic and not sufficiently open to the fact of mystery and risk.

2.7.4.3. His Philosophy of the World

2.7.4.3.1. Creation out of Nothing

St. Thomas was indebted to St. Augustine for his basic understanding of creation. But he went much deeper into it and drew attention to the more positive meaning of the term, as total dependence. That is why he was able to explain not only why no other creature can create - even by "delegation" from God - but also how there could be an "eternal creation". However, his rejection of the Augustinian "rationes seminales" would go a long way to give early twentieth- century Thomists their bias against evolution. It must be admitted that, even if St. Thomas didn't quite expound such a view, his disciples tended to derive from his teachings a rather static understanding of the universe!

2.7.4.3.2. Analogy

Here is another great contribution of St Thomas, elaborated from an Aristotelian intuition and of particular relevance to the Indian scene. If it is true that not all Indian thought is pantheist, it is as much certain that this pantheism or monism derived from the lack of the notion of participation and analogy that obtains among our early metaphysicians, such as Śankara and Rāmānuja.

2.7.4.3.3. The Problem of Evil

Once again, we note Aquinas' indebtedness to Augustine, this time for the latter's definition of evil as privation. And once again we see how St. Thomas could turn his brilliant intellectual vision to good account in this, inasmuch as he led the reflection on the mystery of evil to more profound depths. But once again, too, his intellectualism seems to come in the way. His response to the mystery is plausible and reasonable enough. But it lacks the personal touch which a more human and existential approach - such as that of Lecomte de Navy in his *Of Human Destiny,* for instance. Still, one could hardly expect to work out a better rational vindication of God's goodness in the face of the evil of the world. This is confirmed by the fact that the rationalist Leibniz, five centuries later, when he set about elaborating a 'theodicy' could not improve Aquinas' earlier answer.

2.7.4.4. His Philosophy of Man

2.7.4.4.1. The Human Composite

Here St. Thomas definitely parts company with St. Augustine and rightly so! He makes it very clear that the body is no mere inferior appendage of the mind or soul which comprises man's essence. The body-soul union is something necessary and desirable in man: it is the *sine qua non* of his meaningful relationship with the world. Recent thinkers, such as Donceel, have tried to bring out even more this unity and harmony by speaking of the body as 'the soul made visible' and defining man as 'incarnate spirit'. Yet there are a few thinkers who, inspired by men like Teilhard, still wonder if even there we have not a dualistic tendency. They ask if the presupposition that a soul is required to account for certain activities of man (such as knowledge) is not precisely that! Without denying the superiority of human life to animal and plant activity, and without denying any personal after-life, they claim that we can bring out even more the unity of the human person although the concept of a soul be dropped. Such proposals are interesting and merit our considerations, whatever be our final verdict on their conclusions. (Cf. for example the interesting theory of Piet Schoonenberg)

2.7.4.4.2. Ethics

Aristotle's intellectualism led him to postulate a Supreme Being whose absolute perfection would consist in the fact of his being "thinking thought" and the Stagyrite could not imagine how such a being could busy himself about the world or be interested in it in any way without this involving some imperfection on his part. Small wonder, then, that the ultimate end of man should have been seen, by him, to consist in the act of intellectual contemplation of the highest truths. St. Thomas was also none too little influenced by this attitude and that is why, for him, the final goal of man is the Beatific Vision understood more in terms of knowledge of God, than in loving him, though the latter is by no means excluded. Leslie Dewart felt that, in spite of everything, Aquinas was not able to make ethics advance very far from the hedonism that characterised Aristotelian and all Greek moral thought; true, the angelic doctor, like the Stagyrite, advocated a mere "spiritual hedonism" but, as Deqart suggests, wouldn't it be, not only more wholesome, but also more profound to see "man's purposiveness and striving (to) reside in his seeking creatively, not to be **happy**, but to **be**"? He adds, "The Christian idea of grace can be totally integrated with this idea if we keep in mind that the free self-creation of man takes place in the presence of God not only insofar as it constitutes man's final achievement, but also insofar as it constituted his constant, present being." *(The Future of Belief,* London, 1966, p 32)

2.7.5. Final General Remark

I can think of no better way to conclude this very skimpy introduction to St. Thomas' thought than to quote the late Pope Paul VI who declared that Aquinas' doctrine "belonged not only to the Dominican Order, but to the whole Church, and indeed to the whole world; it is not merely medieval but valid for all times, not least for our own." Most of us would find that remark something of an exaggeration. But if we wish to call it an exaggeration, let us not forget that every exaggeration has a solid core of truth!

2.8. Duns Scotus (1265–1308)

2.8.1. His Life

We appreciate all the more the genius of John Duns Scotus, who earned, for himself the title "the subtle doctor" (*doctor subtilis*) and proffered a philosophico-theologico system well able to rival that of Aquinas ... even though he was to die at the comparatively young age of 43!

Born in Scotland in 1265 (or 1266), he was christened John, to which was added the family name Duns, taken from a place in the old county of Berwick from which the clan originated. By the mid-thirteenth century the name *Scoti* was being exclusively given to Scots, do we need not think that he - along with John Scotus Eriugena, with whom he is often confounded - could have come from Ireland. At the tender age of 12 he entered the Franciscan Order and received the habit two years later!

Duns Scotus studied in Paris and Oxford, where he was later to begin and continue his researches, writings and teaching. Very soon the clarity of his notions (and their subtlety!), the richness of his precise distinctions, the force of his argumentation and the depth of his problematic became known and the Franciscans were happy to find in their ranks someone who could give new power to the Augustinian tradition that they had always upheld and which was being so threatened by the Aristotelianism propounded by the Dominicans, thanks to their luminary, St. Thomas Aquinas. Duns Scotus was an independent thinker and did not hesitate to cross swords with tradition - especially with St. Thomas, whom he criticised freely and frequently. Yet he did not criticise merely for the sake of it, he did it, quite sincerely, for the sake of bringing out and establishing the truth more firmly.

After teaching at Oxford and Cambridge he was called to Cologne, after having fallen out with the French nobility in Paris, on account of his outspoken support for the Papal cause. He died in Cologne and was buried in the Franciscan Church there. Duns Scotus' work was immense, considering the shortness of his life.

The authenticity of some of the writings attributed to him have been questioned, but we are sure that the two great commentaries on the *Sentences* are his. The famous *Opus Oxoniense* (literally, the "Oxford Work") and the *Reportata Parisiensia,* though his originally, seem to contain expository comments added by over-zealous disciples. Another important work that is authentic enough is his *Tractatus de Primae Principia* (or Treatise on the First Principle).

It may not be quite out of place to add that it is to Duns Scotus that is attributed the famous "potui-decuit-fecit" argument in favour of the Immaculate Conception of the Virgin, whatever be the merit of the logical reasoning contained therein.

2.8.2. Bibliography

2.8.2.1. Primary Sources

Following are some of the better translations of the works of Duns Scotus in our Library:

John Duns Scotus, *Philosophical Writings*, selected, edited and translated by Allan Wolter OFM, London, 1962 (Taken mainly from the *Oxford Commentary on the Sentences of Peter Lombard*, but covering a wide variety of topics from the human soul to God)

_______. *A Treatise on God as First Principle*, trans, and edited by Allan Wolter OFM, Chicago, 1966.

_______. *God-Creatures*, trans. of the Quodlibetal Questions with an introduction, glossary and notes by Felix Alluntis OFM, Princeton, 1975.

2.8.2.2. Secondary Sources

Here is a very select bibliography:

Harris, C R S, *Duns Scotus*, 2 volumes, New York, 1959 (a classic; vol I: *The Place of Duns Scotus in Medieval Thought*; vol. II: His Doctrine).

Bettoni, Efrem, OFM, *Duns Scotus: the Basic Principles of His Philosophy*, (trans from the Italian by B. Bonansea OFM), Washington, 1961.

Balic, Charles, OFM, *The Formal Distinction of Duns Scotus*, Ph.D. dissertation from the Catholic University of America, Washington, 1944. (Systematic, technical treatment of a characteristic element of Scotist doctrine).

2.8.3. His Philosophy

2.8.3.1. Philosophy of Knowledge

2.8.3.1.1. Some unusual views

Scotus parted company with St. Thomas as regards not a few points. And he did not hesitate to say so in no uncertain terms, often going to the extent of qualifying some of the latter's views was not only erroneous but downright heretical. It is true that very often his criticism of Aquinas is based on a wrong interpretation of his thought, but ever so often Scotus makes a telling observation that makes us aware that there is another way of looking at the issue and that, sometimes, the Scotist view is not only more modern, but fuller and richer. At any rate, Scotus insisted on the intellectual intuition of the singular object. St. Thomas had consistently and clearly maintained that the immediate object of intellectual apprehension is the universal. Scotus would say, in effect, that this stance amounted to denying that the Apostles believed that Jesus, a singular object if there ever was one, was God - and this was rank heresy. He also held that the concept of being was not analogical but univocal. He honestly felt that this was the only way to prevent natural theology from lapsing into agnosticism. He also introduced into the theory of knowledge - in the sense that he made very extensive use of it - the famous *distinetio formalis a parte rei,* which Copleston translates ably as 'objective formal distinction'. Here, too, he was not just trying to show off his subtle mind. He was convinced that our actual use of concepts demands such a notion. In short, he felt it necessary, on several counts, to correct what he found in Thomism as dangerous and misleading, as capable of landing the unwary thinker into the morass of agnosticism. Not a few Thomists have made out a counter-thesis to the effect that it is precisely the thought of Scotus that opens the door to such developments and cite the philosophy of Occam as a perfect example.

2.8.3.1.2. Intellectual apprehension of concrete things (Intuitive cognition)

Scotus understands intuitive cognition by way of contrast with abstractive cognition. The latter, as we have seen, involves the universal; and a universal as such need not be exemplified. That is, my intelligible species of dog only tells me what it is to be a dog; it doesn't tell me whether any particular dog actually exists. Intuitive cognition, by contrast, "yields information about how things are right now". Scotus held that man can directly apprehend, with his intellect, the concrete particular things of everyday experience. St. Thomas did not deny that we can intellectually "know" the individual object. He said we cannot intellectually intuit it, i.e., we cannot know it directly and immediately, but by means of the universal that we "abstract" from the concrete, leaving aside the particularities that are essentially unintelligible. The issue is complicated, however, by a distinction between what Scotus calls the "common nature" and the universal. The distinction of the two is the distinction between "Socratesness" and the human nature of Socrates. Through an act of (intellectual-sensual) intuition, the agent intellect attains the "common nature" and derives the intelligible species form it.

2.8.3.1.3. Univocal Concept of Being

Thomas Aquinas held that the primary object of the human intellect was material being, that is, the human intellect knows directly and immediately "being realised in matter". Of course, he did not deny that the human intellect can know being in general, but this is so only indirectly and immediately (through material being). Scotus begged to differ. According to him, the primary object of the intellect is being in general. That the soul was dependent on the senses in this life, Scotus did not deny. But he held that this was due to some punishment meted out to the soul, due to original sin or something. St. Thomas held that dependence on the senses belonged to the very essence of the human soul and so, when separated from the body after death, it could not acquire any new knowledge, since it was no longer united to the body through which, alone, it could know. Scotus rejected this view as degrading to the human soul. This dependence on the body is not essential and so the human soul, when separated from the body, is by no means cut off from the possibility of acquiring new knowledge. From all this it should be easy to understand how Scotus came around to holding that the concept of being is univocal. He did not mean that God and creatures are being in the same way. Hence it is unfair to accuse him of anticipating Spinoza. He conceived "being" as simply that which is opposed to non-being. Now, God, as much as creatures, is opposed to non-being. Therefore, each is univocally being, each fulfils the Scotist definition of being in the same way. Scotus would be quite prepared to grant that God and creatures are opposed to nothingness in different ways. But though the way of opposing may be different, the fact of their opposing non-being is incontestibly equally evident. Thus, being can be predicated univocally of God and creatures. Scotus' theory follows logically from his original approach to metaphysics and epistemology. If we grant him the freedom to choose his particular stand-point and approach (and what right have we not to?) we have to say that the univocity of the concept of being is a logical result.

2.8.3.1.4. Scotus and Analogy

We have seen that, from the fact that Scotus rejected the Thomistic theory of the analogy of being, it cannot be said that he was teaching that God and creatures are the same in the real order. He quite explicitly says that they aren't. It cannot too often be stressed that he and Aquinas defined being differently. He even admits, in so many words, that "all beings have reference (attributionem) to the first being, which is God". This is, in effect, what Aquinas would call analogy of attribution. However, he wished to stress that analogy, actually, presupposes some univocity, since we cannot refer creatures to God unless there was a concept common to both.

2.8.3.2. Philosophy of God

2.8.3.2.1. Proof of the existence of God

Since man has no intuitive knowledge of God in this life, it is necessary that man prove God's existence, by reason, and that this proof be a *posteriori.* However, he was far from satisfied with the traditional proofs of Aquinas.

The proof from motion would, at most, force us to postulate a first mover. But there is no reason to oblige me to say that this first mover should transcend the physical order and be the ultimate total cause of creatures. All that the argument has shown is that it accounts for the physical fact of motion. As regards the "chains of causes" argument, the second way of Thomas, Scotus supplies another of his telling distinctions.

Scotus begins by arguing that there is a first agent (a being that is first in efficient causality). Consider first the distinction between essentially ordered causes and accidentally ordered causes. In an accidentally ordered series, the fact that a given member of that series is itself caused is accidental to that member's own causal activity. For example, Grandpa A generates a son, Dad B, who in turn generates a son of his own, Grandson C. B's generating C in no way depends on A — A could be long dead by the time B starts having children. The fact that B was caused by A is irrelevant to B's own causal activity. That's how an accidentally ordered series of causes works.

In an essentially ordered series, by contrast, the causal activity of later members of the series depends essentially on the causal activity of earlier members. For example, my shoulders move my arms, which in turn move my cricket bat. My arms are capable of moving the cricket bat only because they are being moved by my shoulders.

An essentially inter-related (or vertical) series of causes rule out all possibility of an infinite regress (i.e., a chain of causes that are dependent from the point of view of the activity). But this need not be required of an accidentally interrelated series, where the causes depend for their being on the previous ones, not for their activity. Thus, he preferred the proofs from causality or contingency, but added his own refinements and detail.

2.8.3.2.2. The Infinity of God

"Infinity" is, for Scotus, the attribute of God *par excellence.* This is because it is more fundamental than other attributes as goodness and truth, since it is no mere quality (Scotus says *passio)* to be predicated of God, but denotes his mode of being. Other perfections of God flow from and are grounded in his infinity. Scotus presents a series of arguments to bring out God's infinity. For instance, it is not incompatible with finite being that there would be a more perfect being, but it is incompatible with the supreme being that there be a more perfect being. But infinity is greater and more perfect than finitude.

Therefore, the supreme being must be infinite. Indeed, Scotus points out, there is no incompatibility between "being" and "infinite".

2.8.3.2.3. St. Anselm's Argument

Scotus said that the argument of St. Anselm is inadequately expressed. It needs to be "coloured" or improved upon and even then, it can be no more than a *persuasio probabilis,* a probable proof, the only through-going demonstrations of God's existence being the *a posteriori* ones. The particular "colouration" that Scotus had in mind would involve restating the argument thus: "God is that than which, having been thought without contradiction, a greater cannot be thought without contradiction". He then proceeds to show that the greatest conceivable being is not a contradiction, and then he points out that if it is possible it must exist, for a merely possible greatest conceivable being would be less great than something that actually exists! But Scotus immediately adds a caution. Though we might be able to conclude to the existence of the greatest possible being if we can definitively show it is a possible being, it does not follow, from the mere fact that we cannot observe any contradiction in the idea, that in actual fact no contradiction is involved.

2.8.3.2.4. Many Attributes of God are not Demonstrable

Parting company with St Thomas and many medieval, Scotus held that many of the essential attributes of God, such as omnipotence, omnipresence, truth, etc. cannot be proved. All these, he says, come under *credibilia,* things to be believed and we know that God is all these only through faith. Finally, Scotus will differ with St. Thomas once again, when the latter would recognise in God no real distinctions apart from the distinction between divine persons. Scotus recognised an objective formal distinction in God between the various divine attributes. We shall try to explain what this distinction is, in the next section.

2.8.3.2.5. About Creation

Scotus was of the opinion that God's ability to create in the strict sense (i.e., out of nothing) can be proved. As regards an eternal or a temporal creation, he disagreed with those who held that creation from eternity can be philosophically proved. He agreed, with St. Thomas, that creation in time cannot be proved philosophically, either. But he seems to be much more hesitant in speaking out his minds as regards this question.

2.8.3.3. Philosophy of the World

2.8.3.3.1. The objective formal distinction

Though Scotus did not invent the celebrated *distinctio formalis a parte rei* (*'formal distinction on the side of/ in respect of the thing'* which several earlier Franciscan thinkers made use of it), he employed it so extensively that may people think it was his own invention. It is a kind of halfway house between a real and a mental (or logical) distinction.

The real distinction arises when we are concerned with separableness in reality (as between a man's two hands) or when, of two realities, one is not a part of the other (there is a real distinction between matter and form because, though, they can't be physically separated, matter is not a part of form and vice versa). A logical distinction is one that our mind makes (e.g. between a thing and its definition, between a man and his soul). In reality, they are identical or one is a part of the other. The distinction arises from my point of view, is grounded in my mind rather in reality. Thomists would further subdivide logical distinctions into those which admit of a foundation in reality (as between the vegetative and rational "souls" in man) and those which don't (as between the divine attributes). Scotus felt that there were other cases which warrant yet another possibility to which the *distinctio formalis a parte rei* was the sole answer. To understand this, we must grasp what is meant by *the formalitas* or *(ratio formalis*) of a thing: it is its constitutive note, that which makes it to be what it is. Sometimes, as in the case of God's justice and God's mercy, each of two things are identical with the same essence (here, the divine essence), Yet God's justice is, as such, not God's mercy. Their formality is distinct. Scotus felt that it is not merely our mind that makes the distinction and so wouldn't be ready to call this a mere logical distinction. In any case, Aquinas' way of viewing the matter seemed to undermine the objectivity of knowledge, for it appeared to imply that the mind is reading into the object what isn't there. On the other hand, the Scotist distinction, while not impairing the unity of the object, asserted that there was something *a parte rei* (from the part of the object or thing) which corresponded to what the mind was asserting.

2.8.3.3.2. Individuation

We have here one of the best examples of the richness of Scotus' subtle and penetrating mind. Individuation is the fact of a being not being another being and the "principle of individuation" is that which, in the being, brings this about. What "individuates" God from creatures is the fact that his is not a received existence, whereas the creature's existence is a received existence. Again, it is clear that what individuates a horse from a cow is their form. That is how one can "tell them apart". But what individuates one horse from another horse, or one man from another man? It is true that I tell them apart by their "accidents", by their particular height. colour etc. But surely, it can't be these accidents that individuate them. I could conceive, for instance, two men who are identical twins and so possess the same "accidents" and yet they would be individuated. They would be two separate individuals. What individuates them? Not their form, as we have seen and certainly not their accidents. What else is left to individuate them if not prime matter? This what Aquinas says. But, as we have become accustomed to expect, Scotus disagrees.

Prime matter cannot individuate, says Scotus, for it is of itself indistinct and indeterminate, so how can it give distinctness and determinateness to a thing? Not even the Thomistic refinement of the theory is acceptable, for it seems to say that quantity individuates. But quantity is an accident and, as we have seen, an accident cannot individuate.

What then individuates? It is the *entitas individualis or hacceitas* (i.e. the individual entity or the "thisness" of the thing). This is vague and abstruse enough, but Scotus will point out that the "thisness" of the thing is, thus, something positive, for it provides this individuation. Hence knowledge of the particular is vindicated as against the apparent overvaluation of the universal found in Aristotle and Thomas - and, obviously, Plato.

2.8.3.4. Philosophy of Man

2.8.3.4.1. Primacy of the Will

In perhaps no other aspect of Scotus' thought does his Augustinian roots seem so evident as in his insistence of the superiority of the will over the intellect. This follows from the fact that the intellect is a natural power, but the will is a free power. If something is presented to the intellect as true, it cannot but give its assent to it. It is not "free". But the will is ever free. If something is presented to it as good, it still remains free to accept or reject it. St. Thomas holds that when the will is confronted with the supreme good, as is the case with the blessed in heaven, they cannot but choose it and adhere to it. Scotus held that the will is *never* physically determined by the good, not even the absolute good. He agreed that the blessed in heaven cannot sin (in his conception of the term), but because of a positive free inclination of the will due to the "habit of glory" *(habitus gloriae).* Scotus adds other reasons to indicate the primacy of the will. For instance, the corruption of the will implies hatred. Corruption of the intellect is ignorance or refusal to know. Now hatred is a worse corruption, hence it is the corruption of that which is better. And so on.

2.8.3.4.2. Body and Soul

We have seen that, in characteristic Augustinian fashion, Scotus diminished the extent of the dependence of the soul on the body, yet, thanks to his rich cast of mind, he was able to do this in a way which involved little of that scorn of the body that we have come to expect from such an approach. We have already seen how he accepted that the soul is, in this life, dependent on the body, but would not hold that this is something intrinsic to the soul as such. Thus, it could acquire new knowledge when in a state of separation from the body. The here-and-now dependence of the soul on the body and on material being is a kind of punishment added on to the soul, not something that flows from its very nature. Scotus says that St. Thomas, at best, teaches that the soul is united to the body for the good of the soul. The body is there to provide the soul with knowledge and so on. He does not agree with such a conception. The soul is united to the body for the perfection of the whole man, who consists of soul and body. The *de facto* state of the dependence of the former on the latter is because of man's state as way fare, on the road to heaven and not yet arrived there (or perhaps due to sin). After all, it is man, the total composite whom God created and it is man, the total composite, who acts!

2.8.3.4.3. Immortality

That the rational soul is the form of man and that one could prove this "by the natural light of reason" Scotus had no doubt. But it is quite another matter when there is question of the immortality of the soul can, at best, be buttressed by parable arguments, nothing more. It can only be known by faith. As regards the resurrection of the body, that is even less demonstrable. However, faith can assure us of this. He criticised Aquinas' attempts to establish the immortality of the soul, but did not quite say that they were erroneous. That they were probable and even persuasive he would admit. What he denied was that they were fully demonstrative and conclusive.

2.8.3.4.4. Ethics

Scotus is often accused of teaching that the moral law is due simply to the arbitrary caprice of God who decided "just like that" that certain actions be good and others be bad. Though such a charge is understandable, it is not quite fair. Scotus makes a distinction between the primary and secondary precepts of the Decalogue and held that only the first three - the primary precepts - are absolutely binding and not even God can dispense it from their observance. As regards the others, it seems that God had, in fact, dispensed from their observation on specific occasions in the Old Testament. This means that the secondary precepts are not so solidly and immediately grounded in God's nature as the primary. They follow rather from the primary precepts and not directly from God's nature. Aquinas and his disciples held that God cannot dispense from any of the Ten Commandments as they all are grounded in his Eternal Will and, if God did dispense man from serving these laws in certain situations, it was not due to a real repeal of the laws, as it were, but a change in the concrete situations which made it such that the laws concerned didn't apply.

2.8.4. Some Critical Remarks

2.8.4.1. His Philosophy of Knowledge

2.8.4.1.1. Scotus' Originality

It should be clear enough that Scotus was an original independent thinker and that when he differed with St. Thomas, he did not do so just to be difficult, as his penetrating criticisms do show. He firmly believed in the objectivity of knowledge and if he defended some views that others would later use to attack this-very objectivity, paradoxically enough, he, at least, developed and defended them because he felt such an approach would safeguard human knowledge - and the Christian faith - better than Aquinas' approach. One does not brand an approach to reality as right or wrong: one is obliged to admit a plurality of approaches, since reality is too vast, too rich to be approached from one point alone. And each approach, whether we realise it or not, cannot but take a particular frame-work in which to develop its system. And it elaborates a particular language which is relevant to that approach and frame-work. Hence, Scotus' approach is as valid and legitimate as Aquinas'. Perhaps the only requirement that we can exact of any frame-work, of any system, is that it does not distort reality or ignore aspects of it that refuse to "fit into" the preferred approach.

Both Aquinas and Scotus offer us a consistent and logical approach to the mystery of being and their conclusions follow quite legitimately from their promises. Hence, it is up to us to choose between these but on the basis of which for me, given a better, richer and more meaningful picture of reality.

2.8.4.1.2. Intellectual Apprehension of Particulars

This is a very good example of what we have just said. I think it would be foolish and unfair to criticise Scotus from the stand-point of Thomism or to interpret Aquinas in terms of his subtle opponent's philosophy. Those who say that Scotus was degrading the human intellect are viewing the latter through Thomistic spectacles. And those who say that Aquinas' view that we cannot directly and immediately know particulars implies agnosticism are distorting what the angelic doctor said by misrepresenting his views, because they have chosen to understand him from undermining the spirituality of the intellect and Aquinas was no crypto-agnostic! Each of their views are perfectly orthodox and logical, when read within their respective systems. If we wish to choose one of these two ways of viewing knowledge, our choice will have to be on the basis of which of these two approached we find, personally, more rich and meaningful.

2.8.4.1.3. The Univocal Concept of Being

Thomists claim that the Scotist theory of the univocity of the notion of being could lead to a kind of pantheism and there are even a few who try to make out that Scotus was a kind of proto-Spinozist. Nothing 'could be further from the truth - except, perhaps, the charge made by certain Scotists that the Thomistic doctrine of the analogy of being would lead necessarily to the death of metaphysics and of natural theology. Once again, we have to decide which is, for us" the richer and more meaningful definition of being, the Scotist (that which is) or the Thomist (that which is in its own way). For neither of these two great thinkers understood or developed their doctrines in a way that would inevitably lead to the errors people would like to accuse them of. Each doctrine is perfectly orthodox, consistent and takes care of all real and imaginary dangers!

2.8.4.2. His Philosophy of God

2.8.4.2.1. Proofs for God's Existence

The fact that Scotus could uphold the primacy of *a posteriori* proofs for God's existence shows that, convinced Augustinian though he was, he was no blind follower of the great African Doctor. He was quite ready to break with the pronouncedly Augustinian preference for *a priori* proofs. His criticism of Aquinas' ways, on the other hand, do reveal clearly enough, that the angelic doctor had taken not a few short-cuts in his elaboration of the argument and a more careful and deeper treatment of the argumentation was necessary. As for Anselm's proof, he very ably anticipated Leibniz' observations on the same and most likely would have been able to show the latter that perhaps the only way to show that the concept of God is a possible concept would be through an analysis of some activity, some existential activity, which reveals the possibility of the concept as a necessary pre-condition. This, in effect, was what Marechal would do. (Cf. in this connection, Donceel, *Natural Theology,* pp 15-19)

2.8.4.2.2. The "Names" or Attributes of God

It is true that Scotus held that many of the attributes of God could not be demonstrated by reason, though Aquinas was of the view that they could. Most of the time the difference of view, here, is due to the fact that Scotus was much more demanding as to what constituted a demonstration in the full sense of the word. Besides, he had the habit of introducing into the discussion various distinctions and refinements that Aquinas simply did not take into account, nor felt were relevant to the issue. Yet, he did not hesitate to qualify the proofs, when they were forthcoming, as "probable" "more probable" or "persuasive". Still, however, understanding one tries to be, it is difficult to accept, with him, that the infinity of God can be proven whereas other attributes cannot. One cannot help thinking that, even granted his particular framework, many of the: *credibilia* can come within the ambit of philosophy.

2.8.4.3. His Philosophy of the World

2.8.4.3.1. The Objective Formal Distinction

Scotus was convinced, quite sincerely, that unless we admitted such a distinction, we were in danger of undermining the objectivity of the human intellect. He felt that the Thomistic recognition that some merely mental distinctions do have a foundation in reality was not enough for they do not sufficiently bring out conformity of our knowledge with reality. On the contrary, they seem to show that our intellect, in some cases is more subjective and arbitrary than objective. However, the objective formal distinction seemed to save the situation. In as much as it was an objective distinction, it pointed to something inherent in the object. Yet, as a "formal" distinction, it did not entail that the unity of the object be in any way impaired. Thus, he seemed to have found out a better way to speak of, for instance, the distinction between the divine perfections than Aquinas. Scotus' theory, in this respect, seems to offer a richer and more meaningful picture than Aquinas', however orthodox, consistent and defendable though it be!

2.8.4.3.2. Individuation

Scotus' view that it is the "thisness" of the thing that individuates, when taken together with his assertion that man can immediately know the particular, laid the foundation for a new viewpoint, one which is very modern indeed. Scotus was one of the first to underplay the element of the universal in knowledge and stress the importance of the individual, the concrete, the particular. Perhaps the traditional view had given too much importance to the universal and neglected the particular. Scotus will turn attention in this direction, though it may not be altogether his fault if individualism was to become a disturbing problem in the hands of his disciples and indeed in much of recent philosophy.

2.8.4.4. His Philosophy of Man

2.8.4.4.1. Primacy of the Will

Here we are face to face with one of the key oppositions in the two great currents of Scholastic philosophy: the intellectualism of St. Thomas (and indeed of the whole Aristotelian tradition) and the voluntarism of St. Augustine (and the Platonic stream). Let us note, once again, that here too it is more of a question of a different point of view than a regular opposition. The primacy of the intellect in Thomas is a primacy of priority (you must know something before you can will or love it), whereas the primacy of the Will in Augustine is a primacy of fulfilment (love of something is more enriching than more knowledge of it). However, Scotus' understanding of the indefectability of the blessed not only brings out his tremendous respect for the dignity of human freedom, but also affords a fruitful and interesting alternative way of understanding the situation of man whom confronted with the supreme good.

2.8.4.4.2. Body and Soul

Scotus' understanding of the body-soul relationship is interesting and, to say the least, quite original. Though one cannot but recognise a typically Augustinian under-playing of the role of the body (e.g. the soul can still acquire new knowledge after separation from the body), yet - thanks to his nimble mind - Scotus was able to do all this without in any way depreciating or despising the body. If the union of body and soul is not essential to the make-up of the soul, it is nonetheless a good for the whole composite and has a positive value for man's wayfarer condition here and now as *homo viator* (original sin is not the only explanation put forward to explain this condition). From this it is clear to see how Scotus was of the opinion that the resurrection of the body cannot be proved philosophically: after all, the human soul would in no way be essentially incomplete when separated from the body!

2.8.4.4.3. Ethics

It should be obvious enough that it is not fair to Scotus to accuse him of basing his ethical doctrine on some sort of arbitrary divine authoritarianism. The very fact that he made a distinction between primary and secondary precepts show that he did not conceive of the whole moral law as simply based on God's arbitrary choice. The actual discussion and interpretation of the particular Old Testament texts which taxed Scotus and Thomas, inasmuch as they speak of God permitting apparent violations of the Decalogue, is beyond our scope here. Suffice it is to say that modem exegesis does not feel the need to try to hunt up such explanations. Finally, if Scotus did not teach that the whole moral law, including the" entire decalogue, is the arbitrary creation of the divine will, he certainly prepared the way for Occam to say so.

2.8.5. Final Remarks

Scotus certainly helped prepare the ground for the critical philosophy of the fourteenth century. The radical and destructive views of Occam, if they are not the logical outcome of Scotism, sound more plausible to one whom Scotus had schooled. It seems, however, ridiculous to make of the subtle doctor a direct precursor of Occam or even Luther. Nor is one justified to try and make of him a continuator of Thomism, someone in the same line of thought who meant but to correct and polish up a bit the philosophy of

Aquinas. Scotus all too often parts company with St. Thomas for us to be able to justify such a view. He is a deep and original thinker who neither hesitated to attack Aquinas nor break away from his Augustinian tradition, when he felt it necessary. And it was he who inspired the poetry of Gerald Manley Hopkins SJ, which escapes most of us.

2.9. William of Ockham (c.1287–1347)

2.9.1. His Life

William of Ockham (often called simply "Occam") was born somewhere between 1287 and 1300 in either Ockham in Surreyor in Yorkshire, though, as Copleston observes, "it is possible that he was simply William Ockam and his name had nothing to do with (either) village." He entered the Franciscan Order and, by 1310, was studying theology at Oxford. Then a spell of lecturing in philosophy and in theology must have followed. At any rate, from 1319-24 we find him in Europe, where he gave himself up to study, writing and disputation. He had an extensive knowledge of the great Scholastics who preceded him and possessed unusual insight into Aristotle. In 1324 he was summoned to appear before Pope John XXII, at Avignon, on charges of heresy. Thus, he was never able to teach as an official doctor, though he had fulfilled all the academic requirements. This explains the honorific title given him, *venerabilis inceptor,* the first as a mark of respect to the man who founded a new trend or school in thought (Ockhamism or Nominalism), the second because he never got beyond the official beginner's stage (Latin, *inceptor)* in his teaching career. Realising that the process against him was loaded, "Occam" fled to Germany where he sought the protection of Loius of Bavaria. "Protect me with your sword and I'll defend you with my pen," he is supposed to have said. In any case, he certainly earned his royal protection well, supporting Louis' claim to the Imperial throne (as against another pretender favoured by Pope John), and later championing his cause, when he wished to marry a close relative, not to mention various other cases of less moment. When Louis incurred papal displeasure and an excommunication to boot, Occam really leapt into the fray and then began a long polemic on the Church-State issue, a polemic which spanned the reign of three different popes and occasionally strayed into theological questions. Unfortunately, Occam's protector died suddenly 1347 and the intractable Franciscan began to take steps towards reconciling himself with the Church, quite certainly not only for prudential reasons. But he died two years later, in

Munich, a victim of the Black Death, apparently before he was able to sign the formula of submission.

2.9.2. Bibliography

> William of Ockham presents the spectacle (which has had not a few parallels) of a philosopher, generally conceded to be of the first importance, whose reputation seems undiminished by the fact that none of his logical, physical or philosophical works have been published since the seventeenth century. (- McKeon)

No wonder, then, that there are no copies or editions of any Occam's original works in our library, save a few extracts from his *Seven Quodlibeta* edited and translated by McKeon from a 1491 edition published at Strasbourg (in Volume II of *Selections from Medieval Philosophers*, London, 1931.) As regards our stock of secondary sources, these consist, for the most part, of scholarly dissertations on technical points (mainly in French, German and Latin). I cannot but mention a very good study of Occam on the Church-State question, though it is in French (*La doctrine de l'eglise et de l'etat chez Occam*, Adalbert Hammam OFM, Paris, 1942). We have also Ernest Moody's excellent book, *The Logic of William Occam*, which Bertrand Russell read and appreciated. Apart from these, should you wish to deepen your acquaintance with 'Occam", you will have to rest contented with browsing in the more general English manuals (Copleston has some six chapters on him, totaling nigh 80 pages).

2.9.3. His Thought

2.9.3.1. Philosophy of Knowledge

2.9.3.1.1. "Occam's Razor"

Mention of Occam makes almost everyone think of his "razor", a maxim of intellectual economy (it has been called the 'law of intellectual birth control') usually presented, in Latin, as *entia non sunt multiplicanda sine necessitate* (literally; beings must not be multiplied without necessity). It is sound philosophy not to unnecessarily complicate an issue by needless multiplications of notions and subdivisions of notions when one could explain things equally well without them. The problem is that most other Scholastics found necessary a good many 'beings' that Occam eliminated with his ruthless razor. Not only did the universals get slashed, but also, as we shall see, space, time and not a few other 'beings'.

2.9.3.1.2. Universals

Occam was determined to revive what he considered to be a not properly understood thesis of Aristotle that only individuals exist. What have been called universals are mere terms which signify individual things and stand for them in propositions. Since whatever exists is individual, the very idea of an existent universal is contradictory. Occam then sets out to show that there is no common reality existing in the members of a species. For instance, a new man could be created or an existing one annihilated by God, without any other man's essence being in any way affected. In any case, held Occam, there is no need to postulate any universals to explain knowledge. The individual mind and the individual thing can explain all. The fact that the question of universals does arise at all is due to the mere fact of our observing degrees of similarity in individual things. Since Plato and Socrates are more similar to each other than to an ass, we are led to make up the specific concept of man. Yet we must be on our guard against saying that Plato and Socrates share in some thing(s) (for that would imply that there is some common nature that is theirs); we should say, rather, that they are alike by some things. Now there seems to be very little difference, when all is said and done, between this understanding of universal and that of the classical Scholastics. It is certainly not them that Occam is refuting when he says that creating or annihilating one member of a species would not affect the others. Yet, since Occam (as we shall see, presently) denied that there exist any such thing as divine ideas, there was no possibility of any metaphysical reasons for such similarities. There was just the arbitrary divine choice.

2.9.3.1.3. Terministic Logic

With Occam, logic becomes less and less a tool of knowledge, but its very subject matter. The important thing is no longer to find rules for correct thinking, but to analyse, study and classify the use of the term in knowledge. It is true that Occam did not originate this approach. Englishmen, Frenchmen and, above all, a certain "Peter of Spain" had inaugurated such an approach almost a century before Occam took it over. But it was he who hammered such a method into a real scientific discipline which would he put to good use by many a later English logician, all the way down to the Language Analysts and Logical Positivists of our time. Basic to terministic logic is the distinction between the signification and the supposition of terms. The signification of a term, as the word indicates, refers to its status as sign. Though terms may differ in various languages, their signification is the same: "*man*", "*hombre*" and "*ādmī*" are signs for the same reality. The supposition is a property belonging to a term in a proposition. It expresses the function of standing for something definite in a given statement. When I say, "That man is alive", I am referring to a specific person. This is an example of personal supposition. Or I can use also the same term "man" to refer to all of that species, as when I say, "Man is rational". This is a simple supposition. Or can I use the word "man" to refer to itself as a word, as when I say "Man is a monosyllable". This is a material supposition. Terministic logic, then, would proceed to study in more detail, with the help of careful classification and analysis, the supposition of terms in statements.

2.9.3.1.4. A Basic Empiricism

There is a basic empiricism that characterises Occam's theory of knowledge and which will enter the mainstream of British philosophical thought to remain there together with its impact on language analysis. He holds, in effect, that sense-perception and introspection are our two sources of knowledge concerning all that exists. He speaks of our having intuitive knowledge and this, it is true, is something more than sense-knowledge. It refers to the intellectual apprehension of the material things, the individual existent. He denies that we can have intuition of anything else. Like Scotus, he holds that we are able to intellectually apprehend the individual material existent directly, and not by having to pass by the way of the universal or any such thing. This is empiricism, but it can't be put on the same plane as the empiricism of Locke, though it is all "in the family".

2.9.3.1.5. The Universal Concept of Being

Occam agrees with Scotus that the general concept of being is universal. Were this not so, declares the former (echoing the latter), we would not be able to form any concept of God, since we do not have any intuition of his essence. Not that this means we can have a proper concept of the divine being. Like Scotus before him, Occam went out of his way to show that the theory of the univocity of the concept of being does not lead to pantheism. That would be if being were predicated of God and creatures as if they were perfectly alike. But this is not so. Far from even recognising that God and creatures are alike in some way and unlike in other ways, Occam continues, God and creatures are neither accidently nor substantially alike. And yet 'being" is predicated of them. But when we do not in any way imply that the latter are modes of the former or that they both participate in some super-reality called being. All this would lead to pantheism. In fact, Occam - like Scotus before him - was quite convinced that the theory of the analogous predications of being would evitably lead to pantheism. When we predicate "being" univocally of God and creatures, we do not imply that there is some corresponding common reality in them; we just mean that they are wholly different things simply conceived as existing.

2.9.3.2. Philosophy of God

2.9.3.2.1. No Divine Ideas

We have already said that Occam wished to maintain, at all cost, the omnipotence and freedom of God. Now, the famous divine ideas, apart from being one of those unnecessary beings needlessly multiplied by philosophers (and thereby meriting the slash of his terrible *razor*!), seemed to threaten this very divine freedom and omnipotence. It was all Plato's fault: his particular philosophy necessitated the existence of ideal forms and the Augustinian, slavishly following him, thought they had solved the problem by placing these forms in God's mind and making of them the archetypes of creation. But these ideas limited God's freedom and omnipotence. For, inasmuch as they were patterns of reality, he is obliged to make various individuals of a species which resembled each other. It was not because he was being obliged to conform to some archetypal pattern in his mind; it was merely because he had freely chosen to do so.

2.9.3.2.2. Proving God's Existence

Occam is in full agreement with Scotus: the existence of God cannot be known by 'a priori' deduction. However, Occam was rather wary of the principle of causality. All we can know of a thing is that it has a cause; we cannot establish with certainty what this particular cause of it is. Hence, we cannot expect him to be too impressed by the traditional proofs for God's existence. But when he says that conservation, rather than contingency etc., could be a proof for God's existence, we should not feel he has suddenly changed his mind. For here we are concerned with an activity, the here and now fact of things being kept in existence. Now, as Scotus has shown, we cannot have an infinite being kept in a series which involves dependence in activity. This brings us, then, to a conserver, instead of the producer or mover or causer so most we have proven that there is some being conserving this world. We cannot exclude that there be other worlds, each having its own conserver! That his conserver is God and that he is the unique conserver of all things, that can only be known through faith!

2.9.3.2.3. Concerning God's Nature

We have seen that we cannot strictly and conclusively prove, by the light of natural reason, that God exists as the infinite and omnipotent being, creator of all things. Occam would go as a step further. He says that even if one were to grant the concept of an absolutely supreme being, one could not deduce from that concept that he would be infinite and omnipotent, that is universal cause. Neither can one assert that he is omniscient. That he knows other things beside himself can neither be proved nor disproved (one cannot prove, for instance, every cognition depends on an object). At most we can prove that God knows some things other than himself. But these proofs are not conclusive: they have the force of more probable arguments.

2.9.3.3. Philosophy of the World

2.9.3.3.1. Causality Undermined

Occam's empiricistic outlook led him to cast severe doubts on the famous principle of causality. The direct intellectual knowledge we have of one thing cannot give us direct intellectual knowledge of another thing. At most, we can 'intuit' that a given thing must needs have a cause. But what this actual cause is can only be given us through some experience. This arises when we discover through trial and error - by reviving various antecedents and noting whether the result or consequent is also thereby removed - what that cause is. But when we cannot remove an antecedent (e.g. the moon to show it is the cause of tides or God to show he is the cause of creation) we can never prove philosophically that a particular thing is the cause of a particular effect, Causality, then admits of a strictly empirical application only.

2.9.3.3.2. Motion, Place and Time

These are three more 'beings' that fell victim to Occam's merciless "razor". To begin with motion, Occam accepts the Aristotelian sub-division of qualitative motion (alteration or change) and quantitative or local motion (movement). However, neither of these involve positive entities in themselves. In qualitative motion or change, a thing acquires (or loses) a form gradually, part by part. The only "beings" this obliges us to postulate are moments of rest, and we create out of that a being called movement. Again, following Aristotle, Occam makes short work of place and time. Place is not an entity distinct from the surface of a body and the surfaces of other bodies with reference to which the body is said to be in a certain place. As for time, that is not a thing distinct from motion.

2.9.3.4. Philosophy of Man

2.9.3.4.1. The Human Soul

According to Occam, it cannot be proved that man has an immaterial and incorruptible soul, which is the form of his body. We have no reason to postulate a soul to account for such activities as knowing and willing. We may, then, quite reasonably conclude that they are the acts of the extended and corporeal form. Of course, Occam adds, once again, that we do have immortal souls but only through faith.

2.9.3.4.2. Two Forms in Man

Even if we accept, as a datum of faith, that man has immaterial and incorruptible form, we are forced to say that it does not inform our matter directly. For the human body is not incorruptible - which would be the case if it were directly supported by incorruptible form. Hence, we have to suppose that there is in man “another form in addition to the intellectual soul, namely a sensitive form, on which a natural agent can act by way of corruption and production”. This latter is distinct from the former and, ordinarily, perishes with the body unless God should will otherwise. In maintaining that there is a special form of corporeality in man, Occam was continuing the Platonic-Augustinian tradition of the Franciscan school.

2.9.3.4.3. Intellect and Will

Occam put his trusty razor to work again in dealing with the famous faculties. We may distinguish the various sense-faculties from each other - seeing is not hearing (this is confirmed from the fact that the organs of one being impaired do not in any way impair the other). But there is no need to postulate different eliciting principles of the various sense activities. There is but the one sensitive soul that is extended throughout the body acts through different sense- organs. The case is the same with reference to the immaterial and incorruptible soul of man. The intellect is nothing but this soul understanding and the will is naught but this same soul willing.

2.9.3.4.4. Freedom

This is one of the chief properties of the rational creature. Its existence is shown, not *a priori,* but by reflecting on the evident experience that ‘however much (man’s) reason dictates something, his will can will it or not will it.” This is further confirmed from the fact that we condemn or commend people for their actions, which implies that we recognise that they were free to do or not to do these acts. Parting company with St. Thomas, Occam will hold that man remains free even with reference to his last end, happiness. That God alone is able to satisfy the will cannot be proved philosophically, says Occam: it is but an article of faith. And even if we are persuaded of this truth through faith, we can still not will it, as experience shows. Besides, there are men who feel convinced that perfect happiness is not attainable. Erroneous though this view may be, the will of man can refuse to set its sights on the attainment of what it knows to be (or wrongly believes to be, through the intellect) impossible. So, man’s freedom is absolute.

2.9.3.4.5. Ethics

We have already had occasion to mention that Occam’s denial of divine ideas and of created natures would make impossible any kind of morality based on natural law. As a consequence, the only ontological foundation of the moral order would be the free choice of the divine will. Man is obliged to do what God orders him to do and not to do what God orders him not to do. And this obligation is not grounded in human nature, for there is none such. It is directly grounded in God’s free choice, in divine arbitrary authority. Evil arises when one disregards an obligation - and disregard an obligation one can, for one is always physically free. God is under no obligation and so he cannot do evil. He has given man a certain set of obligation - e.g. not to murder or steal etc. And man would do evil were he to disregard this obligation and act in defiance of it. But it could have been otherwise. Had God chosen to give man other obligations, he might as well have created an ethical order where murder and lying were permitted and some other arbitrarily chosen acts were forbidden. There is no immutable natural law upon which morality is founded. Very logically, Occam went on to say that God could totally cause a specific man to elicit an act of hatred. There would, then, be no moral evil in the act at all. Certainly, man is not culpable since the act is not his, nor would God be guilty of an evil act since he is not governed by any moral obligation and evil arises only when one freely disregards a moral obligation. Indeed, were God to order fornication, stealing and so on, it would be evil not to do these things!

2.9.3.4.6. Right Reason

After having presented his case for an arbitrary moral code founded on divine authority alone, Occam also speaks of "right reason" in morality, a concept frequently used by traditional Scholastics and which seems to contradict his authoritarianism. For an act to be moral, it is necessary man is morally obliged to follow his conscience. All this seems to amount to saying that Occam is bringing in through the back door the natural law morality he had banished from his ethical system. And there are not a few critics who accuse Occam of teaching one ethical theory as a theologian and another one as a philosopher. In a sense there may be some truth in it. The point is that Occam didn't want to say that those who reject the Christian revelation (which tells us precisely what God has freely decided should be our moral obligations) or are ignorant of it, are thereby exempt from all ethical standards and can just do as they please. In such a case, a man is obliged to follow a conscience based on "right reason". Still it is not certain how man can discover what this "right reason" entails; after all, the Scholastics who use this phrase found it on that same natural law that Occam denied.

2.9.3.4.7. Church and State

Occam's views on the independence of political sovereignty from the spiritual power as well as his views on the Pope's position within the church (very much in the line of what we would call 'collegiality' nowadays and what was described as 'conciliarism' then) would seem to be very modern. However, we must admit that he was far from being the first to propose such a view. Occam was only upholding a gathering tradition when he maintained a clear distinction between the spiritual and temporal powers, insisting that the supreme head in the spiritual power, the Pope, is not the source of imperial power and authority and his confirmation is not required to validate an imperial election. The emperor derives his authority, not from the Pope, but from the people through their electors. Ultimately, the power of the emperor came from God, through the people. But the people are free to choose their own form of government, be it an elected of a hereditary monarch. Occam also held that papal absolutism, even within the Church, was unjustified. It should be checked and limited through synods and councils. The Pope, then, should not govern the church despotically and monarchically. He should do so in consultation. Occam's polemic against the arbitrary and unrestrained power of the papacy - especially the Avignon popes - had an important part to play in the formation of the Conciliar Movement which we can see as the forerunner of today's theory of Collegiality.

2.9.4. Some Critical Remarks

2.9.4.1. Occam's Theory of Knowledge

2.9.4.1.1. His "Razor"

Scarce anyone would question the soundness of Occam's principle of economy. Even with reference to scientific hypotheses, one always prefers the simplest explanation, provided it explains the facts. Similarly, one should not postulate extravagant entities and special divine interventions to explain what could be accounted for by creatures themselves. This is the principle of subsidiarity. But Occam's empiricism often led him to oversimplify things and take unwarranted short-cuts where certain elements of experience demanded the retention of things, such as the universal idea. One may not necessarily accept the Scholastic theory of universals. But to say that the intellect can know directly the material reality of an individual concrete being does violence to either the nature of the spirit or of matter. Besides, one cannot be surprised that Occam did not make use of his principle of economy to eliminate the plurality of forms in man when even the Scholastics found that one would be sufficient. Yet, we cannot deny that Occam's ruthless razor and his penetrating criticism of so many dogmatically assumed principles of being, has been a real stimulus to clear thinking in philosophy.

2.9.4.1.2. Terministic Logic

Whatever be one's personal views on a logic that seems to stop with the terms of propositions, seeing them as an end in themselves, rather than a tool to study reality, one cannot but admit that much of contemporary British philosophy consists of applying Occam's razor to Aristotle's beard. I suppose the remark implies that language philosophy, inspired by Occam, is making short work of the grand systems of philosophy of Aristotle is a classic example. And one can hardly deny that language philosophy has clarified a lot of conceptual confusion, while the refinement of logic under the skilled hand of, say, a Russel, have gone a long way to exposing our latent dogmatisms.

2.9.4.1.3. Occam's Empiricism

Just as we can trace a basic kinship from present-day British language philosophy all the way back to Occam, it is not too difficult to note the link between the empiricistic slant begum by Scotus and pushed to its logical conclusions by Occam, past the "common sense" philosophy of Locke all the way down to the empiricistic flavour that has characterised the views of British thinkers over the last six centuries. Yet we cannot reduce Occam's empiricism to Locke's. It has its own particular brand. He was more concerned with breaking away from the Augustinian penchant for *a prioris* in the form of innate ideas, divine archetypes and special interventions. He was concerned with taking man and his capacities very seriously. Only, somewhat like Macbeth, he overleapt himself and fell on the other side!

2.9.4.1.4. The Univocal Concept of Being

There is little that we need add here. In responding to Scotus' theory of the univocity of the concept of being, we have already had occasion to mention that we can hardly say that the reality of being forces us to define analogously and univocally. It does seem that the univocal theory, though it does not necessarily lead to pantheism, necessitates plenty of detours and ramifications to avoid that impasse. The analogy theory, it appears, answers all the difficulties and explains the facts in simpler and clearer manner.

2.9.4.2. Occam's Philosophy of God

2.9.4.2.1. No Divine Ideas

It may not be necessary to postulate divine ideas in the mind of the creator. Perhaps these are but a useless appendage of Platonism that has all too slavishly been conserved by the Augustinian tradition. It is not the actual employment of the 'razor" in this connection that would bother us. Occam did this with a specific purpose; to vindicate divine freedom. By making morality depend on the chance whims of divine authority, he may have saved, for himself, a certain concept of divine liberty. But such an approach only confirms many people - especially our youth - in their opinion that God is an arbitrary tyrant who chose, out of sheer spite, to make the most interesting things sins. Sin should then be not a refusal to love and the sinner no longer a coward, unable to accept the consequences of a decision to love. Sin becomes a revolt against an arbitrary tyrant and the sinner a bold rebel who is not afraid of an absolute authority. Occam's notion of divine freedom would buttress a very notion of mortality that is unworthy of man come of age. Is it really necessary that the removal of divine ideas should lead to authoritarian mortality? We are once again faced with the question as to whether something is forbidden because it is evil or evil because it is forbidden.

2.9.4.2.2. Proving God's Existence

Occam has well shown that a really conclusive proof for God's existence should be sought in the order if activity, rather than in that of being. The fact of conservation is in the sphere of dynamic, existential activity and it is easier to see the impossibility of taking refuge in an 'infinite regress', here. Marechal, with his transcendental analysis of intellectual dynamism, would certainly agree with Occam's critique.

2.9.4.2.3. God's Nature

Occam was certainly ruthless in his critique of traditional argumentation and proofs. Perhaps he may have been very demanding, too demanding even, with regard to what makes a conclusive proof. But he and Scotus are a welcome break from the usual medieval procession of pontificating pundits who offer us elaborate dissertations on divine psychology and what not, and who often make us wonder where they have found the naivety or the pride to dare to imagine that they have been able to poke their way in to the inner life of God! I do not mean to say that Occam's objections are unanswerable. Some may be, but they always make us realise how over hasty we have been in our conclusions and force us to better appreciate the complexities of the questions.

2.9.4.3. Occam's Philosophy of the World

2.9.4.3.1. Causality Undermined

Occam's critique of causality anticipates the objections of Hume against the same and it was Hume who woke up Kant from his "dogmatic slumber". Actually, Occam is, in many ways, the direct forerunner of Hume, the father of British empiricism. It would take a Marechal to answer such a mighty challenge.

2.9.4.3.2. Motion, Place and Time

Once again, Occam is anticipating Hume's critique of the sciences. Kant will later subscribe to an understanding of time very similar to Occam's and put it to good use in his *Critique of Pure Reason.* Occam's empiricism would not let him see any continuity or process in things: there was but series of discrete static situations. Kant, too, would have a similar understanding of things. It seems inevitable for one with an empiricistic outlook.

2.9.4.4. Occam's Philosophy of Man

2.9.4.4.1. The Human Soul

Though he did not very much elaborate his arguments - no doubt because of the pressure of his times - Occam's objection against the arguments usually adduced in favour of the existence of the human soul anticipate a very modem difficulty. Recourse is had to a spiritual principle, the very soul, because, it is alleged, the body is not capable of eliciting spiritual activities such as knowing and willing. Is not this begging the question? Nor is a more integrated conception of the human person going to cancel out the possibility of explaining any life after death.

2.9.4.4.2. Plurality of Forms in Man

It is surprising that Occam didn't put his razor to work here, eliminating the unnecessary extra forms in man. A single higher form could assimilate the activities of the lower ones and a refinement of Aquinas' theory of subsistent forms would be able to answer Occam's objection about the corruptibility of the body which is informed by an incorruptible soul, directly.

2.9.4.4.3. Ethics

It is a pity that, though Occam was able to recognise that God's inability to contradict the metaphysical or logical order did not undermine his liberty, yet his inability to go against the moral order (which is founded on the metaphysical order of essences) would. His view that God could actually order or cause murder is, to say the least, horrifying. His inconsistent view of "right reason" itself shows that he was not too comfortable with all the implications of this particular theory. Actually, most of those difficulties arise from a rather one-sided view of (divine and human) freedom, which is a bit too much identified with the mere ability to do whatever one wants or to act otherwise. But there is more to it than that.

2.9.4.4.4. Church and State

Occam's bold views, however, much they might have been aimed at protecting his own skin, went a long way to checking papal absolutism and paving the way for the Conciliar Movement of his times. In this line, many of his writings seem very modem to us, who are just entering the age where Collegiality is becoming a reality and the international synods which Occam envisaged have become the order of the day, though they have yet to be taken seriously.

3. MODERN PHILOSOPHY

3.1. Introduction

3.1.1. "Modern"

Never before in the history of the human race have so many sentences been written, beginning with the phrase "never before in the history of the human race ..." as in our day. After all, every period is, in a sense, a kind of revolt against the one that went before it. It is with the history of mankind as it is with the story of each individual person. We speak of our times as the glorious era where man has, at last, "come of age", comparing this stage in human history to that of a young man just out of the gangling awkwardness of adolescence. Perhaps there is something in the image, after all...

For the beginnings of the "modem period" in Western philosophy (if not the entire span) certainly present several points of reference to the teen-ager's coming to grips with that bitter-sweet discovery of his freedom. One of the characteristics of "modem philosophy" is its consciousness of having broken with an over-protective past, of striking out in bold new directions, untramelled by the strait-jackets of authority and custom. "Immortal God! What a world I see dawning! Why can I not grow young again!" Thus, exclaimed Desiderius Erasmus (whom we will meet soon) in 1517, in anticipation of what many a Catholic thinker would cry in the middle sixties, just after Vatican II (one has only to read the earlier statements of the late Paul VI).

And, as in every adolescent life, great contradictions jostle each other. The "modem age" began with a bang. It all but ended with a whimper. Extremes of pessimism and optimism succeeded each other. Religious revivals, mounting atheism and agnosticism and bloody "holy wars" came and went. New horizons suddenly opened up before man, including a revolutionary understanding of the cosmos, great movements of emancipation and the discovery of new and more efficient weapons - all these were part of the setting. Great wealth began to be amassed by a few at the expense of the many, works of surpassing artistic beauty flourished against a background of dehumanising social injustice, freedom of thought and the overt/covert machinations of 'thought-police' - these were there, too. Small wonder that the same Desiderius Erasmus, in 1526, was but a broken and bitter old man, noting his disappointment and the failure of all his great expectations. But it is precisely out of a coming to grips with the shattering of one's adolescent romanticism that maturity is born. It's not a question of surrendering one's ideals. It's a question of still aiming high while looking the world squarely in the face for what it is. And I think we are not being too presumptious in describing the best and noblest minds of our times as doing precisely that.

3.1.2. Dating the Period

We must be on our guard against hasty generalisations. There is little historical foundation to support the claim that in the "modern period" man was at last being allowed to think for himself, that he had finally learnt to break free from the domination of the Church. Nor would we be justified in dating the birth of the age with the fall of Constantinople and the consequent sudden availability of the sources of Western culture, through salvaged copies of great literature and philosophy. As we have seen for ourself, the recovery of the classics had already begun in the thick of the *media aetas* (middle age) and there had been plenty of original thinking in the middle age - witness an Eriugena, an Aquinas and an Occam, to name just a few.

Yet, for all their divergences and differences, it cannot be denied that the medievals, as a group, offer a picture of unity in diversity. None of the great medieval thinkers questioned the basics of their faith, though they may have criticised each other's interpretations of these. And, if the classics were available, they were all read with a particular slant, namely to see how to make of them a kind of handmaid of theology. All this would change very much with the dawning of the Renaissance. That is why I would like to start our study of Modern philosophy with a glance at the thought and the thinkers of the Renaissance, after a very brief introductory acquaintance with a transitional figure whose life and thought fits in very well with the spirit of our times.

3.1.3. The Renaissance

In 1453, Constantinople fell to the Turks and soon all of Europe was flooded with refugees from that ancient centre of culture where East met West (present-day Istanbul is half in Europe and half in Asia!). These refugees brought with them the literary treasures they had managed to rescue from the great library of the city and thus it was that the term Renaissance was first used (in 1542) to herald the rebirth of art and fine writing.

But it was not just that single event that sparked off a revolution in human thinking. There had been, as we have seen, a growing sense of dissatisfaction with the way things were, and a developing conviction that man must strike out in new directions if his spirit was to survive. Then came a whole series of break-throughs, any of which would have been enough to give a thorough shaking-up to any traditional views. All taken together, they created something like an explosion of human thought.

Suddenly a whole New World was discovered and hot on its heels the earth was circumnavigated and its real size was understood. Next a long forgotten cosmological theory was revived and men knew for certain that our earth was not the centre of the cosmos. Each of these discoveries had devastating religious, sociological and economic implications for the man in the street. Then the printing-press came into being and suddenly 20,000,000 copies of a man's thought poured out of a machine, replacing expensive, tedious, hard-to-come-by hand-written copies of cumbersome manuscripts. Learning to read became a practical and economically viable idea. And we all know what an emancipation that is!

3.1.4. Kant

We will conclude this review with the study of the philosophy of Immanuel Kant (1724- 1804), "the engineer of philosophy's last great revolution, from which stem all subsequent little philosophical uprisings." (Bertrand Russell). Indeed, one can scarce hope to understand the workings of the contemporary western mind if one has not delved a bit into the writings of the sage of Konigsberg. Yet we have kept Kant with the moderns for there is a kind of intellectual kinship between him and all the ups and downs of their times and if Kant is the father of contemporary philosophy, then Descartes is its grand-father for his had rests heavy on the former's shoulder. Still, with Descartes, one is still philosophising in an age charged with theology. Whereas with Kant one can tell that we have entered the scientific, if not quite the nuclear, age.

3.1.5. Bibliography

A General Bibliography for this period

James Collins, A History of Modern European Philosophy, Milwaukee, 1954.

Frederick Copleston SJ, *A History of Philosophy* (vol IV Descartes to Leibniz, 1960, vol V Hobbes to Hume, 1959, vol VI Wolf to Kant, 1960).

Gilson and Langan, Modern Philosophy: Descartes to Kant, New York, 1963.

Johannes Hirschberger, The History of Philosophy, vol II (trans. Fuerst), Milwaukee, 1959.

Frederick Meyer, A History of Modern Philosophy, California, 1951.

Thomas Noill, Makers of the Modern Mind, Milwaukee, 1958 (popular and eminently readable presentation of 12 personalities from Luther to Dewey - includes Luther,

Calvin, Descartes, Locke, Newton, Rousseau, Kant; an un-scholarly presentation, in comparison to the others, but sometimes over-simplifies).

In addition to the above, there are many specialised works on the Philosophy of the Renaissance and on British Philosophy. These are listed separately.

3.2. Nicholas of Cusa (1401–1464)

3.2.1. His Life

Nikolaus Kryfts or Krebs was born at Kues (Latin Cusa), the son of an obscure boatman on the Moselle. His was the first encounter of medieval civilisation with the Renaissance spirit and this was no mere passive one. He had a creative mathematical mind and was one of the first to conceive of maths as "the science of the infinite". By the breadth of his travels, the range of his many interests and the depth of his penetrating, synthetic mind, he is one of the finest examples of that cosmopolitanism that will be the hallmark of the Age of Adventure, as the Renaissance has been called. He was made a Cardinal in 1448 and appointed to the Bishopric of Brixen two years later. He attended the Council of Basle and strove to bring about a reunion of the Eastern Churches with Rome. One of the Church's first great ecumenicists, he published in 1453-4 his *De pace fidei,* wherein he proposed foundations for dialogue between Islam and Christianity, at a time when all Europe was in mortal terror at the threat of an "infidel" invasion. In this work, far ahead of his time, he drew on his extensive knowledge of the Koran, picked up during a sojourn in Constantinople. He worked hard in his diocese for Church reform and actually resided there (an unusual thing in those times). He had a Christo-centric integrated vision of the universe which reminds us, in many ways, of that of Teilhard de Chardin. He was sent as Papal Legate to Germany in 1451 and died at Todi in Umbria.

3.2.2. Bibliography

We have quite a good selection of works by and on Nicholas of Cusa (he is listed in the library index as Nicolaus of Cusa) ... in French, German and Latin, including the three volume *Philosophische-Theologische-logische Schriften*, Vienna, 1964 (published on the occasion of the fifth centenary of his death). There is a copy of his *Learned Ignorance* in English translation (by Germain Heron, OFM), London 1954. To it is appended an excellent introduction by D. J. Hawkins. There is an English biography, *Nicholas of Cusa*, by Henry

Bert, London, 1932, a classic of its kind. *The Modern Schoolman* brought out a special issue in his honour (Nov. 1964, vol 42, No 1) and Copleston has nigh 20 pages on him in vol III of his *History of Philosophy* (p 231-247). He gets a shorter and less sympathetic treatment in the hands of the other standard writers.

3.2.3. His Thought

3.2.3.1. Harmony

A certain "passion for harmonisation" seems to characterise all of Nicholas of Cusa's thought. The key idea that grows on him and is specially developed in his *De docta ignorantia* (on learned ignorance) is that of unity as the harmonious synthesis of opposites. This will be driving force, for him, in fields as diverse as astronomy, politics, mathematics and theology.

3.2.3.2. God

He defines God as the *coincidentia oppositorum,* the coincidence or synthesis of opposites, of things normally considered to be opposed or irreconcilable. God not only transcends all the differences we find operating among finite beings, he is also able to unite them in himself in a mysterious and incomparable way. For instance, in him, existence and essence merge as his "essence is to be". We can call God the greatest being as much as the smallest being, for there is no real size in God and he is in even the smallest of things. Thus, the opposites of essence and existence, of greatness and smallness, are reconciled in him.

3.2.3.3. Learned Ignorance

This, as we have seen, is the title of his most famous work. It is also a phrase that sums up his "negative theology". He holds, with the Pseudo-Dionysius, that we know better what God is not, than what is. We are rather in a state of ignorance when it comes to knowledge of his nature. Yet this ignorance is not the result of any lack of effort on our part, much less is it the fruit of religious indifference. On the contrary, it is but the realisation of our finiteness, the outcome of our positive attempt to fathom God's nature. We discover and humbly admit our limitations, our ignorance. Ours is, then, a learned or a schooled ignorance.

3.2.3.4. Pantheism

Like all gifted men who have a mystical slant, Cusanus (as he is sometimes called) has been accused of pantheism. This is utter nonsense, of course, for one has only to look at the whole thrust of his life and work to see that he is quite orthodox in this line. If he says that "God contains all things and he is contained in all things in so far as he is in all things", he is merely saying that every creature is a theophany or a manifestation of God. Similarly, when he says that a creature is a "created God" he is but repeating the idea, using his penchant for harmonising opposites (here creator-creature)

3.2.3.5. Man

Every individual is a kind of summary or contraction of its species and of the entire universe. The universe, in turn, is a "contraction" of God. But if every creature is a microcosm, then man is *the* microcosm, the mirror of the universe, *par excellence,* for he unites in himself the worlds of organic, sensitive and rational life plus is made up of the same basic elements as the rest of the inanimate universe. And just as man is mirrored in all his parts, but more so in his head than any other, so also the universe is mirrored in all its parts, but most of all in man.

3.2.3.6. Christ

Cusanus provides a final touch to his whole vision, which makes of his an eminently Christian philosophy. Christ, who unites in himself all levels of created existence as man, also synthesises the Godhead in his human nature, for he is the Godman. He is the *concrete maximum,* the unique and necessary means for man and, through man, all creatures to be united with God. Man's highest potentialities are only actualisable through Christ and there is no incorporation into Christ except through the Church, his mystical body.

3.2.3.7. Cosmology

Nicholas of Cusa rejected the crystal-sphere cosmology of the Ptolemaic medieval system, He does not see the earth as the centre of the universe and certainly not as the centre of the (non-circular!) orbit of the planets. He will not accept the Aristotelian contention that the earth is a kind of sub-lunary rubbish dump. It is "a noble star", he avers. The boatman's son even found time to consider the possibility of extra-terrestrial life. That is possible, he says. But, he adds, it would be silly to speculate whether they would enjoy a form of life superior or inferior to ours. Theirs would merely be "a perfection of their own", different from ours. He also revived the Neo-Platonist view of the *anima mundi* or world soul, but with a Christian corrective.

3.2.4. Some Critical Remarks

Nicholas of Cusa was

> not only a thinker, but also an essentially Christian thinker, who was preoccupied with the search for the hidden God and whose thought was definitely Christocentric in character. - (Copleston)

The great German idealists of the eighteenth century, notably Fichte and Hegel, will return to the idea of harmonious synthesis. Within the Catholic fold, there was Teilhard de Chardin SJ who would also strive for an integrated vision of reality, founded on the theory of evolution and St. Paul.

What amazes us is the tremendous openness of this man's vision. He could interest himself in other faiths, other cultures and with none of that patronising attitude that we might expect from a 15th century Churchman. He could consider the possibility of life on other planets without batting an eye-lid, lay the foundations for a new approach to Mathematics and, most of all, show himself a sincere and devoted pastor.

At his native Kues, the hospice that he had founded survived the centuries. The people saw to it that the rules he had laid down were carefully observed and his books, astronomical instruments and personal effects were looked after with loving care. That is, until the "civilisation" of a certain Austrian house-painter named Adolf Hitler put an end to it all in the early 1940s.

3.3. Some Renaissance Thinkers

3.3.1. General Introduction

From an impressive cast we select just a few of the many men who have had their part to play in the making of the modern Western mind or whose names have become common property whenever one has reason to talk of culture or the arts. But let us not forget that if this was "the civilisation shooting forth wonderful sparklers, but out of balance and kilter, full of broken utopias and futile dreams, passionately rehearsing great motifs, but ready to settle down into the immobile splendour of long decadences comforted with splendid dreams." The truth of this other remark will be borne out by the men and the ideas we will now be studying.

3.3.2. Renaissance Philosophers - Montaigne

3.3.2.1 Chaos and Confusion

Intellectual coherence and disciplined thinking cannot always be demanded of thinkers in an age of radical change - as our own times will all too clearly tell us. Chaos, rather than order, helter-skelter advance rather than slow and sober reflection, are more likely to be the traits of such an age. The pedantry of the quack-scholar soon overtook the genius of the man of learning and philosophy soon earned for itself the bad name which it has never quite been able to rid itself of. Sir Thomas Overbury, poisoned in 1613 for having dared to criticise the young Countess of Essex, gives us a neat sketch of these 'pseudos' as we'd call them today:

> A mere scholar ... an intelligible ass, or a silly fellow in black, that speaks sentences more familiarly than sense. The antiquity of his university is his creed and the excellence of his college -- though but for a match of football – is his article of faith. He speaks Latin better than his mother-tongue and is stranger to no part of the world but his own country.

How little times have changed!

3.3.2.2 All sorts

Strange things were happening all over Christian Europe. Italy spawned all manner of decadent Aristotelians who were able to be at the same time loyal Catholics as well as rabid Averrhoists, denying personal immortality. Such was Pietro Pompanazzi (1462-1524). Cremonini was paid twice as much as any other Italian professor and given a palazzo as grand as any cardinals by the Republic of Venice in gratitude for his teaching that there was no such thing as personal immortality. No Inquisition ever took **him** to book, for the Republic had taken him to her heart. He was the man who dismissed an invitation to look through Galileo's telescope with a "Basta! I don't want to know anything more on the subject!"

The tide of anti-Aristotelianism was growing elsewhere. For instance, Francois I of France was so delighted to hear the (premature) claim of one Ramus that he had refuted Aristotle, that he promptly rewarded the servant with a gift of 10,000 livres, a sum several times the value of today's Nobel prize.

Not many thinkers had the balance of a Nicholas of Cusa to preserve themselves from pantheism. If Tomasso Campanella (1568-1639), whose doctrine of innate ideas and of the *cogito* anticipated Descartes, was able to remain a devout Catholic and a good Dominican friar in spite of his apparent pantheistic views, his co-religionist Giordano Bruno didn't have it quite so easy. Hounded everywhere he went by what he called the three-headed monster of Aristotle, Ptolemy and dogma, he was pursued and persecuted by Catholic and Protestant alike and finally met his end at the stake, a victim of the Roman Inquisition. A rationalist who attenuated supernatural faith, he was to have a great influence on Spinoza, Leibniz and Schelling. Like Erasmus, he was wooed by Protestantism but, like him too, pronounced Luther's determinism a "corruption of laws and religion" which would only make of men "greater barbarians".

Given such a barrage of conflicting theories and counter-theories (there were ever so many more) propounded by eminent men as well as academic mediocrity, we should not be surprised to find some sceptics among the finest of Renaissance minds. Among these we may mention the converted Jew, Francis Sanchez, who published, in 1581, his *Quod nihil scitur* (i.e. that nothing is known - perfectly).

3.3.2.3. Montaigne

This background was necessary to present Michel Eyquem, Seigneur de Montaigne, in Gascony (1553-1592), lest we too lump him with the other so-called sceptics of the time. Truly a "wonderful neighbour to have", as Mme de Lafayette wistfully remarked two centuries after his death, he was more a reactor against the pedantic dogmatism of his age than a full-blooded sceptic.

If his favourite phrase was ***Que sais-je?*** (What do I know?), this, his motto was engraven on a balance! "To be sincerely true is the beginning of great wisdom," he wrote. And if he wrote, "There is no animal in the world so treacherous as man," we should read this in the context of his rejoinder to the pretentious and proud claims being made about human intelligence and the human person, at the time. One should not forget the fact of his close friendship with Etienne de la Boettie, of which he wrote in glowing terms. Nor was he remiss in calling for tolerance and fairness, of the need for weighing all claims in the balance of good judgement.

His famous Essays are a classic in French literature, a literary form in their own right. They are more a style of musing aloud, in a form more spoken than written and would influence many a would-be philosopher of France, all the way to Descartes and beyond. "This, dear reader," he announces in the preface, "is a book about myself." And so it is. All his foibles, quirks and limitations are here laid bare, coalescing into the portrait of a very real man - a man who is so very much like ourselves. We understand what he means when he professes, "Others fashion man. I repeat him."

In spite of his unconventional, curious mind and his "sceptical bent", Montaigne had no sympathy for Protestantism which he considered as subversive and wished ever to be considered a good Catholic. "The ancientest evil, if it be known to us," he observed, "bears always lighter upon us than a new one of which we know but little." Indeed, for all his daring, Montaigne had little sympathy for novelty and spoke rather disparagingly of the "new" heliocentric theory.

3.3.3. Renaissance Scientists: Copernicus, Galileo, Kepler

A corrective: There is a current enough view that scientists are immune from that particularly human failing to which philosophers and theologians are fatally prone. Arthur Koestler, in his excellent and readable book, *The Sleepwalkers,* has exposed this fallacy. Scientists can be as much sleepwalkers as any other. They, too, can be as blind and dogmatic when it comes to defending their pet theories or feathering their own nests. They, too, do not hesitate to distort or overlook uncomfortable facts that do not quite square with their neat little systems. If the scientists of the Renaissance laid the foundations of modern science, it was often through abrupt turns and dizzy gyrations, in spite of (and sometimes because of) their prejudices and the opposition of others and they often did all this without being aware of what they were up to. The heliocentric controversy is an excellent example of all this.

3.3.3.1. Niklas Keppernik (1473-1543)

When this obscure German ecclesiastic from the Polish border regions entered the scene, astronomy was one big mess. Everyone blindly accepted the Ptolemaic- Aristotelian cosmology according to which the earth was the centre of the cosmos with the planets moving around it in neat circular orbits. This was false and the evidence was clearly against it. But rather than scrap their presuppositions, the greatest scientists and mathematicians of the age preferred to try and puzzle out how to make the facts agree with their theory. Finally, someone had a great insight. The planets paraded around the earth in neat little circles: but, in so doing they also swung around the paths of their orbit round the earth ... in neat circular orbits. It was assumed that by various combinations and permutations one would more or less arrive at a system of orbits around orbits or wheels within wheels which would save the theory by making the disobedient planets behave. Aristotle had offered a system where there were some 30 spheres. His disciples improved on this by adding 20 more. But still the stubborn facts refused to agree with the theory. Thus, it had been for nigh two thousand years with some of the world's finest mathematical brains sweating at their desks and torturing their refined minds to come up with device after device of inter-acting, inter-locking cycles and epicycles - each one improving upon the approximations of his predecessors, but none ever getting things to square exactly. So, we are not surprised to hear Alphonso X (surnamed "the Wise") declare, in desperation, when, in his studies, he had been introduced to the complicated whirligig of the Ptolemaic system, "If the Lord Almighty had consulted me before embarking upon creation, I should have suggested something simpler."

And then along came Copernicus with his heliocentrism and saved astronomy from being speculation and made of it a real science - or so everyone, as rule, thinks. The historical facts, however, are somewhat different.

First, Copernicus (the Latinised version of his name) was far from having those qualities which would make of him the intrepid patron of scientific research. Koestler has shown that the epithet that befits him most is "timid". Apart from that, he was an extremely niggardly and careless scientific researcher. He used the erudest instruments, even though the finest could be had for the asking in nearby Nuremburg. His notes were carelessly scribbled in the margins of books he happened to be reading at the time (among various other marginal notes). He was extremely slovenly in his observations, preferring to take for granted the nigh prehistoric data of ancient Chaldean, Greek and Arabian astronomers than do any work for himself. In fact, he made only 27 observations of his own in 32 years.

Secondly, his *On the Revolutions of the Heavenly Spheres* did not advocate strict heliocentrism (it was the only other book he published during his life-time, besides a translation of a third-rate Greek writer) and it only saw the light of day due to the constant harassment of a small coterie of his friends. When at last, after much prodding, he agreed, he was nigh upon his deathbed and too far gone to acknowledge or approve of its original form. A forged preface was duly added later, alleged to have come from the hand of Copernicus himself. It claimed for his theory the rank of hypothesis, but we cannot be too sure as to how seriously the timid canon took this idea.

Early in the book (Bk I, Ch X) he writes, "...in the midst of all dwells the sun ... Sitting on his royal throne, he rules the fly of the planets which turn round him... We thus find in this arrangement an admirable harmony of the world." Very heliocentric indeed. But, when he comes to setting his theory to accord with observed facts (in Bk III), we find he has made the earth and everything else turn, no longer round the sun, but about some mysterious vacant spot somewhere in mid-space, as far from the sun as a distance equal to thrice its diameter. And this empty spot is the centre of the earth's orbit, not the sun's. This new version of the old system improved a bit on some of the approximations of some of the predecessors of Copernicus. But not all. And it was still far from the facts.

No wonder the timid canon hesitated to publish his weird theory which, apart from its novelty, had so little arguments in its support. He had ended up by substituting an arbitrary empty spot for a solid "earthy" centre of the system and couldn't say why that spot, rather than any other, should be postulated. So, nobody took his unreadable book very seriously, least of all the Church. It has remained, to today, one of the most unread books in the world. Seventy years had to pass before the ecclesiastical authorities took any notice of any such theory, and this was due to a man of quite a different stamp from our "timid canon". Nor should it surprise us that, though the alleged contents of the book became public property, it was mainly through rumour and second-hand report, hardly from a first-hand acquaintance with it. Such is the fate of most revolutionary books. Few Communists have read *Das Kapital* from cover to cover and not every Christian has gone through the entire Bible. Yet every "common man" will be able to tell you something of the contents of these tomes. The very fact that Copernicus is credited with advocating a heliocentric universe, when he actually proposed an inane vacuocentric one, is proof of the same!

3.3.3.2. Galileo Galilei (1564-1642)

Here is another Renaissance man of science about whom it is very easy to cherish misconceptions and very hard to write about in an objective manner.

Let us remark, at the onset, that not all those who have ranged themselves against Galileo have been Catholics or would-be defenders of the faith. Some of the silliest charges against him came from the anti-religious French encyclopaedists and one of the most irresponsible anti-Galileo accounts of the celebrated case has come from the pen of the eighteenth-century Protestant writer, Mallet du Pan. On the other hand, many reputed Catholic scholars have taken up eudgels in defence of the great Florentine - l'Espinois, Reusch and Fr James Brodrick SJ.

A popular misconception casts Galilei in the classic role of "the scientist" coming to grief in the face of obdurate religious dogmatism, "the Church". Galileo, however, was more than a scientist, he was a humanist and was not merely satisfied with advocating a new scientific theory. He wanted to integrate it into his whole culture, a fact that both friend and foe alike were not so slow in recognising. And a harnessing of new perspectives to a revolutionary shake-up of the old established order of looking at things always meets with the severest opposition from vested interests. Now a glance at the dedication of Galileo's book (to Pope Paul II) or a letter of his to Paolo Guido (May, 1612), makes it pretty clear as to where he expected his opposition to come from: not the Church, but the old die-hard Aristotelians and their ilk, who commanded great respect at the Universities.

The villain of the piece was, then, not the Pope, the Cardinals, the Roman Curia and so on. It was academic conservatism, "The inertia of the human mind and its resistance to innovation are most clearly determined not, as one might expect, by the ignorant mass - which is easily swayed once its imagination is sought - but by professionals with a vested academic interest in tradition and in the monopoly of learning. Innovation is a twofold threat to academic mediocrities: it endangers their oracular authority and it evokes the deeper fear that their whole, laboriously constructed edifice might collapse." Brodrick might have also added that it also makes them fear for their jobs. It was academic mediocrity that men of genius, from Socrates to Freud, had to fight, it is academic mediocrity that have ever succeeded in bullying men of insight into silence and it was such a solid rear-guard phalanx, firmly entrenched in academic chairs and preachers' pulpits, that brought Galileo to grief.

I would not take too much time to go into all the details. Suffice is it to say that, as historical research seems to have shown, pretty conclusively, the tragedy of Galileo was the result of a carefully engineered plot, of which the hierarchy turned out to be as much a victim as Galileo. It was the work of a group of obscure and desperate characters (all luminaries of that academic mediocrity we have spoken of), who planted false documents in the Galileo file, falsified others and, in general, misinformed the pope, presenting him slanderous information on which to make his decision. Galileo's ventures into Biblical exegesis, however, in which he tried to defend himself against charges of contradicting the Scriptures, still read today as pretty modern and sound. They could almost have been taken out of the paragraphs of the Vatican II document ***On Revelation***.

Still, to be perfectly objective, we must say that Galileo cheated a bit, too. He was too eager to "sell" his theory and his famous *Dialogue on the Great World Systems* contains some defects and insincerities! He brazenly pretended that the Copernican system was ever so simple and had been proven beyond doubt, whereas, with its 40-odd epicycles and its empty-spot centre had little to recommend itself by. Most of all, he was blindly following another dogma of the ancients - the belief that the planetary orbits were circular, not elliptical. Had he given less than scurvy treatment to the findings of the brilliant Kepler, he would have been able to clinch his arguments far better - instead of alleging that the fact of tides proved heliocentrism when it was evident that, if they did, there would be only one high tide a day and that at noon. Whereas every coastal dweller knows that this is far from the case!

3.3.3.3. Johannes Kepler (1571-1630)

This ex-Lutheran-seminarian, scientist, mystic and Court Astrologer to the Duke of Wallenstein, offers a very interesting study of contrasts and contradictions, so typical of an age of transition. Theology, physics, philosophy, astronomy and astrology all trip lightly across the pages of his works, entitled - significantly enough - ***Mysterium Cosmographicum*** *(The Cosmographical Mystery)* and ***Astronomia Nova*** *(The New Astronomy),* jostling and influencing each other till it is difficult to tell which is which. His painstaking researches showed that the orbits of the planets trace an elliptical path, contrary to the current popular scientific dogma. Thence he went on to formulate his famous three laws of interplanetary motion which were to provide Newton with the starting-point for his physics, in 1666.

Kepler's grandfather was a much-respected man and went on to become the local mayor. Thereafter, the reputation of the Keplers began to slump a bit. Johannes' father was a mercenary pirate who almost ended up on the gallows. His mother had been brought up by an aunt who was later burnt as a witch and she too came to be accused of consorting with the devil in her old age, almost suffering a similar fate. Of the seven children, three died in child-birth and the nearest in age to Johannes turned out to be an epileptic and succumbed to the psychopathic streak in the family. Johannes got off lightly. He was merely born with defective eye-sight and was saddled with constant ill-health and a hatred of self that was almost neurotic. Yet it was this myopic youth, who sometimes saw the world doubled or quadrupled, who laid the foundations of modern optics. This man, who could not see clearly, gave us the modern astronomical telescope.

Only one problem needs attention. How could such a mind let himself be pulled into astrology? It is true that he was not very proud of this sphere of his intellectual activity, but there it was. After all, how would one account for the different events and character traits to be observed in people - especially in an innocuous family as his own? He had rejected Calvinistic pre-determination and knew nothing of our sophisticated alternative explanation about the interplay of genes and chromosomes. And Freud was yet to be born. Nor had people thought about blaming it all on the class struggle. Was it so very illogical to assume that man's condition and fate were influenced by the very same celestial motions that accounted for the seasons, the quality of harvests and the fertility of plants, not to mention tides?

Anyway, as we have remarked at the beginning of this section, it is out of such meanderings, half-guesses and nigh superstitions, that the foundations of the scientific era were laid!

3.3.4. Renaissance Humanists: Erasmus, More

Humanism: The word 'humanism', as the historians tell us, was coined in ancient Rome of 150 BC, within the circle of the Scipios. It came to stand for the new imperial civilisation, the heir to that of ancient Greece. It was opposed to *barbaritas or fereitas,* the "way of the wild ones", that is, the uncivilised manners and customs of the so-called barbarian nations. In the Christian era, to "humanism" was added the connotation of man's misery and transcience, consequences of our fallen state. Finally, in the Renaissance, both these ideas come together. The word 'humanism' came to denote man's "high estate" which ranked him above all of visible creation. Yet it also included the elements of human fallibility and frailty. From here stem the connotations of darings, risk, freedom, responsibility and tolerance which emerge as the hallmark of the humanistic movement of the fifteenth and sixteenth centuries.

3.3.4.1. Desiderius Erasmus (1464-1536)

This ex-Augustinian monk of Rotterdam, who was ordained in 1492 (though he never got round to saying Mass), was certainly one of the most cultured men of his times. A true "citizen of the world", he travelled extensively and was welcomed everywhere on account of his acquaintance of the letters. He was an intimate friend of St Thomas More, Lord Chancellor of England, and was a frequent caller at that other humanist's house at Chelsea. His friendship was sought after by as different persons as Henry VIII of England, Charles V and Francois I of France, the Popes Julius II and Leo X, and Martin Luther. But Erasmus broke with the rebel, upholding free-will against the latter's determinism, in a 1525 conflict that stirred all Europe.

Erasmus was a bit of a dreamer and a romanticiser, fine subject-matter for the amateur psychoanalyst. He fantasised about his parents and his early life and seems to have ended up believing some of the very stories he spread around concerning his childhood and youth.

Erasmus never tired of belabouring the "religion of the common people", laying bare its hollowness and superstition. Like the other humanists of his time, he endeavoured to offer to the layman a kind of alternative to the monastic ideal. He, too, wanted to guide the Christian layman as to how to live up to the ideals of his faith right in the midst of his secular environment. To this end he published three important works which enjoyed immense popularity and expressed one of the best Christian responses to the Renaissance spirit. Judged by the perspectives and vision of Vatican II's *The Church in the Modern World,* these three works are a bit too negative and overly pious, but we know that every Christian worthy of the name, at the time, carried a copy of one or two - sometimes all three - of these tracts in his satchel for frequent meditation. The titles give us some inkling of their contents: *Enchiridion militis Christiani (The Handbook of the Militant Christian), De Contemptu Mundi (On Contempt for the World)* and *De praeparationem ad mortem (On Preparation for Death).* As we have noticed, these booklets were written in Latin, in the flowing Latin that is typical of an eminent stylist of the age.

Ignatius of Loyola was understandably surprised at the casual, almost flippant manner in which Erasmus referred to theologians and traditional devotional practises in the first (and most read) booklet, though he was, naturally, pleased with the military idiom. The militant Christian is summoned to battle with the world, the flesh and the devil. His main weapons are to be prayer ("which lifts our hearts to heaven, as a citadel which the enemy cannot reach"), wisdom (i.e. knowledge of wholesome thoughts regarding Christian warfare, to be found not only in the Scriptures, but also in the moral maxims of pagan writers), self-knowledge (for the Christian soldier's greatest enemy is himself). There are listed as many as 22 "general rules" of combat. Chief among these is the injunction to seek after Christ alone, rather than lose oneself in a multitude of devotions and pious practices. Erasmus frequently speaks of the necessity of detachment and renunciation as the best way to avoid being contaminated by the evils of the time.

Another popular little work of Erasmus which, not too surprisingly, has a special message for our own times of conflict and transition, is his eminently readable *In Praise of Folly.* Here he mercilessly lambastes all manner of pompous and pretentious learning and hits hard at all quacks and charlatans - wherever they be found. Churchmen get the worst blows. "I may well conceive," he averred, "that the apostles, had they been to deal with these new kinds of divines, would need to have sought in prayer the aid of some other spirit."

3.3.4.2. Thomas More (1478-1535)

For his good friend, Erasmus, he was a man "whose soul was more pure than any snow, whose genius was such as England never had - yea, and never shall have again, mother of good wits, though England be." For himself, as he declared on the gallows, he was but "a good servant of the king, but God's first." These famous last words sum up his life and ideals and make of his biography the blue-print for the committed Christian of today's world, as Hans Kung, in a profound but simple little pamphlet, has shown.

Seriousness, amiability and humour - these were the characteristics of Thomas More, as his contemporaries bear witness. Erasmus adds that he seemed to have an almost innate passion for jokes. It was particularly touching to see this great mart, so laden with affairs of state, romping with his children and pet animals in a house filled with music and laughter. And yet he was not only one of the most cultured men in XVI century Europe, but also the prophet and apostle of a new civilisation. He could be hailed as the founder of the modem English school system and all his life he worked to replace the outdated stronghold of medieval learning, with its useless logic and sterile intellectualism, by means of a system of formation more geared to life. Like Erasmus, he too, was great champion of freedom and reform but, like him, again, refused to break with orthodoxy. Though his king was his close and personal friend, and though Henry VIII had showered on him all manner of favours, Thomas More would not go against his personal (and lonely) convictions, though it undoubtedly cost this lovable and loving, very human man a great deal not to go along with his friend. And so, perished on the scaffold one of England's wealthiest, saintliest and most loved of all sons, a saint whose universal appeal is rivalled only by Francis of Assisi.

It was from the pen of this versatile genius that came the little book which, with Machiavelli's Prince, became one of the most influential writings on the State in the sixteenth century. "The position of More's **Utopia**," wittily writes Paul Turner, "is rather like that of the baby in the judgment of King Solomon. One school of thought claims it as a Catholic tract, in which anything resembling Communist propaganda should be interpreted as moral allegory. Another claims it is a political manifesto in which all references to religion should be firmly ignored. Both claimants seem more concerned with the rights of ownership than the work itself, and cast from it any part of its anatomy that offends them." Evidently, the truth about this "really splendid little book, as interesting as it is instructive" (as proclaims the first edition 1516 folio), is somewhere in between. It is aimed at conveying some much-needed home-truths to More's contemporaries and that, without laying himself open to too much peril in a highly intolerant age, by hiding behind a smokescreen of fantasy and humour.

Utopia mixes genuine autobiographical data (More's actual visit to Flanders, in 1515), real personages (Peter, Gilles, real-life town clerk of Antwerp) with fiction. A serious problem is raised in the course of a familiar conversation and then the genre changes to the popular literary form of the traveller's tale, recounted by one Raphael Hythlodaeus (whose name, in Greek, means dispenser of nonsense!). The hero's imaginary adventures and his visit to Utopia (in Greek, Nowhere) are grafted onto the historical voyages of Amerigo Vespucci and further semblance of reality is provided by the specimen of Utopian literature (in Utopian characters), with a free translation, to boot.

More touches upon various things. Should philosophers advise princes, he asks and then goes on to present some very modern theories about the penal system. He questions the value of capital punishment and says that rehabilitation should be the basis of it all. The surest way to end thievery would not be to hang thieves, but to reform the social structure that obliges men to steal to find food.

Utopian society amuses, instructs and startles us. The model is communal, not familial. There is a six-hour working day, so that everyone will have ample time for leisure and the arts. It is a well-organised welfare state which takes care of all man's basic needs. In revenge, everyone is obliged to wear the same colourless garb and there is a drastic limitation of consumer goods. In fact, More seemed to have recommended, in Utopia, what George Orwell in 1984, feared. There is a strict moral code. Pre-marital sex is usually punished with enforced celibacy for life and adultery brings slavery and, if repeated, death. Women's libbers will be enraged to find that Utopian women are required to go on their knees, once a month before their husbands and "confess all sins of omission and commission and ask to be forgiven." There is no such corresponding rule for men.

More is surely joking when he tells us that prospective Utopian couples are required to inspect each other naked before giving their consent. He is being barbedly satirical when he says that gold is used in Utopia merely for making chamber pots and children's baubles. But when he says that the Utopians have a married clergy and practice euthanasia and divorce, people are shocked. "Can a devout Catholic really have meant that?" asks Donner.

The truth of the matter is most likely that More did not intend to offer us, in Utopia, a blue-print for a perfect society. He was writing, in a realistic vein, of a place which had many improvements to offer to a decadent and religiously intolerant European society, but which could do with some enlightenment, itself. Finally, if few moderns would pronounce Utopia, with its dreary Spartan atmosphere, as fit for human habitation, let us not overlook its timely message to a harsh authoritarian society with a corrupt and unjust social system, where poverty and persecution were taken for granted in a land infested with robbers and thieves and where destitute and starving people were strung up "by the twenties". And perhaps there has never been written a more revealing definition of capitalism than those prophetic lines of St. Thomas More, "I can perceive nothing but a certain conspiracy of rich men, procuring their own commodities under the name and title of the Commonwealth."

3.3.5. Religion in the Renaissance: Luther, Calvin

3.3.5.1. The Background

3.3.5.1.1. Religion

Religion was a burning question during the Renaissance. If your religious views didn't square with those of your local political leader, you burned. The Catholic Church had its Inquisitions which hustled heretics off to the stake. The Church of England prescribed being hanged, drawn and quartered for her adversaries. John Calvin put to death anyone in Geneva who interpreted the Bible differently from the way he did. Martin Luther exhorted the German princes to "cut and thrust, strangle and strike him at random, as if in the midst of mad dogs" the recalcitrant Anabaptists. These were indeed grim times, when Christian could maim, kill and torture Christian and think that by so doing he was doing an act pleasing to God.

3.3.5.1.2. Weariness, not reason

No wars are more brutal than those fought in the name of religion. And this was the time of such wars. "Christians attack Christians with the very weapons of hell!" cried Erasmus (and this at a time when gun-powder was still the most murderous weapon known to man). A few lone voices protested but were lost in the carnage. "Oh, if only the Christian spirit informed the Lutheran attitude to the Romans and the Roman attitude to the Lutherans - verily, then our Churches would be spared these tragedies of which no end can be seen ... Truly the wild beasts deal more kindly with each other than Christian deals with Christian." So wept Copernicus' good friend, Canon Giese. But such lone calls were unable to prevent "the horrible nurses itching to boil each other's children". In 1648, the Treaty of Westphalia put an official end to all the bloodshed. By then, the population of Germany had been reduced by half. "Weariness was to deliver more than reason ever could," observed Santillana acidly.

3.3.5.2. Martin Luther (1483-1546)

The religious revolt, as everyone knows, was spear-headed by the Augustinian monk from Wittemberg, Martin Luther. Yet, the root cause of Luther's break-away was not, as is often thought, the scandals and corruption in the Church (and their name was legion), but a very personal religious problem. Beset by terrifying doubts as to his salvation - and no doubt disgusted with the simoniacal selling of indulgences to well-nigh purchase one's heavenly visa - Luther solved the issue by reposing his entire redemption wholly and entirely in God's hands, without any scope for human intervention in this regard. He took his stand on **Romans** 1:17. "Without this doctrine," he wrote, I would be constantly tortured by uncertainty ... My conscience would never enjoy certain ease." And, just to make sure, that "human intervention" not sneak in through the back door, he denied freedom altogether. "If free-will were offered to me, I would not accept it at all," he averred. "The human will stands like a saddle-horse between God and the devil. If God mounts the saddle, man wills and goes forward as God wills ... But, if the devil is the horseman, then man wills and acts as the devil wills. He has no power to run to one or the other of the two riders and offer himself to them. But the riders fight for the possession of the animal." Erasmus was horrified at this determinism which made of man the mere passive stage on which the two great personages in the drama of salvation battle it out. And he engaged Luther in debate, eventually breaking with him altogether on this issue. It is interesting to compare the polite, reasoning of the erudite humanist, Erasmus, with the earthy vituperative of the miner's son, Luther. However, most writers today are inclined to underplay this element of Luther's ideas. Indeed, one wonders if he really meant it to be taken so seriously. It was an extreme position into which he was forced by his clever adversary. He was not so much interested in denying man's free will as in affirming the totality of divine causality in human salvation. Nor can we deny that, if Luther had exaggerated a truth, he was doing so in reaction to the Catholic emphasis of man's part in "working out his salvation". If Luther ever-stressed the 'personal commitment to Jesus' aspect of faith, Catholic gave the impression that faith was a matter of accepting certain propositions and that 'good works' (especially the buying-of- indulgences shortcut) practically 'earned' man his salvation, as a right.

If Luther really ever said anything like "believe firmly and sin boldly", the emphasis was certainly meant to be on the first part. The belief he spoke of, as we have seen, was no mere intellectual assent to divinely revealed propositions. It was a personal commitment to Christ, as ones Saviour, a word that we might better render as 'trust' or 'confidence'. In his over-anxiousness to ensure that there would be absolutely no scope left for human causality in the work of salvation, he not only undermined free-will (as we have seen), but also launched one of the most scathing attacks on human reason that history has ever known. Philosophers were anathema. Aristotle is "an urchin that must be put in the pigsty or the donkey's stable", the Sorbonne is "that mother of all errors", the theologians of Louvain are "cursed donkeys, coarse sows, bellies of blasphemers, epicurean swine, heretics and idolaters, putrid puddles, the cursed breath of hell" and reason is "a prostitute whose face must be smeared with dung". All his life long, Luther fought a (losing) battle against reason, "the devil's greatest whore". "Alas," he lamented, "in this life, reason is never completely destroyed." It was not a very noble concept of man that Luther handed on to his disciples. For, bereft of his reason and his free-will, what is man? Still, once again, we must draw attention to the fact that polemic is dangerous: it tends to make us overstate one aspect of the truth. But however, understanding we try to be, reminding ourselves that Luther was but reacting to the opposite extreme, it cannot be denied that Luther has had no small part to play, at least, in the anti-intellectualistic prejudice that characterises so much of contemporary thought.

Luther would liberate the Christian from the domination of the mercenary machinations of priestcraft. The sole duty of the Christian is to trust in Christ "Everything is founded upon this article which we teach and by which we live, in defiance of the pope, the devil and the world," declared Luther. Catholic critics usually question whether this Christo-centrism is all what it is claimed to be. Is it not a kind of veiled anthropocentrism? After all, writes Neil, "man's need for spiritual security was (Luther's) starting-point and man's desire for spiritual satisfaction was its purpose ... Man reigns supreme within the system." Whether Luther really meant God to be a kind of spiritual crutch or prop for man, it is certain that this is how he was commonly understood. And this is precisely the type of religious belief that sincere thinkers like Freud hold up to ridicule.

St. Paul had said that Christians have a vocation to liberty. But, he added, do not let your liberty become an excuse for your selfishness, a kind of licence to indulge yourself. Use your freedom to serve and love each other all the more fully (Cr. Gal 13:15). But not all the German peasantry were able to make these conclusions. Finding themselves free from all religious authority, and encouraged to despoil the rich monasteries, they had little inclination to cease their plunderings and settle down. And there was no force to check them... except the secular arm. Thus, it came about that Luther, who had once said things like, "neither the pope, nor the bishop, nor any other man has the right to dictate even so much as one syllable to the Christian believer, except with the latter's consent," had to eat his own words. Five years later he was calling upon the civil authority to hand over Anabaptists "to their proper master, to wit, Master Hans (the hang-man). Having thrown religious authority overboard, the only place he could turn to for the enforcement of order and conformity to the appointed norm was the State. And that he did with a vengeance. "The ass wants to be beaten and the mob ruled by force," he declared. "No one need think that the world can be ruled without blood. The civil sword shall and must be red and bloody." Thus, in effect, Luther helped lay the foundations of the totalitarian state. For he ended up by granting to the state all the authority that he denied to the religious authority and added a few more that the Church had never ever claimed for herself! In his treatise *On Secular Authority* he wrote things like: "There are no better works than to obey and serve all those who are set over us as Superiors. For this reason, also disobedience is a greater sin than murder, unchastity, theft and dishonesty ... It is in no wise proper for anyone who would be a Christian to set himself up against his government, whether it act justly or unjustly ... A Christian ought to be ready to suffer violence and injustice more particularly from his own ruler... The princes of this world are gods, the common people are Satan... I would rather suffer a prince doing wrong than a people doing right." All this must be read in the context of the marauding, pillaging hordes of the Peasants' Revolt. Luther had struck a blow for freedom and emancipation in calling upon the people to break away from the exploitation of the Churchmen. Suddenly, he found himself with unruly mobs, exulting with their new freedom, which they understood as licence. The only way to restrain them was the civil authority. Thus, whether he intended it or not, Luther laid the foundations of the totalitarian state. There seems to be an unbroken link connecting Luther, Fichte, Nietzsche ... and Hitler.

It would be grossly unfair to suggest, with Neill, that Luther just happened to come along at the right time. It is even questionable that he wanted to break away from the Church. He was a prophetic figure and, had the Pope of that times been less interested in boar-hunting and more concerned for the People of God, he might have realised that Luther was but stressing an aspect of faith that had been sorely neglected by the money-grabbing ecclesiastics. Had Luther not protested, abuses would have limped on for a longer time. It is largely to him that we owe the calling of the Council of Trent, long overdue, which took up - with all the limitations of that age and its polemies - the reform of Church order and discipline.

3.3.5.3. John Calvin (1509-1564)

If Luther came from rough peasant stock, John Calvin came from the upper crust bourgeoisie of Noyon, in France. Like his father, the latter was a lawyer and he carried his cool, methodical legal brain, with its talent for rebuff and repartee, into the reformation he engineered. When Lutheranism was settling down to go on a mere defensive before the challenge of a revived Catholicism, Calvinism became militarily aggressive.

Actually, Calvin did little more than draw the main ideas of Luther out to their logical and fullest conclusions. Luther knew how to start a revolt, but once he had roused the masses into revolutionary fury, he was quite unable to take the helm and direct the turbulence to any goal. Calvin could never have been able to whip up the rank and file into revolt, but he knew how to step in, once they had been stirred up, assume command and lead the hectic rush towards victory. Calvin was able to add to Protestantism what Luther never could: a thoroughly systematic body of doctrine, coolly thought out and logically arranged.

Calvin was only 27 when he wrote his *Institutions De La Religion Chretiennes* (Institutions of the Christian Religion). During his own life-time it went through six editions and grew from the original six to eighty chapters, gathering various beliefs into a coherent system, and trying to give some sort of rational foundation to a movement that, until then, had been largely emotional and voluntaristic. "Everything that the controversialist with Rome needs, is here," declared an enthusiastic reviewer. "Scholarship, argument, scripture proof, inventive, denunciation, ridicule, and above all the systematic exposition of fundamental principles."

Luther's God had been an overindulgent father, who overlooked man's weakness and sin. Calvin's was an arbitrary tyrant, who lorded it over despicable, degenerate man with a ruthless severity and had scant love for his wicked creatures. Luther's was a God of mercy, Calvin's was one of strict justice.

Central to Calvin's reform was the doctrine of predestination, which he had inherited from Luther and then pushed to relentless conclusions. "If we are not ashamed of the Gospel," he wrote, "we must confess what is plainly there declared. God, by his eternal goodwill, which has no cause outside itself, destined those whom he pleases to salvation, rejecting the rest; those whom he dignified by gratuitous adoption, he illumined by his Spirit, so that they receive the life offered in Christ, while other voluntarily disbelieve, so that they remain in darkness, destitute to the light of faith."

Calvin founded his predestinationism on certain texts, mainly from St John, which, taken in isolation, do seem to imply some such idea. But, should not one interpret an individual text or passage in the light of the general thrust of a book? Anyway, Calvin had no intention of preaching a cruel, heartless and whimsical God. He was convinced that allowing man to make some sort of contribution towards his salvation - be it the free decision of committing himself to Christ's call - would undermine God's absolute sovereignty. And it was God's absolute sovereignty that he wished to proclaim. However, the message that most people got was that of a heartless and arbitrary tyrant. And it is this type of God that most early American revivalist preachers would uphold: "We're all sinners in the hand of an angry God. We all deserve damnation. In his mercy, he spares some of us." And this is precisely the God that some of the finest American writers defied. For, under the aegis of the Puritan founding fathers, this was the kind of Christian God first preached in the New World. Mark Twain, Herman Melville and Nathaniel Hawtherne - these are but few of the "early generation Americans" who, in their writings, rejected this God, the only one they had ever known.

When Calvin finally won control of Geneva, "Protestant Rome", he ruled it with an iron hand, propounding a harsh legalism that was perhaps more inhuman than anything ever enforced by the earlier Christian authorities. A child was beheaded for striking its mother and men were burnt at stake for interpreting the Bible otherwise than did John Calvin. One may mitigate the charge of cruelty against Calvin, by pointing out that he saw any rebellions against himself as a rebellion against God and his Elect. But this only would high-light the man's insufferable presumption and intolerance. The same things could be said about the Inquisition, of course!

One final question, naturally, presents itself. Is there any way of knowing whether you belong to the Elect? Calvin offers a two-fold answer: one is through "the witness of the spirit", which consists in a deep and overwhelming assurance that you are saved. But this is only good for oneself: would there be a way of letting others know this, a way of telling who else has been included in the Glory Ride? Well, there was the "sign" of prospering in this life. Calvin would have been one of the first to point out that this was not a fool-proof way. Besides, there are many passages in his Institutions, where he seeks to put checks on the thirst for material success and prosperity. But thrift, diligence, industry, respectability - and above all Success (with a capital "S") became key virtues in the Puritan moral code as well as highly prized values in most of The American Way of Life. Calvin's injunctions to frugality, industry and so on were heeded, his warnings against avarice were forgotten. The explanation lies in the almost irresistible power of economic forces and in the tendencies of human nature. Competition and acquisitiveness very often take over what the noblest teachings have begun.

3.3.5.4. The Council of Trent (1545-1563)

Undoubtedly one of the greatest councils in the history of the Church (at least from the point of view of the repercussions it would have on the life and worship of the Christian Community for centuries), this stormy and long-drawn out assembly sought to come to grips with the challenges of the Reform Movement and to correct abuses of long standing. This Council was long overdue and it is true that it did a lot to stem the revolt. Seminary education was put in order, commissions clamped down on the evil practices that had become tied up with indulgences, religious life was renewed and so on. But there was an over-reaction against what the Reformers were stressing. The Church became very centralised and legalistic. Faith was presented more as orthodoxy - belief in the right propositions and the power of the clergy was stressed over against the Lutheran affirmation of the priesthood and responsibility of the laity. We had to wait for Vatican II and the spirit of dialogue that good Pope John had ushered in, before all the excesses (on both sides) could begin to straighten themselves out.

3.3.6. Political Thought in the Renaissance: Machiavelli

3.3.6.1. Nicolo Machiavelli (1469-1527)

John Donne, the English "metaphysical" poet, represented him as one of the devil's councillors. He was taken to be the very incarnation of Satan himself (mothers still scold errant children by telling them that "old Nick" will get them if they don't behave). The shadowy figure of that sixteenth century Florentine has become a synonym for all that is darkest and shadiest in "the dirty game" of politics. As we might be beginning to suspect, this does scant justice to the facts.

Nicolo Machiavelli was assistant Secretary of State to the Republic of Florence from 1498 to 1512. When the Republic fell, he had to retire to private life on his small farm, and it was there that he wrote his *Prince* and *Discourses*. When the ruling Medicis relented somewhat, they commissioned him to write a History of Florence. Asked his advice, he boldly said that the only method of government that would ever succeed in Florence, would be the Republican one. In 1527, Florence regained her liberty, though for a rather short time, and Machiavelli's name was proposed for his old job. But his reputation as the author of the Prince was catching up with him and he was passed over. He died not long after, unwept and forgotten, at the age of 59. Machiavelli's is the tragedy of a statesman who did himself out of his job by being too bold a thinker.

The Prince was never really published during Machiavelli's own life time. But its contents "got around" in various garbled and plagiarised forms. Interpretation of the text is still very much in dispute. The book is traditionally looked upon as a devilish work of unscrupulous immorality, which teaches all manner of intrigue and supports every evil machination, inventing a few tricks of its own, in the bargain. It might be truer to describe it as a tongue-in-cheek phenomenological study of how politicians behave and what principles they use in their exercise of their duty. It is not always easy to tell what Machiavelli's own position, in all this, was. He gives us the impression that he prescinds from all moral considerations: he just looks at the history of various European principalities to see what lessons can be learnt from their actions and which could active as guidelines for those who wish to follow in their footsteps.

For instance, he observed the machinations and outcome of the 1503 papal elections. From this he drew a lesson: he who thinks new favours will cause great personages to forget old injuries, deceives himself. Charles VIII invades Italy, with his tiny army, and topples the Italian princes before him. "Our Italian rulers thought that it sufficed a prince to know, from his desk, to make a smart retort and to indite an elegant letter, to be subtle in argument, quick in repartee ... and lead a life of unmitigated lascivousness. Whence, in 1494, the great fright, and the sudden flights, and the well- nigh inordible losses." The Dominican Savanarola stirred up a movement of religious reform. The tide turned and he was burnt at stake as a heretic. Lesson: "unarmed prophets have always been destroyed; whereas armed prophets have succeeded." Chairman Mao could scarce have put it better.

Such passages are harmless enough. But what of the following: "When on the decision to be taken depends wholely the survival of one's country, no consideration should be given to justice or injustice, to kindness or cruelty, or to its being praiseworthy or ignominous, but rather, any other thought being set aside, that alternative should be followed utterly which will save its existence and preserve its freedom." In other words, whatever helps further the cause of the party, is good. Or, again: "A wise lord cannot, nor ought to keep faith when such observance may be turned against him, and when the reasons that caused him to pledge it exist no longer. If men were entirely good, this precept would not hold. But, because they are bad, and will not keep faith with you, you, too, are not bound to observe it with them." Such attitudes would completely undermine all national and international order. Nor should we hesitate to say that those politicians who would most violently denounce these policies, are most likely the ones who practises them most. As someone once said, politicians dislike Machiavelli because he gave away their secrets. On the other hand, let us not forget that Machiavelli regarded mass deportations and liquidations (so much a part of our political scene) as something quite beyond the pale of mankind; "these means are cruel and destructive of all civilised life and are neither Christian nor human and should be avoided by everyone," he wrote. Besides, there is the fact that he ever remained a loyal Catholic all his life though he once made a wry remark to the effect that Christianity would never work as the established religion of mankind as it is built on justice and love, whereas temporal society thrives on hypocrisy and deceit. Was Machiavelli serious when he advocated deceit or was he being cynical?

3.3.7. A Select Bibliography of Some Renaissance Thinkers

3.3.7.1. In General

Giorgio de Santillana, *The Age of Adventure*, New York, 1959 (Contains also some basic texts from leading Renaissance thinkers; excellent introduction and notes).

Frederick Copleston SJ, *A History of Philosophy*, vol. III, London 1953 (This volume has a whole section - Part II - comprising some 1330 interesting pages, on the times and the thinkers).

You may also consult the other standard texts: Hisrchberger, Thonnard, etc. Note that Renaissance thinkers are usually classified with Medieval Philosophy.

3.3.7.2. Philosophy

Montaigne, *A Book of Good Faith*, trans. Bullett, London, 1928 (includes a very good introduction).

_______. *Essays*, 3 volumes, Florio's edition, with an introduction by Desmond MacCarthy, London, 1938.

Philip Halie, *The Scar of Montaigne: An Essay in Personality,* Middleton, 1966. (very good!).

3.3.7.3. Science

Galileo Galilei, *Dialogue on the Great World Systems*, revised, annotated and with an introduction by Giorgio de Santillana, Chicago, 1953 (a regular 'labour of love', painstakingly done!).

James Brodrick SJ, *Galileo: The Man, His Work, His Misfortunes*, London, 1964.

_______. *Robert Bellarmine, Saint and Scholar*, London, 1961 (A re-working of his earlier 2 volume edition, *The Life and Work of Blessed Robert Francis Bellarmine*, London, 1928. There is a treatment of the Galileo case. since Bellarmine was one of the personae involved. Brodrick acknowledges some correctives and criticisms, including those of Santillana).

Giorgio de Santillana, *The Crime of Galileo*, Chicago, 1955 (very fair, though the author is not at all pleased with Galileo's scurvy treatment of his hero, Kepler).

Arthur Koestler OP, *The Sleepw*alkers, Harmondsworth, 1964 (Eminently readable account of how the scientific era began; interesting and popular presentations of the work of men like Copernicus, Galileo, Kepler).

3.3.7.4. Humanism

Desiderius Erasmus, *The Enchiridion*, London, 1943.

_______. *In Praise of Folly*, trans. John Wilson, New York, 1958.

_______. *Luther and Erasmus on Free Will*, London, 1969 (Interesting study of the actual texts of the controversy).

St. Thomas More, *Utopia*, Harrnondsworth, 1961 (Includes excellent critical introduction).

Froude, *The Life and Letters of Erasmus*, London, 1894 (A classic; text of lectures delivered at Oxford University, 1893-4).

Christopher Hollis, *Erasmus*, London, 1933.

Huizinga, Erasmus of Rotterdam, New York, 1952 (includes a selection of his letters; gives very well the spirit of the age. There is also a fine introduction by G N Clark).

Reynolds, *More and Erasmus*, London, 1965 (One of best recent studies).

Hans Kung, *Freedom in the World: St. Thomas More*, trans. Cecily Hastings, London, 1965 (A world famous theologian brings out the relevance of the "Man for all Seasons").

Reynolds, *St. Thomas More*, New York, 1958.

Chambers, *Thomas More*, Ann Arbor, 1959.

3.3.7.5. Politics

Nicholas Machiavelli, *The Prince*, London, 1965 (With very good critical introduction)

Hale, *Machiavelli and Renaissance Italy*, Harmondsworth 1972 (Gives the spirit of the times in a very vivid manner).

Pasquale Villari, *The Life and Times of Nicolo Machiavelli*, trans Linda Villari, London, 1929 (A classic: over 1000 pages!).

Count Carlo Sforza, *The Living Thought of Nicolo Machiavelli*, London, 1949.

3.4. René Descartes (1596–1650)

3.4.1. His Life

Born on March 31, 1596, at La Haye in Touraine, the third child of a provincial gentleman, René Descartes Duperron, was expected to die along with his mother (she expired not long after his birth), but, thanks to the care of a devoted nurse, he survived, though his health was never of the best.

In 1606, he was enrolled at the newly found Jesuit school of La Fleche and there picked up his great love and admiration for Mathematics at the feet of the great mathematician Christopher Clavius who held that this discipline should be conceded "the first place among Sciences" for it alone is able to give "the most solid reasons" for all it teaches. Small wonder, then, that young René, when he moved on to the University of Poitiers, in 1614, was already convinced that Mathematics was the Queen of the Sciences and the only one worthy of the name. In 1616 he graduated from the University with the degrees of bachelor of, and licentiate in, law.

Then began a long period of travel and adventure that took him almost all over Europe in the army of Maurice of Massau, in the Netherlands. His interest in mathematics was broadened and intensified due to his new contacts and slowly he began to consider the possibility of applying himself to solving the age-old problems that have ever tormented the mind of man, using a mathematical approach which would provide a sure and evident answer.

On the night of November 10, 1619, he is supposed to have dreamt three epoch- making dreams in which he saw himself being called by God to seek after truth and to offer the fruits of this his vocation to mankind, thereby uniting the different schools of philosophy, which had ever been at variance with each other. Forthwith, he made a vow to Our Lady, resolving to go on pilgrimage to Loreto and dedicate his newly found vocation to her. He would have to wait four years to fulfil this pledge. Descartes certainly had a very high concept of his philosophical vocation. This was one of the reasons why he never married - he felt that this required of him the total dedication one expects of the celibate priest. Human nature being what it is, he fathered an illegitimate son, but was not remiss in his bringing up of the boy nor in providing for the lad's mother.

In 1626, he was back in Paris, where he resided for two years and received plenty of encouragement from Cardinal Berulle.

In 1628, he went to Holland, where he composed most of his works, including the *Rules for the Direction of the Mind* (published posthumously). He cautiously delayed publication of his *Treatise on the World,* well aware of the Galileo affair. In 1637, he wrote his *Discourse on the Method* and several of his scientific works. These were followed by the famous *Meditations on the First Philosophy,* published in 1641.

He fell out with the University of Utrecht, on account of some of his views and had to appeal to the Prince of Orange for protection, in 1642. He was considering returning to France (no great model of toleration, herself), when he received an invitation become private tutor in Philosophy to Queen Christina of Sweden.

Thither he repaired in 1649, and there he wrote his *Principles of Philosophy* for his royal pupil. Unfortunately for Descartes, her royal highness insisted on having her daily Philosophy class at 5 a.m. when, in her opinion, her mind was freshest. The cold Scandinavian air was too much for Descartes and scarce a year later he was dead of a chill he had contracted on an early morning visit to the Palace. He had just managed to complete his *Passions of the Soul.* He left behind him several unfinished works.

Descartes was one of the first modern philosophers to prefer his vulgar tongue to the traditional Latin of the scholars, to expound his ideas. This is because he took his vocation as apostle of reconciliation very seriously indeed. "I wish to make myself understandable, even to women," he (rather unchivalrously) declared.

His remains were carried to France and they reposed for a long time in the Pantheon. In 1819, they were transferred to the Church of St. Germaine des Pres. Gustave III erected a monument to him in Stockholm.

3.4.2. His Thought

3.4.2.1. Philosophy of Knowledge

3.4.2.1.1. The Challenge

Philosophy, lamented Descartes, has been "cultivated for many years by the most distinguished men and yet there is not a single matter within its sphere which is not still in dispute." (Disc. On Method, Pt I) Was there any hope of ever giving it as certain and universally-accepted a foundation as mathematics which, in spite of its certainty, had been used to provide the basis of "no loftier edifice ... than the mechanical arts"? (Ibid.)

3.4.2.1.2. Sensation can't provide us with a starting-point

What we need is a starting-point that is so sure and unassailable that not even the most radical scepticism would be able to shake it. Then we would be able to build our edifice of philosophy on this solid foundation. Now, such a starting-point could not be found in the realm of sensible experience, for it is a fact that our senses sometimes deceive us (e.g. a distant object looks small, etc.) and "it is wiser not to trust entirely to anything by which we 'have once been deceived."(Med. I) As for more immediate and apparently so obviously certain sense data - such as, for example, that I have a body and am seated here - even they could be the object of doubt: I could be dreaming all these things and there seems to be no way of telling that I am not!

3.4.2.1.3. Neither can the "eternal and necessary truths"

Alas, not even mathematics itself can provide us with an unshakeable starting-point, though it is not directly concerned with sensible objects and is not tied up with sense experiences. For, who knows, perhaps there exists some "evil genius, not less powerful than deceitful" (Med. I) who is constantly corrupting and disturbing my thinking processes in such a way that he actually makes me think that "eternal and necessary truths", such as '2 + 2 are 4' and 'the whole is greater than the part' are true, whereas they are, in fact, false. Let us not forget that we are seeking a starting-point that not even the wildest sceptic doubt could upset.

3.4.2.1.4. The Cartesian doubt

And so, Descartes begins his philosophy with a universal doubt - a doubt about everything. Yet his is not like the sceptic's attitude. The latter doubts, too, but his doubt is born of despair: he never hopes to get out of it. Descartes, however, described his doubt as **methodical**: he doubts in order to know. It is part of his method of philosophising. In the **Discourse on the Method**, he adds other precisions concerning this doubt. It should remain in the theoretical order and does not imply that, in practice, we call into question and disregard the laws of the State or the Church. This seems only sound practical advice!

3.4.2.1.5. The Solution: *cogito ergo sum*

Archimedes of old had said that, given an appropriate fulcrum and lever, he would be able to move the whole world. Descartes, falling back on this image, wonders if he could be able to find a starting-point "certain and indubitable" from which he'd be able to move himself out of the morass of universal doubt. And then, suddenly he has found it. Deceived though I may be as to whatever knowledge I am persuaded to believe in through my senses or the machinations of the evil genie, still I assuredly exist, since I was persuaded, he exults. As he puts it in the **Discourse**, "This truth, *I think, hence I am* (cogito ergo sum), was so certain and of such evidence, that no ground of doubt, however extravagant, could be alleged by the sceptics, capable of shaking it, that I concluded I might, without scruple, accept it as the first principle of the philosophy of which I was in search." (Pt. IV)

3.4.2.1.6. Other forms of the Cogito

Descartes' cogito (I think) was open to embrace any conscious experience: it is not limited to intellectual affirmations as such. In his *Principles of Philosophy* (and elsewhere) he says that one equally well say *I understand, therefore I exist* - or *I will, I imagine, therefore I exist*. In fact, any conscious experience would do. I could even say, I walk, therefore I exist - provided that by "I walk" I refer not to the bodily activity, as such (which is an activity of the body, whose existence may be doubted, since I could be dreaming all this) but to the mental activity of being conscious of this alleged activity. This takes me back to the mind and its activity and I can base my starting-point on that!

3.4.2.1.7. The Criterion of Truth

I am in possession of at least one item of certain truth: I exist, derived from the fact that I think. Now, the characteristic qualities of this idea are that it is a clear and distinct perception. Hence, "it seems to me that I may now take as a general rule that all that is clearly and distinctly perceived is true." (Med. III) What does Descartes mean by "clear" and "distinct"? It would seem that a thing is clear, when we can tell what it is; 'It is distinct when we can tell it apart from other things which it is not. "I call that clear which is present and manifest to the mind giving attention to it, just as we are said clearly to see objects when, being present to the eye looking on, they stimulate it with sufficient force, and it is disposed to regard them; but the distinct is that which is so precise and different from all other objects as to comprehend in itself only what is clear." (Principles, I, XV)

At the beginning of the *Fourth Meditation,* Descartes claims that the will to deceive is "undoubtedly evidence of malice or weakness" so as to be an imperfection. But, since God has all perfections and no imperfections, it follows that God cannot be a deceiver. For to conceive of God with the will to deceive would be to conceive him to be both having no imperfections and having one imperfection, which is impossible; it would be like trying to conceive of a mountain without a valley. This conclusion, in addition to God's existence, provides the absolutely certain foundation Descartes was seeking from the outset of the *Meditations*. It is absolutely certain because both conclusions (namely that God exists and that God cannot be a deceiver) have themselves been demonstrated from immediately grasped and absolutely certain intuitive truths.

This means that God cannot be the cause of human error, since he did not create humans with a faculty for generating them, nor could God create some being, like an evil demon, who is bent on deception. Rather, humans are the cause of their own errors when they do not use their faculty of judgment correctly. Second, God's non-deceiving nature also serves to guarantee the truth of all clear and distinct ideas. So, God would be a deceiver, if there were a clear and distinct idea that was false, since the mind cannot help but believe them to be true. Hence, clear and distinct ideas must be true on pain of contradiction. This also implies that knowledge of God's existence is required for having any absolutely certain knowledge. Accordingly, atheists, who are ignorant of God's existence, cannot have absolutely certain knowledge of any kind, including scientific knowledge.

3.4.2.1.8. Types of Concepts

Descartes started what would become almost a mania for moderns: the habit of classifying and dividing up our concepts. According to him, these are of three basic types. First, there are purely ***representative facts*** or images of things and to these alone properly belongs the name ***idea***, "as when I think or represent to my mind a man, a chimera, a sky, an angel or God." (Med. III). Secondly, there are purely ***active facts*** of consciousness: these consist of **volitions** (acts where the soul seems to be the efficient cause, e.g. to love God, to desire a reward, to hate ones enemy) and **sentiments** (acts where the soul appears to be acted upon by something, e.g. the pleasure one experiences from seeing a friend or the pain one feels from a wound). Finally, there are ***judgments***. These are a combination of the above and occur where a connection is made between two of them. Finally, the first group, ideas, are sub-divided into three types according to their origin. There are ***adventitious*** ideas, those which come to me (Latin advenire) from outside (e.g. a man, the sky). Then there are ***factitious*** ideas, ideas I fabricate or make myself (Latin facere) by piercing together or combining different adventitious ideas (e.g. I put together two adventitious ideas; woman and fish, and I get the factitious idea of a mermaid). Finally, we have the ***innate*** or ***in-born*** ideas (Latin-natus). These, as the name indicates, are in-born in us from birth. Such are the idea of God and of extension.

3.4.2.1.9. Innate Ideas or Dispositions?

An obvious objection was made to Descartes to the effect that it would be difficult to explain *how* there could be atheists in the world if man has an innate idea of God. Replying to such a question in his ***Notes Against a Programme***, Descartes said that what he really meant is that man has a "certain disposition or propensity" to form such an idea. An atheist is one who has not actuated this potentiality. But if it is a mere capacity or disposition or propensity, why call it an idea?

3.4.2.1.10. The Problem of the Bridge

In his third Meditation, Descartes raises an important question: "Are ideas which I find in myself... similar or conformable to things which are outside of myself?" This is the foundation of the famous 'problem of the bridge', as it has been called by later thinkers. The problem is how does one bridge the gap between the world of ideas within me and the external world. Descartes had an answer. God, our good and wise Creator, would not let us be deceived. If we know some 'internal ideas' which claim to refer to the external world, then we can quite safely assume that there is such a world, corresponding to these ideas. "It is impossible for (God) to deceive me," writes Descartes, "for in all fraud and deceit there is a certain imperfection; and although it may seem that the ability to deceive is a mark of subtlety or power, yet the desire to deceive testifies to malice or weakness; and such accordingly cannot be found in God." (Med. IV)

3.4.2.2. Philosophy of God

3.4.2.2.1. Proofs from Within

We have just seen how Descartes used God's existence to guarantee the reality of the external world. Obviously, then, he wouldn't be able to take as his starting-point for proving God's existence, some observable fact from the external world, such as finality or motion. That would be a blatant vicious circle. Descartes will follow the Augustinian approach. He was convinced that we are able to form an idea of God wholly from within, on the basis of our self-consciousness and without any reference to created reality outside of us.

3.4.2.2.2. A Proof from Our Idea of the Perfect Being

We have a clear and distinct idea of a being that is perfect in every way (so runs the argument in Meditation III and elsewhere). This is confirmed from the fact that I realise in me several imperfections (such as to doubt). From here I become aware that I have an idea of the perfect being. Now this perfect being must exist, how else could I explain the origin of this idea in me? After all, "there must be at least as much reality in the efficient and total causes as in their effect." Now, neither the external world nor I are perfect. The former isn't because it is corporeal and changeable (in any case, I can't be sure of its existence in itself) and I am not because I doubt, for one thing. Therefore, there must exist a perfect being who has put in me this idea of himself.

3.4.2.2.3. A Proof from the Indication that I Did not Create Myself

This argument is most clearly given in the ***Principles of Philosophy***, (I, XX). It runs thus: a being which is capable of both forming the idea of the most perfect as well as of producing itself, would make itself perfect. But we have the former capacity and yet, as we know too well, we are not perfect. Therefore, we cannot be our own cause. Hence, ultimately, God exists as our cause.

3.4.2.2.4. The Cartesian version of the Ontological Argument

Descartes really added nothing new to the ontological argument of Anselm, except that he called the idea of the greatest conceivable being an innate one. And he added the simile of the valley and the mountain. "I cannot conceive a God unless as existing, any more than I can a mountain without a valley." This is because "the mountain or valley, whether they do or do not exist, are inseparable from each other" and because, similarly, "we cannot conceive God unless as existing." This is brought about not "by my thought, nor does it impose any necessity on things. On the contrary, the necessity which lies in the things itself, that is, the necessity of the existence of God, determines me to think in this way." (*Meditation* V; of also *Principles of Philosophy*, where he uses the image of a triangle and the necessity of its three angles totalling two right angles).

3.4.2.3. Philosophy of Man

3.4.2.3.1. The definition of man

Having established indubitably that he exists, Descartes turns his mind to the consideration of ***what*** he is. The primary and certain datum, *I think – I exist*, provides the answer. Obviously, I am nothing else but "a substance, whose whole or nature is to think" (*Discourse on Method*). In the second meditation, he puts it more bluntly: "I am only a thinking thing, that is, a mind." Note carefully that "only"!

3.4.2.3.2. What, No Body?

"I am only... a mind," says Descartes. And that is his definition of man. But surely, he did not mean that man was a pure spirit? When he wrote, "I am not the assemblage of members called the human body," he meant the stress to be on am not. That I have a body is "a teaching of nature". Yet Descartes was adamant in denying that the body is part of man's nature. Man's mind or soul is purely rational. There is no vegetative or sensitive aspect to it, nor are universal ideas formed, by it, through abstraction.

3.4.2.3.3. The Unity of the Human Composite

So, man is a soul and he has a body. If the latter is not part of man's nature, how are the two connected to each other? "It is necessary for (the soul) to be united and joined more closely to the body, in order to have sensation and appetites similar to ours," admitted Descartes (Discourse, V) How do we explain the high degree of intimacy between the two, while yet denying any substantial unity? "At this point, Monsieur Descartes withdrew from the game," wrote Leibniz angrily. Finding himself in difficulties, Descartes characteristically evaded the issue. He would try to convince us that there was a special *pineal gland* somewhere in the head where the two met. But nobody was fooled by this explanation. In a later letter to Princess Elisabeth, Descartes actually admitted a substantial union in so many words, but here he was emptying the scholastic formula of all meaning, for he kept maintaining that the body is not part of man's nature!

3.4.2.3.4. Sensations and Passions

In his last published work, *Passions of the Soul*, Descartes provides accounts of how various motions in the body cause sensations and passions to arise in the soul. He begins by making several observations about the mind-body relation. The whole mind is in the whole body and the whole in each of its parts but yet its primary seat is in a little gland at the centre of the brain now known as the "pineal gland." The main point was that the soul makes a human body truly human; that is, makes it a living human body and not merely a corpse.

Descartes maintains further that all sensations depend on the nerves, which extend from the brain to the body's extremities in the form of tiny fibres encased by tube-like membranes. These fibres float in a very fine matter known as the "animal spirits." This allows these fibres to float freely so that anything causing the slightest motion anywhere in the body will cause movement in that part of the brain where the fibre is attached. The variety of different movements of the animal spirits cause a variety of different sensations not in the part of the body originally affected but only in the brain and ultimately in the pineal gland. So, strictly speaking, pain does not occur in the foot when a toe is stubbed but only in the brain.

These sensations may also cause certain emotions or passions in the mind. However, different sensations do not give rise to different passions because of the difference in objects but only in regards to the various ways these things are beneficial, harmful or important for us. For example, the sight of an ice cream parlour, caused by the movement of the animal spirits in the eye and through the nerves to the brain and pineal gland, might also cause the passion of desire to arise. These same animal spirits would then dispose the body to move (for example, toward the ice cream parlour) in order to attain the goal of eating ice cream thereby satisfying this desire. Descartes goes on to argue that there are only six primitive passions, namely wonder, love, hatred, desire, joy and sadness. All other passions are either composed of some combination of these primitives or are species of one of these six genera.

3.4.2.3.4. Ethics

It appears that Descartes wanted to go down in history as a great ethical teacher. In his prefatory letter to the Principles of Philosophy, he declared that morals is "the highest and most perfect" of all the sciences that sprout, like branches, from the tree of philosophy whose root is metaphysics and whose trunk is physics. But he had to leave to his great disciple and admirer, Spinoza, to fulfil his great dream.

3.4.2.3.4.1. The Provisional Moral Code

In Part 3 of the *Discourse on Method*, Descartes lays out a provisional moral code by which he plans to live while engaged in his methodological doubt in search of absolute certainty. This code of "three or four" rules or maxims is established so that he is not frozen by uncertainty in the practical affairs of life. These maxims can be paraphrased as follows:

1. To obey the laws and customs of my country, holding constantly to the Catholic religion, and governing myself in all other matters according to the most moderate opinions accepted in practice by the most sensible people.
2. To be as firm and decisive in action as possible and to follow even the most doubtful opinions once they have been adopted.
3. Try to master myself rather than fortune, and change my desires rather than the order of the world.
4. Review the various professions and chose the best (AT VI 23-28: CSM I 122-125).

The main thrust of the first maxim is to live a moderate and sensible life while his previously held beliefs have been discarded due to their uncertainty. Therefore, the first maxim is intended to provide Descartes with guides or touchstones that will most likely lead to the performance of morally good actions. The second maxim expresses a firmness of action so as to avoid the inaction produced by hesitation and uncertainty. By following this maxim, Descartes hopes to avoid the regrets experienced by those who set out on a supposedly good course that they later judge to be bad. The third maxim enjoins Descartes to master himself and not fortune. This is based on the realization that all that is in his control are his own thoughts and nothing else. In this way, Descartes hopes to avoid the regret experienced by those who have desires that cannot be satisfied, because this satisfaction lies beyond their grasp so that one should not desire health when ill nor freedom when imprisoned. It is difficult to see why the fourth maxim is included. Indeed, Descartes himself seems hesitant about including it when he states at the outset that his provisional moral code consists of "three or four maxims." This seems to imply the correct choice of occupation can ensure a degree of contentedness that could not be otherwise achieved if one is engaged in an occupation for which one is not suited.

3.4.2.3.4.1. Generosity

After the *Discourse* of 1637, Descartes did not take up the issue of morality in any significant way again until his correspondence with Princess Elizabeth in 1643, which culminated in his remarks about generosity in part 3 of the *Passions of the Soul.* Given the temporal distance between his main reflections on morality, it is easy to attribute to Descartes two moral systems – the provisional moral code and the ethics of generosity. At *Passions*, part 3, section 153, Descartes claims that the virtue of generosity "causes a person's self-esteem to be as great as it may legitimately be" and has two components. First is knowing that only the freedom to dispose volitions is in anyone's power. Accordingly, people should only be praised or blamed for using one's freedom either well or poorly. The second component is the feeling of a "firm and constant resolution" to use one's freedom well such that one can never lack the will to carry out whatever has been judged to be best.

3.4.2.4. Philosophy of the World

3.4.2.4.1. The notion of substance

Descartes borrowed from Scholastic philosophers the notion of substance and used the term quite extensively. But he defined it in a peculiar way. "By substance, we can conceive nothing else than a thing which exists in such a way as to stand in need of nothing beyond itself in order to its existence." (Principle of Philosophy. I, LI) In that case, only God could strictly verify the meaning of substance. And so, Descartes admits, "And, in truth, there can be conceived but one substance which is absolutely independent, and that is God." He got out of pantheism, however, by adding that we could call created realities substances though they can exist "only by the help of the concourse of God." This is because substance is not a univocal term.

3.4.2.4.2. Extension

Towards the end of the first part of his Philosophical Principles, Descartes noted that every substance has "one principal property... which constitutes its nature and essence, and on which all others depend." (I, LIII). If thinking was the characteristic of the spiritual or ego-substance, then extension was the attribute of the corporeal substance. Extension is one of the clear and distinct ideas.

One of the more controversial positions the *Principles* forwarded, at least according to Newton, was that a vacuum was impossible. Descartes's rejection of the possibility of a vacuum followed from his commitment to the view that the essence of body was extension. Given that extension is an attribute, and that nothing cannot possess any attributes (AT VIIIA 25; CSM I 210), it follows that "nothingness cannot possess any extension" (AT VIIIA 50; CSM I 231). So, any instance of extension would entail the presence of some substance (AT VIIIA 25; CSM I 210). In other words, vacuum, taken as an extended *nothing*, is a flat contradiction. The corporeal universe is thus a plenum, individual bodies separated only by their surfaces.

3.4.2.4.3. Animals and plants have no life

Descartes denied all forms of sub-human life. Animals were merely sophisticated machines - all the more so were plants - intelligently created by God. Their movements and their sounds were no more than the smooth running of cleverly constructed mechanical parts. They were life-like robot, not feeling, living things. Part of the reason for this strange conviction was, no doubt, his determination to fight those who wanted to reduce the difference between men and animals to one of degree only. But the real reason is the logical conclusion of his strict separation of the worlds of spirit and matter. True, in his correspondence, there occur phrases like, "I do not deprive the animal of life." Yet, a paragraph later he will say that by "life" he means a mere "warmth of the heart", in other words, certain purely material processes, analogous to our own. The human body, too, in as much as it is corporeal, is a mere machine. As Koestler wittingly sums it up, for Descartes, man is but a "ghost in a machine".

3.5. Blaise Pascal (1623–1662)

Blaise Pascal was a philosopher of very different stamp of mind. He was different from Descartes in many a sense. Pascal was concerned with showing how the Christian revelation solves the problems which arise out of the human situation. Some writers (Henry Bergson, Jacque Chevalier) see in him one of the greatest of French philosophers; others refuse to call him a philosopher. These judgments are obviously partly dependent on personal decisions as to what constitutes philosophy and a philosopher.

3.5.1. Life

Pascal was born in 1623 at Clermont in France. Following his mother's death when he was three years old, Blaise was reared by his father, Étienne, in the company of his two sisters, Gilberte (b. 1620) and Jacqueline (b. 1625). Pascal's father was an accomplished mathematician, and he provided the only formal education that his son enjoyed. The decision to educate Pascal at home was motivated by the fact that he suffered from very poor health for most of his life, beginning at the age of two. Although his sister, Gilberte, may have exaggerated in her hagiographical biography, *La vie de M. Pascal*, she reported Pascal as claiming that 'from the age of eighteen, he never passed a day without pain'.

From childhood he displayed signs of outstanding intelligence and mental power. In 1639 he started writing essays and publishing them. In 1654 Pascal underwent a spiritual experience of realization of God. And from this time his life bore a profoundly religious stamp which turned his mind toward theological themes rather than scientific and mathematical interests. He was to a certain extent in sympathy with Jansenists who emphasized the corruption of human nature after the Fall and the powerlessness of man to become or to do anything pleasing to God without divine grace. He attacked the moral theology of the Jesuits for their casuistry, laxity and hypocrisy in the controversy of Jansenism.

3.5.2. His Thought

3.5.2.1. His Philosophy of Knowledge (Epistemology)

3.5.2.1.1. Knowledge from Experience

Although Pascal was a Cartesian to the extent that he asserted the supremacy of the mathematical method within the field of deduction and demonstration, he by no means shared Descartes' convictions concerning the extent of its applicability and usefulness. We cannot, for example, develop the natural sciences in a *purely a priori* manner. In establishing empirical facts experience, or rather the experimental method must be our guide. Experience is the sole principle of physics. Our knowledge is limited by our experience. Authority is the source of our theological knowledge; the mysteries of faith surpass the reach of the human reason. The geometrical method is inefficacious in the metaphysical field.

3.5.2.1.2. Reason and Faith

By natural reason we cannot prove the existence of God. By faith only we can know the existence of God. If there is a God, He is infinitely incomprehensible. So, the metaphysical proofs of God are so remote from men's reasoning and so complicated that they have little effect. Again, while proofs based on the marvels of nature may serve to draw the attention of believers to the work of God, they are of no service to atheists. On the contrary, to attempt to convince atheists by an argument based on the movement of the heavenly bodies is to give them reason for thinking that the proofs of our religion are very weak, and Pascal sees by reason and by experience that nothing is more calculated to excite in them this contempt. In other words, if the object of proving the existence is to convince agnostics and atheists, the abstract metaphysical proofs are no use, while physical arguments are worse than useless. Reasoning of both types are inefficacious.

But Pascal had a profounder reason for rejecting the traditional proofs of God's existence. The knowledge of God which he had in mind was the knowledge of God as revealed in Christ, mediator and redeemer, a knowledge which is the response to man's intimate consciousness of his own misery. All those who seek God apart from Jesus Christ and who stop at nature either find no light to satisfy them or arrive at forming for themselves a way of knowing God and of serving him without a mediator; and thereby they fall either into atheism or into deism.

Reason has its own sphere, mathematics and the natural sciences or natural philosophy; but the truths which it is really important for man to know, his nature and his supernatural destiny, these cannot be discovered by the philosopher or the scientist.

3.5.2.1.3. Reason and Truth

When Pascal depreciate 'reason', he is using the tern in a narrow sense, to mean the abstract, analytic, and deductive operation of the mind as it is found in geometry. Pascal wishes to make two points: first, mathematical method and scientific method are not the only means by which we come to know truth. Secondly, mathematical and scientific truths are not those which are most important for man to know.

3.5.2.1.4. 'The Heart' (le Coeur)

His famous statement: "Heart has its reasons which reason does not understand" (Le cœur a ses raisons que la raison ne connaît point) needs to be explained. 'Heart' (Le Coeur) here does not mean emotion. Sometimes it is used as synonymous with 'the Will'. At times heart designates a kind of knowledge or an instrument of knowing. And this is Pascal's characteristic use of the term. It is exemplified in his statement that we apprehend first principle by 'the heart'. When Pascal says that principles are felt by the heart, he is obviously talking about intuition. When he asserts that 'it is the heart which feels (perceives) God, and not the reason', he is thinking of a loving apprehension of God, apprehension which is open to those who have no knowledge of metaphysical arguments for God's existence or even of historical and empirical arguments in favour of Christianity. He does not refer to mere emotion, but a loving *apprehension* of God, which is found in Christian believer. Thus, heart refers to instinctive, immediate, unreasoned apprehension of a truth.

On the level of geometry, we have an immediate awareness of principles; and even though these principles cannot be demonstrated our certitude is legitimate and lies at the foundation of deductive reasoning. On the level of moral life there is a spontaneous and direct apprehension of values, though this apprehension can be obscured or corrupted. And on the level of religious life the devout believer possesses a loving apprehension of God which is immune from the attacks of skepticism. In general, 'the heart is a kind of intellectual instinct, rooted in the inmost nature of the soul.

3.5.2.1.5. Method of Pascal

If we have to speak about the method of Pascal, we have to speak of both heart and reason. In mathematics deduction and demonstration would be deprived of certainty, were it not for the immediate apprehension of evident first principles. But without the work of the discursive and deductive reason there would be no mathematics. Again, though the simple and devout Christian possesses legitimate certitude through his loving apprehension of God, this certitude is a personal matter; and it by no means follows that arguments in favour of the Christian religion are not required. We cannot satisfy sceptics and agnostics by appealing to the simple and devout Christian's interior appropriation of the truth. And Pascal himself projected an apology for Christianity with arguments. The arguments to which he appealed were based on empirical and historical facts, the presence of the Christian faith as an empirical fact, miracles, prophecy and so on; but arguments were reasoned arguments. In Pascal's opinion we cannot prove the truth of Christianity by 'geometry', by *a priori* deductive reasoning. We have to turn to empirical data and show how their convergence points infallibly to the truth of Christianity.

The concept of 'heart' has an important part to play even in his reasoned defense of the Christian religion. For while the heart does *not,* indeed, supply the proofs, it discerns the significance of the facts cited in the proofs, and it discerns the significance of the convergence of probabilities. Of the two men who listen to the arguments and understand the word one may see the cumulative force of the arguments while the other does not. If all the arguments have been mentioned, the difference between the two men is not that the one has heard an argument which the other has not: it is rather that one has an intuitive grasp of the force and significance of the converging arguments which is lacking to the other. In the development of an apologetic therefore, it is essential to display the arguments in the most persuasive form, not in order to persuade people to embrace a conclusion repugnant to the mind, but in order to facilitate the working of 'the heart'.

3.5.2.2. Philosophy of Man

Man is the embodiment of a contradiction of wretchedness and greatness. Man's intellectual capacity is limited; he is also liable to be led astray by the senses and the imagination. He is dominated by self-love, and this self-interest blinds his eyes to true justice and is origin of disorder in social and political life. Again, man is riddled with contradictions, and he is a riddle to himself. He can be satisfied with nothing less than the infinite, but in point of fact he finds no complete satisfaction.

3.5.2.2.1. Wretchedness of Man

Pascal said that Montaigne is invaluable for confounding the pride of those who attribute too much to human nature and who ignore man's corruption and weakness. But we have to remember that what Pascal wishes to show is the wretchedness of man, *without God.* Pascal was very conscious of the powerlessness of mere argument to convince those who lacked requisite disposition.

3.5.2.2.2. Greatness of Man

But there is another aspect of man to be considered, his greatness. And this greatness can be inferred even from his wretchedness. The greatness of man is so evident that it can be inferred from his wretchedness. Man is only a reed, the frailest thing in nature, but he is a thinking reed. Were this universe to crush him, man would still be nobler than that which slays him. For he knows that he dies and that the universe has the better of him. But the universe knows nothing of this. "Spatially the universe encompasses and engulfs me like a point. But by thought I encompass the universe." Man is filled with an insatiable desire for happiness, and this desire is a source of unhappiness. But the infinite gulf can be filled by an infinite and changeless object that is by God Himself. So here again man's wretchedness reveals his greatness, his capacity for God. The greatness of man is so evident that it is even proved by his wretchedness. He experiences the three profound needs of, truth, happiness and justice, which he does not succeed in satisfying. His faculties never completely attain these, and if all this is wretched, at least he has these needs and these faculties and this is his greatness. On the other hand, man is aware of his misery and this implies the memory of a passed greatness. "What a chimera then is man, what a novelty! What a monster, what a chaos, what a contradiction, what a prodigy!"

3.5.2.2.3. Jesus Christ - Answer for the Enigma of Man

Only the Christian religion may solve the enigma that is man. Now, two words summarize the whole Christian religion: Adam and Jesus Christ. The knowledge of God without that of our wretchedness produces pride. The knowledge of our wretchedness without the knowledge of God produces despair. The knowledge of Jesus Christ forms the middle point; for there we find both our greatness and our wretchedness.

3.5.2.3. His Philosophy of God

3.5.2.3.1. The Wager Argument

In the *Pensées* there occurs the famous wager argument. Pascal did not develop the wager argument as a proof of God's existence. Nor did he intend it as a substitute for the proofs of Christianity. It appears to a particular class of people, namely, to those who are not yet convinced of the truth of the Christian religion. Pascal wants to show to these people that to believe is to their advantage and happiness, and if it depended entirely on their own will's belief would be the only reasonable course of action. But it does not follow that he demands of them faith simply as an outcome of the wager argument. What he seems to have in mind is rather the preparation of their minds and the production of disposition favourable to belief, dispositions which are not hindered by the passions and by attachment to things of this world. He did not consider that belief is simply a matter of a self-interested wager, of a betting on an objective uncertainty because, if it were true, it would be to one's advantage to have staked in favour of it. If you win, you win all; if you lose, you lose nothing. There is here an infinity of an infinitely happy life to gain, one chance of gain against a finite number of chances of loss; and what you stake is finite.

Now the finite is nothing in comparison with the infinite. There is no need, therefore, for further deliberation.

It may be said that wagering for God means risking what is certain for what is uncertain. To risk a finite good for a certain infinite good is clearly advantageous; but the certainty of loss balances the possibility of gain when there is question of abandoning a certain finite good for an uncertain infinite good. In such a case it is better to retain what one actually and certainly possesses than to abandon it for an infinite good when one does not even know that there is an infinite good which could possibly be gained. But Pascal answers to this by stating that every gambler stakes a certainty to gain an uncertainty, and he does this without sinning against reason. Moreover, even though the man who wagers for God abandons some pleasures, he will acquire others, and he will win true virtue. The prime requisite is to wage, to begin, not by piling up arguments for God's existence, but by lessening one's passions and following the behaviour of those who believe.

Pascal's words do indeed sometimes imply that religion lacks rational support. But we are constantly running risks for the uncertain, in war, in commerce, in journeys. Moreover, nothing human is absolutely certain. It is not certain that we shall see tomorrow, but nobody thinks it irrational to act on the probability of his being alive the next day.

3.5.3. Was He a Philosopher?

The answer depends on what we understand by a philosopher. If we understand by a philosopher a man who sets to create a system by the use of reason alone, a system which is supposed to represent reality as a whole, then we certainly cannot call Pascal a philosopher. For, he believed that problems arise, which reason, unaided by faith, cannot solve. And he also believed that there are mysteries which transcend the comprehension of the mind even when it is enlightened by faith. The notion of omnipotent human reason was abhorrent to him. But we have seen he had a reasoned view of the different modes and methods of human knowledge (epistemology). We have in his writing philosophy of values. There is a philosophy of Man too. Pascal was a philosophical analyst and an existential thinker, because he is a religious thinker, a thinker who primarily interested in the relation between man and God and in the lived appropriation of this relation. Not all feel the stimulus of his writings, some find him repugnant. Others rank him with Descartes, as one of the two greatest of French philosophers, and feel for him the profoundest admiration.

3.6. Gottfried Wilhelm Leibniz (1646–1716)

3.6.1. Life

Gottfried Wilhelm Leibniz was born at Leipzig (Germany) in 1646. Like Descartes, Leibniz held theological views which do not differ greatly from those of traditional Christian theologians. He also shared Descartes' concern with what he called 'the improvement of the sciences' - meaning the advancement of knowledge which would render it secure against the possibility of serious doubt and error. Like Descartes, he felt that the various sciences and our so-called knowledge generally are not properly grounded and lack the certainty and freedom from the possibility of error and so wanted to provide for a foundation for knowledge. As Descartes, he too was very much impressed with Mathematics. His philosophical method was modelled on Mathematics, hoping to get a comparable exactness and certainty of our reasoning about reality.

3.6.2. Leibniz's Thought

3.6.2.1. His Method

He was critical of the method and procedure of Descartes on a number of counts. Leibniz believed that it is necessary to take certain assumptions or principles to be taken for granted:

1. *Principle of contradiction,* by virtue of which we consider as false what implies a contradiction and as true anything the denial of which is contradictory or false. In simple, "If a proposition is true, then its negation is false and vice versa". For example, God could not create a universe in which there are *both* more sheep than cows *and* more cows than sheep.
2. *Principle of sufficient reason,* by virtue of which we hold that no fact can be true or existing and no statement truthful, without a *sufficient reason* for its being so and not different. In simple, "the principle that

everything which happens has, at least in principle, an explanation of why it happened as it did and not otherwise".

3. *Principle of the identity of indiscernibles.* If any objects are in every way the same, but actually distinct, then there would be no sufficient reason (that is, no possible explanation) for why the first is where (and when) it is, and the second is where (and when) it is, and not the other way around. Leibniz is fond of using leaves as an example. Two leaves often look absolutely identical. But, Leibniz argues, if "two" things are alike in *every* respect, then they are the same object, and not two things at all. So, it must be the case that no two leaves are ever *exactly* alike.

From these principles Leibniz contends that the *rules of common logic* may be derived. To avoid all errors, it is enough that one sticks to *common rules of logic* with great constancy and rigour. It is not necessary first to prove that existence and goodness of God, which is not possible without these rules anyhow. The fact that these rules presuppose the validity of the two basic principles mentioned is no cause for worry, and the fact that they themselves cannot be proven valid is no reason to retreat into scepticism. The latter course is simple to lay our basic assumptions on the table, observe the absurdity of questioning their validity, and then get on with the business of seeing what follows from them together with our immediate experience.

For Leibniz there was not only the principles and indeed something more to start with than Descartes' *'cogito, ergo sum'*. There are other truths. That is the particular contents of our immediate experience. What is immediately given is not simply that I think (and exist), but also that I have the *particular thoughts or perceptions* I do. They do not guarantee that there exists anything independent of them, corresponding to them; but they themselves are not subject to doubt. There are as many primary truths of the act as there are *immediate perceptions.*

3.6.2.2. His Philosophy of Knowledge

Leibniz criticizes Descartes for carrying his systematic doubting further than it is reasonable to carry it. The 'evil genius' hypothesis renders them at least initially untrustworthy. Descartes has no satisfactory criteria of what it is for an idea to be clear and distinct. And secondly Descartes' plea that whatever I perceive clearly and distinctly of a thing is true and can be predicated of it, is useless, unless we add the criteria of clearness and distinctness. This is a point with which one cannot but agree.

Rather than simply abandoning all talk of clearness and distinctness, Leibniz attempts to give these notions more precise meaning. All knowledge is either obscure or *clear* and clear knowledge is again either confused or *distinct;* distinct in its turn is inadequate or *adequate,* and again either *symbolic or intuitive.* The more perfect knowledge is that which is both adequate and intuitive (only God has it). But what do these terms mean? I do not apprehend something *clearly* unless I am able to distinguish it from other things which resemble it. This is the criterion of *clarity.* Next, I do not apprehend something *distinctly* unless I am able to identify the various features of a thing which distinguish it from other things. This is the criterion of *distinctness.* The notion of *adequacy* is really only an extension of the notion of distinctness. The possibility of inadequate apprehension arises only in connection with things having a complex nature; if I only apprehend some of the components of a complex thing distinctly, but not others. My apprehension of the complex things falls short of complete distinctness and so is *inadequate.* Finally, Leibniz distinguishes between symbolic and intuitive apprehension. If a thing is relatively simple, I may have no trouble directly envisaging each of its distinguishing features simultaneously when I think of it. In such a case my apprehension is *intuitive.* But because most things are very complex, and because my ability to envisage different features simultaneously is limited, I very commonly must make use of *symbols* to hold the place of some of the component features of things when I think of them.

Perfect knowledge in most cases is something reserved to God alone. We can have perfect knowledge of 'primitive natures' and of very simple complexes formed from primitive notions; but for the rest, the most we can attain knowledge that is less than perfect - *symbolic knowledge.* Leibniz has a rather *low opinion* of the importance of *empirical knowledge.* He is much more interested what can be discovered about *general nature of things through the use of reason* alone. It is this main reliance upon reason as opposed to experiment, and his conviction that reason can reveal to us the basic structures of reality despite the limitation applying to empirical knowledge which accounts for the traditional designation of Leibniz and Spinoza as rationalists.

Leibniz makes the distinction between knowledge *a priori* and Knowledge *a posteriori. Knowledge a priori* is truth of reason discovered by the operation of reason alone, either by drawing a logical consequence of some principle of reason or by logical analysis of some concept. *Knowledge a posteriori* is a matter of fact, discovered in the course of experience.

3.6.2.2.1. Truth

There are *two kinds of truths:* those of *reason* which are necessary and of which the opposite is impossible, and those of *fact* which are contingent and of which the opposite is possible. This is a distinction which applies primarily to our knowledge; for at least a great many things while are contingent truths for us, given the limitations upon our cognitive abilities, are necessary truths for God.

As things stand, it is only within a relatively limited class of cases that we can see certain things are *necessarily* true. But when we do see something is necessarily true, because its *opposite is impossible,* then we can rest assured that it is *really true;* and neither God himself nor Descartes' evil genius could cause matter to be otherwise. If we know what God knows, we would see that these things are not *contingently* true, but *necessarily* true. So, whatever we discover to be necessarily true about the world through the use of reason, we know actually to be true about the world. And through the discovery of such necessary truths, Leibniz holds that we can come to know a good deal about the basic structures of reality.

And idea can be true or false. It is *true* when the notion is possible and false when it involves contradiction. An idea is 'true' if only it is not logically self-contradictory, if only it is logically possible.

3.6.2.2.2. God and World

With Descartes, he considers it indubitable that I think and therefore also that I exist. And he points out that within the general broad category of 'thinking' there are essentially three basic types of conscious activities: *perceiving, conceiving* and *willing.* And from this it follows that at least while I am engaged in these kinds of conscious activities, I exist. Leibniz follows Descartes in taking it to be given that among the ideas he has is the idea of an all-perfect being; though it remains to be seen whether such a being exists.

To Leibniz it is simply obvious that things cannot just happen to exist. If they exist, there must be reason for their existence as opposed to their non-existence. Finally, Leibniz regards two things indisputable:

1. *Truth of mathematics and the rules of common logic,* which he calls it 'eternal truths', since he holds them to be necessarily and universally valid.
2. There is *the existence of the world.* That the world exists - that there is something rather than nothing, whatever its true nature be - is a point Leibniz regards as just as indubitable from the outset as is his own existence.

3.6.2.3. Philosophy of God

3.6.2.3.1. Existence of God

Like Descartes, Leibniz offers three proofs of God's existence but none of them is identical with any of Descartes three proofs, all of which he criticizes. Two are similar to two of Descartes, but his third proof is quite different. He attempts no proof that we have an idea of all-perfect being that there must be an all-perfect being as its cause. He finds this proof defective to the point that he feels that not even some modified form of it will work. He does believe that modified version of Descartes' other two proofs are sound; and that a third, based on the so called 'eternal truths' of mathematics and logic, is also possible.

Leibniz's point is that we have no right to conclude from the definition of God that God exists unless it can be shown that the definition of God is internally consistent, and contains no hidden contradiction.

In God there are three characteristics: his *power* (source of everything), his *knowledge* (which contains the particular of the ideas) and *will* (which is the source of change or production) and *acts according to the principle of the best possible.*

These three characteristics are all logically compatible with each other, and also with the idea of existence. And, second, it follows from the very idea of such a being as a being who is the source of all that exists that there could be *no limitations* upon him which would be *inconsistent with his omnipotence and omniscience.* Consequently, the idea of God is logically sound; it involves no self-contradiction. And now Leibniz says we may conclude with certainty that God does in fact exist - indeed that he *necessarily* exists.

Now we ask, can existence be regarded as a predicate? Is it legitimate to treat existence as a perfection, and therefore as one of the essential features of the very idea of God? Leibniz's other two proofs are essentially two versions of a single general proof, which differ only in that which is cited as something presupposing and therefore entailing the existence of God. These are similar to Descartes' proof which argues that existence of God is entailed by *my* existence; my existence must have a cause, the ultimate cause of my existence must be God, who must therefore exist, since I do.

The difference of Leibniz proof is in that they are cast in terms of *'sufficient reason'* rather than *'ultimate cause'* and also in that it is *not the 'I' or self* for whose existence a sufficient reason is sought. Rather in one proof it is the *world,* and in the other the *'eternal truths'* of mathematics and logic. This proof is commonly known as 'cosmological argument'.

Since the ultimate root of the world must be in something which exists of *metaphysical necessity,* and since furthermore the reason for any existent can only be another existent, it follows that a unique entity must exist of metaphysical necessity, that is, that there is a being *whose essence implies existence.* Hence there exists a being which is different from plurality of beings, that is, from the world, for it has been granted and proved that world does not exist of metaphysical necessity.

And out of all possible worlds God might have created, he created this. Argument: since in the divine ideas there is an infinity of possible universe of which only one can exist, the choice made by God must have a sufficient reason which determines him to the one rather than another. This reason can be found in only the degree of perfection contained in these worlds. This is the cause for the existence of the best, which is disclosed to God by his wisdom, determines his choice by his goodness, and is produced by this power.

So, while we as yet know little about the particular nature of finite things (ourselves- included) we already know *a priori* that the world has a rational structure according with the principles of non- contradiction, sufficient reason, and the great perfection. Whatever these principles logically imply must also in fact be true of the world.

3.6.2.4. His Philosophy of the World

3.6.2.4.1. Finite Things

In place of Descartes' division of finite thing into thinking substances and extended substances, Leibniz proposes a distinction between *souls* or *spiritual substances* and *bodies* or corporeal substances. Leibniz is using 'soul' in a very general way, to refer to not only to the human mind, but more generally to what might be termed the life principle. What distinguishes human souls from others generally, and from animal souls in particular, is that they have a feature which others lack: they are capable of attaining knowledge of *necessary truths.* Knowledge of necessary and eternal truths distinguishes us from animals - we have *a priori* knowledge rather than empirical knowledge. Empirical knowledge even animals can have. So, he denies that animals are machines.

Turning to Descartes' notion of 'body', he holds that 'extension' does not adequately express its essential nature any more than 'thinking' adequately expresses the essential nature of soul. Body is adequately characterized only if reference is also made to *'force'.* This force of action is inherent in all substances ... corporeal substance itself is never inactive. Bodies move; and their movements can be explained neither by reference to the activities of the souls, nor by reference to an initial impetus given to them externally by God when he created the universe. Their movements can be explained only by assuming that a certain active force was implanted in them as part of their nature when they were created. And subsequently, they move in accordance with laws different from those which govern the activities of souls.

So, while there is no soul without a body, and no body without a soul, the two operate distinctly, without interacting with each other at the pineal gland or elsewhere. They do have something in common – both are active, both are characterized by in terms of the concept of *force.*

Now every finitely existing thing, according to Leibniz, consists of a *unity* of corporeal substance or body and spiritual substance or soul. In fact, this must be, given that neither body nor soul is ever to be without the other. They meet by virtue of a pre-established harmony prevailing among all substances. But we are mistaken in thinking that they actually *influence* each other and this mutual interaction is what explains the correspondence between them. Still it is true that when I write something, for example, I have a certain thought, and my hand makes certain movements; and so, we say that I wrote down what I had in mind.

In short, Leibniz, like Descartes, is a *dualist.* Leibniz holds that precisely the same situation exists where *all* finite things are concerned, and not just in the case of man, for the same duality of body and soul exists in all cases.

Now living beings and extended objects generally are composed of parts, even though as a whole they must form a functional unit, or a single complex machine. In fact, they are composed of infinite numbers of parts, since anything extended is infinitely divisible. And each part may itself be viewed as a functional unit or smaller machine.

3.6.2.4.2. Monad

But despite this infinite divisibility of everything extended Leibniz considers it to be self-evident - in fact, logically necessary - that there must be some ultimate irreducible elements out of which all compound substances are formed. This he calls simple *monads.* They are not something one could ever discover. Their existence is simply a logical necessity, which one discovers by the use of reason alone. It is a logical necessity that every existing complex substance must ultimately consist of real, simple elements. There must be simple substances since there are composites. His initial definition of a monad is simply that it is such a simple substance. The monad is simple substance, which enters into composites; 'simple' meaning which has no parts. Many of the things Leibniz goes on to say about monad are merely logical consequences of the fact that, as completely simple substances, they can have no parts. Nothing which does not have parts can be affected by the action of something else, since to be affected means at a minimum to have arrangement of one's parts altered; therefore, monad cannot be affected by anything external to them. Monads have no windows through which anything could come in or go out. Each monad is thus completely self-contained, and has no way of interacting with any other monad.

Yet monads must have qualities otherwise they would even be beings. Each monad must differ in at least some of its qualities from every other. Logically, if their descriptions are identical then *they* are identical, one and the same. This is the so called principle of identity of indiscernibles; and since it is logic which leads Leibniz to conclude that monads exist, he feels it to be necessary to follow the rules of logic in inferring what their natures are. He takes for granted that all created beings, consequently the created monads as well, are subject to change, and that this change is even continual in each one.

3.6.2.5.2. Best World

At any rate, monads for Leibniz are the simple elements of which all finite things are complexes. They are what God created, when he created the world. And when he created, he created them in such a way, (one might say, he programmed) that they relate to each other as they do, and form the complex they do, in a pre-established harmony. Since they are incapable of interacting, influence of one monad on another can take effect only through the intervention of God. No monad - and therefore no soul - is capable of being affected by anything external to it. And so, while Leibniz speaks of 'perceptions', in both cases, no monad - and no soul - is really perceiving anything external to it when it perceives. Each is like a person alone in his own movie theatre. What each sees correlates with what every other sees, because the movies they are all seeing are correlated. But the perceptions of each are really only the unfolding of the inner nature of each. Each sees only what it has been programmed at the outset to see; only, in creating the world, God has correlated the programme in such a way that the programme of each is integrated with the programme of all.

3.7. Baruch Spinoza (1632–1677)

3.7.1. Life

Baruch Benedict Spinoza was born in 1632 at Amsterdam (Netherlands). He was a Portuguese Jew.

He was the middle son in a prominent family of moderate means in Amsterdam's Portuguese-Jewish community. As a boy—known to his fellow Portuguese as Bento—he had undoubtedly been one of the star pupils in the congregation's Talmud Torah school. He was intellectually gifted, and this could not have gone unremarked by the congregation's rabbis. It is possible that Spinoza, as he made progress through his studies, was being groomed for a career as a rabbi. But he never made it into the upper levels of the curriculum, those which included advanced study of Talmud. At the age of seventeen, he was forced to cut short his formal studies to help run the family's importing business.

And then, on July 27, 1656, Spinoza was issued the harshest writ of *cherem*, or excommunication, ever pronounced by the Sephardic community of Amsterdam; it was never rescinded. We do not know for certain what Spinoza's "monstrous deeds" and "abominable heresies" were alleged to have been, but an educated guess comes quite easy. No doubt he was giving utterance to just those ideas that would soon appear in his philosophical treatises. In those works, Spinoza denies the immortality of the soul; strongly rejects the notion of a providential God—the God of Abraham, Isaac and Jacob; and claims that the Law was neither literally given by God nor any longer binding on Jews. Can there be any mystery as to why one of history's boldest and most radical thinkers was sanctioned by an orthodox Jewish community?

To all appearances, Spinoza was content finally to have an excuse for departing from the community and leaving Judaism behind; his faith and religious commitment were, by this point, gone. Within a few years, he left Amsterdam altogether. By the time his extant correspondence begins, in 1661, he is living in Rijnsburg, not far from Leiden. While in Rijnsburg, he worked on the *Treatise on the Emendation of the Intellect*, an essay on philosophical method, and the *Short Treatise on God, Man and His Well-Being*, an initial but aborted effort to lay out his metaphysical, epistemological and moral views. His critical exposition of Descartes's *Principles of Philosophy*, the only work he published under his own name in his lifetime, was completed in 1663, after he had moved to Voorburg, outside The Hague. By this time, he was also working on what would eventually be called the *Ethics*, his philosophical masterpiece. However, when he saw the principles of toleration in Holland being threatened by reactionary forces, he put it aside to complete his "scandalous" *Theological-Political Treatise*, published anonymously and to great alarm in 1670. When Spinoza died in 1677, in The Hague, he was still at work on his *Political Treatise*; this was soon published by his friends along with his other unpublished writings, including a *Compendium to Hebrew Grammar*.

3.7.2. Spinoza's Thought

Baruch (or Benedictus) Spinoza is one of the most important philosophers—and certainly the most radical—of the early modern period. His thought combines a commitment to Cartesian metaphysical and epistemological principles with elements from ancient Stoicism and medieval Jewish rationalism into a nonetheless highly original system. His extremely naturalistic views on God, the world, the human being and knowledge serve to ground a moral philosophy centred on the control of the passions leading to virtue and happiness.

He expounded part of Descartes philosophy. In Spinoza's view the proper order of philosophical argument demands that we should start with that which is ontologically and logically prior, namely with the divine essence or Nature, and then proceed by logically deducible stages. In adopting this approach Spinoza separated himself from Descartes. In this endeavour to give a rational explanation of the world speculative metaphysicians have always tended towards the reduction of multiplicity to unity. Explanation in this connection means explanation in terms of causality and so they have tended to reduction of multiplicity to unity. In this sense, Spinoza was a metaphysician with the ambitious aim of explaining reality or making the universe intelligible. He may have anticipated hypothesis which have commended themselves to many scientists; but he concerned himself with metaphysical problems with which the scientists as scientists are not concerned.

3.7.2.1. Metaphysics

3.7.2.1.1. Substance

Descartes begins the study of metaphysics by defining what substance is. Substance is that which is in itself and is conceived through itself, the concept of which does not depend on the conception of another thing from which it must be formed. But that which can be known through itself alone cannot have an external cause. Substance is cause of itself. "I understand that to be cause of itself the essence of which involves existence and the nature of which cannot be conceived except as existing." In Spinoza's view of substance we perceive that existence pertains to the essence of substance. "If anyone says that he has a clear and distinct (true) idea of substance and doubts whether such substance exists, he is like one who says that he has a true idea and yet doubts whether it may be true or false." Since existence appertains to the nature of substance, its definition must of necessity involve existence, and therefore from its mere definition its existence can be concluded.

3.7.2.1.1. Substance is Infinite

If substance were finite, it would be limited by *some* other substance of the same nature that is, having the same attribute. But there cannot be two or more of them possessing the same attribute. For if there were two or more of them, they would have to be distinguishable from one another; and this means that they would have to possess different attributes. By attribute Spinoza means that which the intellect perceives as constituting the essence of a substance. Given this definition, it follows that if two substances possessed the same attributes, they would possess the same essence. In this case we cannot speak of 'two', for we should be able to distinguish them. But if there cannot be two or more substances possessing the same attribute, substance cannot be limited or finite. It must be infinite.

3.7.2.2. Philosophy of God

Infinite substance must possess infinite attributes. And this infinite substance with infinite attributes is called God. And Spinoza goes on to argue that infinite divine substance is indivisible, unique and eternal and that in God existence and essence are one and the same. But his view of God is not the same as scholastics. God and Nature are not distinct in Spinoza. If God were distinct from Nature, and if there were substances other than God, God would not be infinite. "Whatever *is,* is in God and nothing can exist or be conceived without God." Finite beings are modifications of God. Nature is not ontologically distinct from God. God possesses infinity of attributes, each of which is infinite; and of these two are known to us: thought and extension. Finite minds are modes of God under the attribute of thought and finite bodies are modes of God under the attribute of extension. Nature is not ontologically distinct from God and the reason why it cannot be ontologically distinct is that God is infinite. He must comprise in Himself all reality.

3.7.2.2.1. God and Nature (Universe)

In the logical process of deduction Spinoza does not proceed straight from the Infinite substance to finite modes. In between there are infinite and eternal modes, immediate and mediate which are logically prior to the finite modes. The intellect can discern certain changeless and eternal properties of the universe when it considers the universe under the attribute of thought and extension. Logically prior state of substance under the attribute of extension is motion-and-rest. For Spinoza there is no question of movement being impressed upon the world by an external cause. Movement is characteristic of Nature itself; for there is no cause distinct from Nature which could confer or impress upon Nature. Motion-and-rest is the primary characteristic of extended Nature and the total proportions of the motion-and-rest remain constant, though proportions in the case of individual bodies are constantly changing. Today we speak of total amount of energy in the universe is an intrinsic property of the universe and that is constant. The physical universe is thus a self-contained system of bodies in motion. This total amount of motion-and-rest or of energy is what Spinoza calls the infinite and eternal immediate mode of God under the attribute of extension.

3.7.2.2.2. God and Mind

The immediate infinite and eternal mode of God or Nature under the attribute of thought is called by Spinoza 'absolutely infinite understanding'. The mode of thinking, such as love, desire or any other name by which the modifications of the mind are designated, are not granted unless an idea in the individual is granted of the thing loved, desired. But the idea can be granted although no other mode of thinking can be granted. If this account of the immediate and eternal mode under the attribute of thought is correct, it means that thought in general includes all conscious activity as such. Spinoza does not make it clear what mediate infinite and eternal mode under the attribute of thought is. It is the total system of minds. It is apparent that our mind, in so far as it understands, is an eternal mode of thinking, which is determined by another of thinking and this one again by another and so on to infinity: so that they all constitute at the same time the eternal and infinite intellect of God. It should be noted that eternal and infinite intellect of God belongs to *Natura Naturata* and not *Natura Naturans.* We cannot speak of God as He is in Himself as having an intellect, distinct from the infinite system of minds.

3.7.2.2.3. God and Finite things

According to Spinoza, infinite things in infinite modes must necessarily follow from the necessity of divine nature. It is assumed in other words, that substance must have modes; and the conclusion is drawn that as substance is infinite it must have infinite modes. For him finite modes are caused necessarily by God. In the nature of things nothing contingent is granted, but all things are determined by the necessity of divine nature for existing and working in a certain way. Again, things could not have been produced by God in any other manner or order than that in which they were produced. It is true that the essence of things produced by God does not involve existence. For, if it did involve existence, they would be causes of themselves. Finite things can be called contingent therefore, if by giving them this name one means that they follow contingently, and not of necessity, from the divine nature. God causes them, but He causes them necessarily in the sense that He could not omit to cause them.

3.7.2.2.4. God's Freedom

At the same time Spinoza states that *God is free.* This statement may sound surprising at first. But for Spinoza 'free' does not mean what we mean. That thing is said to be 'free', which exists by the mere necessity of its own nature and is determined in its existence and actions by something else in certain fixed *ratio.* God then is free in the sense that He is self-determined in His actions. But He is not free in the sense that it was open to Him not to create the world at all or to create other finite beings than those which he has created. Hence, it follows that God does not act from freedom of will. The difference between God, the infinite substance and finite things is that God is not determined in His existence or actions by any external cause (there is no cause external to God which could act upon Him) whereas finite things, being modifications of God, are determined by Him in respect of their existence, essence and actions.

God's necessary production of finite things may suggest a most misleading interpretation of Spinoza's thought - an emanation theory. God is identified with Nature. We can consider Nature as an infinite substance without reference to its modifications or as a system of modes. The first way of considering Nature is being logically prior to the second. If we consider Nature in the second way (as *Natura Naturata)* we must recognize according to Spinoza, that a given mode is caused by a preceding mode or modes, which are caused by other modes, and so on indefinitely.

3.7.2.2.5. Elimination of Final Causality

There is no question of a transcendent God 'intervening' as it were to create a particular body or particular mind. There is an endless chain of particular causes. On the other hand, the chain of finite causes is logically and ontologically dependent on Nature considered as a self-dependent and self-determined unique substance *(Natura Naturans).* Nature necessarily expresses itself in modifications, and in this sense, Nature is the immanent cause of all its modifications or modes. God is the indwelling and not the transcendent cause of all things; for all things exist in God or Nature. But this does not mean that God exists apart from modes and can interfere with the chain of finite cause. The chain of finite causality is divine causality, for it is the modal expression of God's self-determination.

As God is infinite being, He must include within Himself all beings, all reality. And that as God is infinite substance, finite beings must be modes of this substance. It is not empirical Nature which is identified with God, but rather Nature in a peculiar sense, namely, as the infinite substance, which lies behind the transitory modes.

Logical deduction *Natura Naturata* is possible under the initial assumption is made that substance must express itself in modes. Scholastic substance as that in which accidents inhere is applied to infinite being. It is true Spinoza is claimed to have a clear and distinct idea of the objective essence of substance or God.

Things were produced by the consummate perfection of God, since they followed necessarily from a given most perfect nature. This may be misinterpreted to mean God as creating things for a purpose, such as manifestation of divine perfection or the wider diffusion of good. But Spinoza will not allow that. The order of nature follows necessarily from the nature of God and there could not have been any other order.

3.7.2.3. Philosophy of Man

3.7.2.3.1. Relation between Mind and Body

The system is one system. There are not two systems, a system of minds and a system of bodies. To every mode under attribute of extension there *corresponds* a mode under attribute of thought (Idea). 'Corresponds' suggests two orders- the order of bodies and order of ideas. But in reality, there is only one order of Nature. If there is only one order of Nature, it is inadmissible to speak of the human mind as belonging to one order and of the human body as belonging to another. The human being is one thing. Human body is man, considered as a mode of the attribute of extension, and human mind is man, considered as a mode of attribute of thought. They are two aspects of one thing.

Mind is the idea of the body. Mind is the counterpart under the attribute of thought of a mode of extension, namely, the body. The idea which constitutes the formal being of the human mind is not simple but composed of many ideas. Memory is nothing else than a certain concatenation of ideas involving the nature of things which are outside the human body and this concatenation takes place according to the order and concatenation of the modification of the human body. Besides, the idea of the body, i.e. the Mind, there can also be idea of the mind; for human can form an idea of his mind - self-consciousness. If human mind is idea of body, it follows that perfection of the mind corresponds to perfection of body. This means we depend on perception for our ideas.

3.7.2.3.2. No Finality for Human Beings

Human beings act according to purpose is also not allowed by Spinoza. Belief that one is free is the result and repression of ignorance of the determining causes of one's desires, ideals, choices and actions, just as belief in finality in Nature is due to ignorance of real causes of natural events. Thus, belief in final cause in any form is simply the fruit of ignorance.

3.7.2.3.3. Ethics

At least at first sight it seems strange that a philosopher like Spinoza, rejecting traditional ethical views, and believing in determinism should write an ethics in which he proposes an ideal of human nature to strive for, prescribes what is good and bad, and exhorts us to organize our lives according to his ethics. This is because he denies certain traditional features of ethics, like free- will, teleology, responsibility.

In as much as we desire to form an idea of man as a type of human nature to which we may look up to there is ethics. To set up an ethics means to conceive of an ideal of human nature and to establish guidelines of what one should do and should not do in order to attain that ideal as closely as possible. People are conscious of their desires for what is useful to them, but not the causes of these desires. Therefore, they think they are free, i.e. they not determined by anything else. At the same time, they know that they are acting in view of an end. The difficulty is that they think they are free and yet determined by and attraction of the ideal human nature. All our volition and desires included, absolutely determined.

The first question to be asked: where does the desire to form an idea of man as a type of human nature to which one may look, come from? Man is a *conatus,* endeavour to preserve his own being and to realize himself as fully as possible. The endeavour of a conscious being is informed by his past experience. But must not man, in views of his knowledge of universal determinism, regard as meaningless his whole striving for more and more understanding? Although we know in general that everything is determined, yet we are not capable of reconstructing nor of predicting the precise concatenation of causes. So, he does not know what his future will be. Secondly, he may reach more and more adequate understanding cannot be ruled out *a priori,* especially not, since he did already come to grasp the absolute value of understanding.

In view of this 'sign of election' and in view of the said ignorance, it is by all means rational to strive for more and more understanding. But still determinism remains. But Spinoza says that determinism does not mean fatalism. Whether particular ideas and strivings are present or not makes a real difference in the chain of causes. The construction of the ideal, the giving of prescriptions to attain it, and our strivings as 'informed' by all this, will have quite determined consequences, leading inevitably to the coming about of more freedom, unless of course our thinking and striving are overpowered completely by external factors.

So, the construction of the ideal, the examination of what is good and bad, the striving towards the ideal, all this makes sense in view of the facts that man does not have at his disposal knowledge of the real chain of causes.

Still the traditional freedom is missing in his ethics. But Spinoza has different concept of freedom: responsibility. One cannot really be held responsible either for one's freedom or for one's lack of freedom: it all depends on the predetermined power one has, or on what the 'conjuncture' of external causes allows. If man comes to form the idea of true perfection particular consequences will inevitably follow in the field of our strivings and actions, and he will be saved; if man does not come to experience from inside the value of rationality, as inevitably his soul will be lost.

For the sake of the clarity and brevity of the argument concerning the compatibility of determinism and ethics in Spinoza we need to further reflect. At certain point of man's life, he comes to experience the incomparable usefulness of real understanding. We do not want to be rational because of something else. Rationality is not looked for in view of something else, but for its own sake; yet, to strive for more rationality for its own sake, is to realize oneself. The effects rational consideration can have on our desires and on our actions, mean the breakthrough of purely internally determined power in an existence which is for the greatest part the result of the influence of external things upon our endeavour, leading to effects which cannot be explained through ourselves alone (which is the reason why such effects cannot constitute real self- realization).

Directives concerning good and bad are by no means simply commands to be obeyed for their own sake, or because a lawmaker so requires. Directives concerning good and bad are simply rational insights into certain causal connections transformed into imperatives, which rational man, as far as it is in his power, will obey inevitably, driven as he is by his urge towards more rationality. Only the wise man knows the real meaning of the commandments; the others look at the law as something external, which they obey out of fear, out of hope for a reward, sometimes because of certain beliefs concerning God. Yet in obeying these rules, the wise man is free. Striving for the ultimate end and the obedience of commandments is a matter of virtue following from man's rational nature. The way to arrive at freedom or rationality is by mastering our passive affects resulting from inadequate ideas. This mastering can come about through rational knowledge of these affects. If one succeeds in organizing one's life into a largely rational life, then this is 'thanks to' our predestination to become a free man.

3.7.2.4. Epistemology

Spinoza's ideal of knowledge recalls to a certain extent the Platonic ideal of knowledge. We find in Spinoza as in Plato a theory of degree of knowledge. Spinoza distinguishes 4 levels of knowledge.

First and lowest level of knowledge is perception through 'hearsay' - e.g. certain people are my parents, I have been told.

Second level of knowledge is that which is vague and confused experience - e.g. I know that I shall have to die. Oil is good for fire.

Third level is knowledge we get by inferring from the essence of one thing the essence of another, but not adequately.

Fourth level of knowledge is perception through the essence alone of a thing or through knowledge of its proximate causes. In order to know a thing, one must know its cause. The knowledge of effect depends on knowledge of cause.

In **ethics** Spinoza gives only 3 levels and does not give the first level of knowledge: perception by hearsay. It is not mentioned as a distinct kind of knowledge. Human body is affected by other bodies and every modification or state so produced is reflected in an idea. Ideas of this kind are more or less equivalent, therefore to ideas derived from sensation and Spinoza calls them ideas of imagination. They are not derived by logical deduction from other ideas and in so far as the mind consists of such ideas it is passive and not active. For these ideas do not spring from the active power of the mind but reflect bodily change and states produced by other bodies. Thus, it is not scientific and coherent knowledge.

There is association of ideas but on the level of sense perception or confused and vague experience. These associations are determined by associated modifications of our bodies and not by clear knowledge of objective causal relation between things. For Spinoza, general or universal ideas belong to this level of experience. A human body is frequently affected by, say, other human bodies. And the ideas which reflect the bodily modifications so produced coalesce to form a confused idea of man in general.

The second level of knowledge is scientific knowledge which involves adequate ideas and is called reason (ratio) as distinguished from the level of imagination. All men have some adequate ideas. All human bodies are modes of extension and all minds are ideas of bodies. All bodies agree in certain things which must be adequately or clearly and distinctly perceived by all. So, we have common notions. These common notions must not be confused with universal ideas. Knowledge as reason is necessarily true and is based on adequate idea. This means an idea without regard to the object has all properties or intrinsic mark of a true idea. Criterion of truth is its own criterion. He, who has a true idea, knows at the same time that he has a true idea; nor can he doubt concerning truth of the thing. Truth is thus its own standard and criterion. A deductive system of general propositions is abstract. Philosophical deduction is deduction of general propositions. It deals with timeless truths rather than transitory individual modes as such. Knowledge of second kind is not the highest and most comprehensive.

Third level is intuitive knowledge, by which the whole system of Nature in all its richness is grasped in one comprehensive act of vision. It arises from second kind. It seems that Spinoza thought of the logical deduction of the essential and eternal structure of Nature from the divine attributes as providing the necessary framework for seeing all things, that is, the whole of Nature in its concrete reality, as one great system causally dependent on infinite substance. The more we understand individual things the more we understand God. The greatest endeavour or desire of knowing things according to the third class of knowledge is accompanied by the highest satisfaction and emotional fulfilment. Vision of all things in God is not something to which the mind can approximate. The vision in question is an intellectual contemplation of the eternal and infinite system of Nature and of one's place in it, not a contemplation of a transcendent God.

3.8. John Locke (1632–1704)

3.8.1. Locke's Life and Works

John Locke was a contemporary of both Leibniz and Spinoza. He was born at Wrington, near Bristol in 1632. John Locke's mother died while he was still in infancy. His father was a "country lawyer" and a captain in the Parliamentary Army during the Civil War; he died while John was still young.

John Locke was elected to a life of studentship at Christ Church, Oxford. As a young man Locke cast about somewhat for a position in life. He might have become a cleric except for the fact that the authorities did not appreciate his anti-Aristotelian views that matter and life was static, was not something to which Locke could subscribe.

Having studied medicine (he did not receive a degree) Locke was willing to help out those who saw him with a medical problem, indeed, he become known as "Dr Locke." In 1666, Anthony "Ashley" Cooper was referred to Locke with a medical complaint. (Ashley was Locke's senior by eleven years.) "Dr Locke" successfully operated, much to Ashley's relief, and cleaned out "an abscess in the chest." This was to be a most fortunate turn of events for Locke, for Ashley was no ordinary man, he was the first Earl of Shaftesbury, a Lord of the realm. Thus, Locke was swept into the halls of power, perched confidently on the tails of Lord Shaftesbury (1621-83). In 1672, Shaftesbury became the Lord Chancellor and Locke, his friend, was appointed to be the secretary of a very powerful Board.

These were interesting historic times; political fortunes would shift in and out (more than once was Shaftesbury sent to the Tower). Locke -- he did not subscribe to the "Divine Right Theory" -- found it, at times, best to put some distance between himself and the political foes of Lord Shaftesbury; indeed, Locke, during the years 1684-1689, was out of the country, in France and in Holland.

Upon his return to England, in 1689, Locke adopted a life style that allowed him to compile his works and make them ready for the press. Thus, we see, in 1690, the publication of Locke's two principal works: *Essay Concerning Human Understanding* and *Two Treatises of Government*.

On October 28th, 1704, Locke died; he was buried in the church yard of High Laver.

Much of Locke's work is characterized by opposition to authoritarianism. This opposition is both on the level of the individual person and on the level of institutions such as government and church. For the individual, Locke wants each of us to use reason to search after truth rather than simply accept the opinion of authorities or be subject to superstition. He wants us to proportion assent to propositions to the evidence for them. On the level of institutions, it becomes important to distinguish the legitimate from the illegitimate functions of institutions and to make the corresponding distinction for the uses of force by these institutions. The positive side of Locke's anti-authoritarianism is that he believes that using reason to try to grasp the truth, and determining the legitimate functions of institutions, will optimize human flourishing for the individual and society both in respect to its material and spiritual welfare. This in turn, amounts to following natural law and the fulfilment of the divine purpose for humanity. Locke's monumental *An Essay Concerning Human Understanding* concerns itself with determining the limits of human understanding in respect to God, the self, natural kinds and artifacts, as well as a variety of different kinds of ideas. It thus tells us in some detail what one can legitimately claim to know and what one cannot. Locke also wrote a variety of important political, religious and educational works including the *Two Treatises of Government*, the *Letters Concerning Toleration*, *The Reasonableness of Christianity* and *Some Thoughts Concerning Education*. He was more original than Leibniz and Spinoza.

3.8.2. Locke's Thought

3.8.2.1. Epistemology (Theory of Knowledge)

Locke holds that all of the ideas we have, are derived from *experience*. But this does not mean that all of our ideas are derived solely from sensation. Some of our ideas are not simply ideas of sensible qualities; for experience affords us also a number of ideas of the operation of our minds upon the ideas we derive from sensation. E.g. we have the ideas of *perception;* and this is not simply the idea of this or that thing which we perceive, but rather the idea of a mental process or operation, which may have all sorts of sensible things as its objects.

Locke holds that the mind is a *tabula rasa* or blank sheet until experience in the form of sensation and reflection provide the basic materials — simple ideas — out of which most of our more complex knowledge is constructed. While the mind may be a blank slate in regard to content, it is plain that

Locke thinks we are born with a variety of faculties to receive and abilities to manipulate or process the content once we acquire it.

3.8.2.1.1. Perception

There are a number of these sorts - a number of operations of the mind or mental faculties - of which we find ourselves to be capable through experience. He takes *perception* to be the most basic of these; for it is through perception that we acquire the various ideas of sense which provide the materials for our other mental operations. He regards it simply as that operation whereby we acquire particular simple idea. Perception is only when the mind receives the impression. He observes that in perception our sensations are often coloured by our judgments, so that our perceptions to this extent are not strictly identical with our sensation. (Kant later works on this idea).

It is interesting to observe that unlike Descartes, though like Leibniz and Spinoza, Locke does not consider *perception* to be something *distinctively human.* Locke grants animals have ideas since they are capable of sensation, and therefore perception. But while they perceive, it does not follow that they are capable of knowledge. For while he holds that perception is the *first step and degree* towards knowledge, and the inlet of all materials of it, it does *not of itself constitute* knowledge.

Knowledge is attained only through operation of a *number of other faculties* upon the simple ideas derived from it.

1. The first of these further faculties or mental operation Locke calls ***'retention'*** which subsumes both our power of 'contemplation' and our power of 'memory'. But these are only the powers of keeping in mind or recalling to mind some idea acquired through perception.
2. The next faculty is that of ***'discerning'*** and distinguishing between our various simple ideas - in other words, being able to notice that one simple idea differs from another and what its character is. This operation too leaves our simple idea essentially as they were when we first perceived them, as does the next operation he mentions.
3. ***'comparing'*** simple ideas one with another in respect of extent, degree, time, place or any other circumstances. These also are found in animals too, but man distinguished and compares better.
4. Beyond these, there are only two further mental operations of which Locke holds us to be capable. The next operation in the mind about its ideas is ***'composition'*** whereby it puts together several of those simple ones it has received, and combines them into complex ones. It is through composition, and only through it that we arrive at our idea of particular things, which involve a variety of simple characteristics. Animals also do this, but not as well as we do.

5. It is only with respect to the final operation of ***'abstraction'*** - that there is a qualitative difference between us and animals. Abstraction involves the use of *words.* But here again, even in this most distinctive operation the mind is limited to a kind of modification of its simple and complex ideas of sense; and does not really generate any radically new ones.

Locke here is advancing the thesis that all our abstractions or general ideas are simply abstractions from various particular ideas we have acquired through perception. The support for this thesis Locke gives is a rather simple-minded theory about the way in which language is acquired.
This completes Locke's inventory of the mental operations which the mind is capable of performing upon ideas acquired through experience.

Next, he shows the *distinctions* between ideas. We will see the first two distinctions in ideas.

3.8.2.1.1.1. Distinction between Real and Fantastical

Real idea is an idea of something that really exists, and fantastical or false idea is an idea of something that does not really exist. This means that Locke presupposes that there is a world existing independently of our thoughts, and that it is meaningful to speak of whether our ideas conform to it.

The main use to which Locke puts these distinctions is to mark off simple ideas as a class from complex ideas of particular things. Since he takes the mind to be completely passive in its reception of simple ideas, he holds that simple ideas in general are both real and adequate. Complex ideas are voluntary combinations. Mind of man uses some kind liberty in 'forming them. And from this it follows that our complex ideas may or may not be real ideas.

3.8.2.1.1.2. Distinction between Real and Adequate Idea

Locke holds that *none* of our complex ideas of particular things can be known to be adequate. Adequacy means perfect representation. No complex idea completely captures all of its features. All our simple ideas are both real and adequate.

3.8.2.1.2. Knowledge

Now knowledge obviously must have to do with ideas. Knowledge is inseparable from thought. Indeed, it is nowhere to be found except as thought - and thought is an activity of the mind, whose only content are ideas. At first it may seem to imply that knowledge is strictly a matter of the 'connection and agreement' of some of our ideas with other ideas. But this is not what Locke intends. He does maintain that the greater part of our knowledge is simply a matter of *observing* the connection and agreement of some idea with others. If there were no more to our knowledge than this, then none of our knowledge would be knowledge of anything independent of our thoughts; and so, we would have no knowledge of things in the world, let alone of the world in general. So, when he speaks 'connection and agreement' of our ideas, he has in mind not only their 'connection and agreement' with other ideas, but also with actually existing things. Four sorts of such agreement are there: i. *Identity,* ii. *Relation,* iii. *Co-existence* iv. *Real Existence.*

3.8.2.1.2.1. Identity or diversity

When he speaks of *identity* what Locke has in mind is simply our awareness of the nature of our various ideas and of their differences from each other. Knowledge here, simply knows each idea to agree with itself and what it is, and all distinct idea to disagree.

3.8.2.1.2.2. Relation

Relation means thinking of the fact that some of our ideas are associated with others in various ways. White and black are related to each other in a way in which triangles and trees are not related to them.

3.8.2.1.2.3. Co-existence or necessary connections

Co-existence means the connection of various ideas in mind. For here Locke is thinking of the fact that a complex idea, for example, the idea of a chair, consists of the conjunction of a number of simple ideas, which we think of together when we think of a chair. The sort of knowledge here is knowledge of what simple ideas are inseparable parts of a given complex idea; it is knowledge of what sensible ideas necessarily 'co-exist' in a given complex one.

3.8.2.1.2.4. Real Existence

This is only when he comes to his fourth category, of *real existence,* that he speaks of knowledge in connection with anything other than the relation of ideas to themselves and to each other. The first three sorts of knowledge are purely conceptual rather than existential (i.e. pertaining to existing things). This sort of knowledge is knowledge of the actual real existence agreeing to any idea. E.g. The proposition: *God is,* is of real existence. Only propositions of the form *'X exists'* or *'there are Xs'* in the world are propositions implicitly presupposing some such assertions, pertain to real existence, rather than simply to the connection of one idea with another.

3.8.2.1.3. Ways of Arriving at Knowledge

Locke says that there are three different ways we can come to the four kinds of knowledge:

1. *Intuitive knowledge:* is had in those cases in which the mind perceives the agreement or disagreement of two ideas immediately by themselves, without the intervention of any other. E.g. white is not black, or circle is not a triangle.
2. *Demonstration:* It does not differ from 'intuition'. The only difference is that the connection of one idea with another is not made directly, but rather by means of the intervention of a number of other intermediary ideas - each of which, however, is intuitively connected with the previous one. Each step must have intuitive evidence. And if each step in a demonstration is itself a matter of intuited agreement, then the operations involved are simply those involved in intuition. This is Locke's analysis of 'that which we call *reasoning'* and of 'what is involved in rational proofs'. The two, Intuition and Demonstration, are degrees of our knowledge; whatever falls short of these is *but faith* or *opinion.*
3. *Sensation:* To this knowledge Locke assigns a rather inferior position.

Locke's idea of knowledge sounds like the rationalists. For him, as well as for Rationalists what counts as knowledge only if it is completely *certain* and it has to be arrived either through intuition or demonstration. The principal difference is that he redirects the ideas upon which intuition and demonstration may be brought to bear to those which derive ultimately from particular perceptions.

When Locke comes to consider how far our knowledge extends, insofar as it is allowed either through intuition or demonstration, he comes up with results which are much narrower than those of the rationalists, because of the restrictions he places upon the ideas we have to work with. With regard to *'identity or diversity'* he holds that we have an intuitive knowledge of the *identity* of all of our clear ideas and of the differences between them. With regard to *'relation'* he contended that while this is the largest field of our knowledge, it is confined to the demonstration of relations of ideas which they have in virtue of their conceptual interconnections and implications (truth of mathematics or analytical truths). As for *'co-existence or necessary connections'* of ideas Locke says that in this our knowledge is very short. We may observe that a variety of simple ideas occur together, and our idea of certain kind of complex thing may involve a collection of certain simple ideas, but for the most part we cannot know whether these ideas are *necessarily* connected with each other or *simply happen* to occur together. Finally, with regard to *'real existence'* Locke holds that intuition and demonstration together assure us of the existence of *only two* things: ourselves and God. He does not stop here; for he maintains that we also have knowledge of another kind of 'sensible' knowledge of object present to our senses through sensation. But this knowledge does not reach very far, because our knowledge of this sort does not extend to objects which are not *now* present to our senses and second, he says that while we can have knowledge *that* these objects exist, we can know relatively little of their true nature.

Thus, for Locke scope of knowledge is quite restricted, since he supposes

a) that all we have directly aware of is ideas rather than things themselves,
b) that all our ideas either derive from perception or are devoid of significant content,
c) that a general proposition cannot be said to constitute knowledge unless it is either intuitively or demonstrably certain.

3.8.2.2. Metaphysics (God, Man and Things)

We have the ideas but of three sorts of substances:

a) God,
b) finite intelligence,
c) bodies.

Even in principle, therefore, we can only have existential knowledge of these three sorts of things. We have knowledge of our own existence by *intuition,* of existence of God by *demonstration,* and of other things by *sensation.*

As for our existence we perceive it is so plainly and so certainly that it neither needs nor is capable of any proof. For nothing can be more evident to us than our own existence. Locke is not reasoning as Descartes. Descartes had argued that my existence is *necessarily* established by the fact that I think; but my existence is asserted as the conclusion of an argument. For Locke, my existence is not something I *infer* from the fact that I think, rather it is something I *perceive* and it is something as directly and immediately as I perceive that I think or reason or doubt.

3.8.2.2.1. Philosophy of Man (Self)

Self for Locke is something like Descartes 'thinking substance' or 'spiritual substance'. Self is not something we actually perceive, but rather is merely *substratum* we are led to *suppose* exists in order to 'support' the various mental processes we perceive with ourselves. Then it is not possible to have a direct and intuitive knowledge of its existence; it would seem that its existence is something which we can only *infer* at best. In short, if what Locke says the status of our idea of 'spiritual substance' is right, then it is not what his remarks about our knowledge of our own existence establish.

3.8.2.2.2. Philosophy of God (Theodicy)

The existence of God is something Locke holds may be established by demonstration. His proof is not a form of ontological argument but a form of cosmological argument. In brief, he argues that existence of God can be established, along with a number of his characteristics, given only that we ourselves exist, and are capable of perception and knowledge.

Locke holds that there are two radically different sorts of beings in the world: 1. *purely material* without sense, perception, or thought *(incogitative),* 2. *sensible, thinking, perceiving beings,* such as we find ourselves to be *(cogitative beings).*

And because he supposes that something produced by something else cannot have any features which that which produces it does not have, he concludes from the fact there are 'cogitative' beings (namely ourselves) that which produced us must itself be 'cogitative'. So eternal being must be cogitative. For it is impossible to conceive that even bare incogitative matter should produce a thinking intelligent being.

The argument depends only if, one assumes that things cannot by themselves come into existence out of nothing, *and* that an effect can have no perfection which its cause does not have. In short argument depends on the validity of a strong version of the principle of sufficient reason. But given his views about nature and origin of our ideas, and the nature and limits of our knowledge, it is not easy to see how he can justify his reliance upon this principle. Locke warns time and again against reasoning from abstract principles which are not derived from and established by experience, but it would certainly seem that he is doing just that in his argument concerning the nature and existence of God.

3.8.2.2.3. Philosophy of the World (Cosmology)

With regard to things other than ourselves and God, Locke holds that their existence can be established *neither* by simple intuition nor by logical demonstration but by *sensation.* Locke feels sure that the ideas we have of them are in some way produced by their action on our *senses.*

3.8.3. Critical Remarks

1. A few words on Locke's view of Human nature. In discovering his enumeration of various operations of our minds, we find that the only qualitative difference between man and animal is that man has the ability of *abstraction,* and therefore man is capable of certain kinds of knowledge which lower animals are not.
2. Locke would accept the Cartesian dualism of material and spiritual substance with Leibniz's modification. But since he holds that sensation

and perception, no less than abstract reasoning are marks of 'cogitative' beings, it would seem that animals are also cogitative beings.

3. No solution to the problem of how mind and body are capable of interacting; though he takes it to be obvious fact that they do. He winds up by saying that all-wise Agent who has made them to be and cooperate as they do.
4. Locke's discussion of our nature suffers from a failure to distinguish between the ideas of a *thinking or spiritual substance,* a *person,* and a man. The idea of thinking substance makes no reference to a body; whereas that of a man makes reference both to a thinking substance and to extended or material substance. And the idea of a thinking substance differs from that of a person, in that the former is completely impersonal, whereas the latter contains the notion of individuality.

3.9. George Berkeley (1685–1753)

3.9.1. Life and Works

George Berkeley was born in Ireland in 1685, eight years after Spinoza's death. Locke was then 53, Leibniz was 41. He was raised in Dysart Castle. Although his father was English, Berkeley always considered himself Irish. He entered Trinity College, Dublin on 21 March 1700 and received his B.A. in 1704. He remained associated with Trinity College until 1724. As was common practice for British academics at the time, Berkeley was ordained as an Anglican priest in 1710.

The works for which Berkeley is best known were written during his Trinity College period. In 1709, he published *An Essay towards a New Theory of Vision*. In 1710, he published *A Treatise concerning the Principles of Human Knowledge*, Part I. In 1712, he published *Passive Obedience*, which focuses on moral and political philosophy. In 1713, he published *Three Dialogues between Hylas and Philonous*. In 1721, he published *De Motu*.

He was consecrated Bishop of Cloyne in St. Paul's Church, Dublin, on 19 May 1734. As bishop of an economically poor Anglican diocese in a predominantly Roman Catholic country, he was committed to the well-being of both Protestants and Catholics.

He died on January 14, 1753 while his wife was reading him a sermon.

3.9.2. Berkeley's Thought

3.9.2.1. Programme and Method

The chief causes of error and difference in the sciences, with the grounds of skepticism, atheism and irreligion are inquired into by Berkeley. His philosophy is reminiscent of Descartes. His main programme was analysis and nature of human knowledge, providing knowledge with a firm foundation. Philosophy should be built on rational proofs, not on revelation.

Existence of God and immortality of soul were *rationally demonstrable,* and not merely matters of *faith.* He was against meaningless nonsense of metaphysicians. It is meaningless and even self-contradictory to suppose that there is anything more to things which make up the world than what we experience. But with the rationalists, he holds that there is no good reason for metaphysical skepticism and that we can know all there is to know about the nature of things. But with Locke, he holds that we can have no knowledge of things except that which our senses provide.

Berkeley, like Locke, is an empiricist in that he holds that we can have no knowledge of things which does not derive from the ideas we have through sense perception or direct experience. But he rejects Locke's conclusion that we must therefore sit down in quiet ignorance of these things which are beyond the reach of our capacities.

3.9.2.2. Theory of Knowledge

3.9.2.2.1. Ideas as the Object of Knowledge

The most interesting and original part of Berkeley's thought is his theory of knowledge. He accepts the Empiricist teaching of Locke that the immediate object of our knowledge is ideas (subjective impressions) but rejects the distinction of Locke regarding primary (objective) and secondary (subjective) qualities.

The primary qualities (time, space, motion) are not perceptible separately from the secondary qualities (colour, sound, tactile qualities, etc.). Indeed, we know the primary qualities only in conjunction with and through the secondary qualities. If we know means to perceive subjective impressions, such impressions cannot be divided into two categories, one subjective and the other objective; all must be impressions felt by the subject, and hence all are subjective.

3.9.2.2.2. No Objective Substance

Berkeley refuses to accept Locke's concept of substance as a mysterious objective substratum which would be the cause of our impressions. Berkeley asks whether such a material substratum, separate from our sensations, can exist. If it is separate from our impressions, then it is not perceptible, is reduced to a term void of significance, and is unknowable and inconceivable. If it is connected with our impressions as a support of those impressions, then it resides in the subject and material substances are cognitive phenomena and hence are subjective.

It is impossible, therefore, that matter be something existing in itself, objective, inert, devoid of thought. When we say that a thing exists, we mean nothing more than that such a thing is perceived by us. The being of things consists in this act of perception: "Omne esse est percipi." (To BE is to be PERCEIVED.)

Primary or secondary qualities, substance and impressions are nothing other than acts of perception, that is, mental facts; and their existence signifies their being perceived as mental acts. Berkeley's theory of knowledge thus reduces all reality to phenomena: The material world exists only as a cognitive act, produced and existing in a mental act, and hence is subjective and not objective.

3.9.2.2.3. No Universal Ideas

Berkeley also denied the existence of what are called abstract objects — or what the medievals called "universals" and what Plato called "forms" or "ideas." For instance, if someone said that redness exists apart from any red thing or that goodness exists apart from any good action or person, then he is saying that redness and goodness exist as independent entities. For Berkeley this is impossible, since nothing that is not being perceived can exist. The idea of redness without a red thing or goodness without a good action is a nonsense idea, every bit as much as matter without a sensation of it.

Hence, only particular, determined ideas exist. The so-called universal ideas are names, not ideas, and exist neither in the mind (because they are not ideas) nor outside the mind (because it is absurd that there be a colour which is not determined).

Berkeley's nominalism is more radical than Locke's in so far as he denies all value to general and abstract ideas, whereas Locke had only imposed restrictions upon them.

3.9.2.2.4. *To be is to be Perceived*

Many philosophers will forever be associated with a single statement.

For René Descartes "I think; therefore, I am" (or cogito ergo sum) is a starting point for metaphysics and epistemology. John Locke said that each of us is a "blank slate" (or tabula rasa) prior to sensation. For Berkeley that phrase is, *"To be is to be perceived"* (or *esse est percipi*). His philosophy is called idealism, for he argues that, strictly speaking, only ideas have existence.

His philosophy and other philosophies that take the view that the external world is somehow produced by the mind is known as idealism. There are only two kinds of things that exist: spirits and ideas. Spirits perceive and ideas are perceived. Ideas are passive, but spirits are active and able to cause ideas. Human beings are finite spirits, but God is an infinite spirit who causes many of their ideas.

For example, if you perceive a rose, your idea of the rose has existence. But the rose has no existence separate from your idea of it. Berkeley's startling and provocative formula — "To be is to be perceived" — means that things exist only if they are being perceived or can be perceived. It follows from this that if something were not being perceived, it would not exist. The only sense that can be made of the word existence is connected with the perception of that thing. He wrote:

> All the choir of heaven and furniture of the earth, in a word all the mighty frame of the world, have not any subsistence without a mind, that their being is to be perceived or known; that consequently so long as they are not actually perceived by me, or do not exist in my mind or that of any other created spirit, they must either have no existence at all, or else subsist in the mind of some eternal spirit.

Thus, to those who argue that material things have some kind of absolute existence without any relation to their being perceived, Berkeley replies, "that is unintelligible." He explains: "The absolute existence of unthinking matter are words without meaning." This says that sensible things exist only insofar as they are perceived. "The only thing whose existence we deny is what the philosophers call matter or corporeal substance."

The upshot is that when philosophers such as Locke label things substance and others use terms like matter, they are using words that denote nothing. If you mean by matter or substance some independently existing thing out in the world, then you are referring to something that does not exist. Also, Locke's distinction between primary and secondary qualities (between such structural properties as figure, motion, and shape, on the one hand, and colour, door, and sound, on the other) on the ground that the former are objective, the latter subjective, cannot be maintained; the primary qualities depend on the secondary; they are equally subjective.

Berkeley also denied the existence of what are called abstract objects — or what the medievals called "universals" and what Plato called "forms" or "ideas." For instance, if someone said that redness exists apart from any red thing or that goodness exists apart from any good action or person, then he is saying that redness and goodness exist as independent entities. For Berkeley this is impossible, since nothing that is not being perceived can exist. The idea of redness without a red thing or goodness without a good action is a nonsense idea, every bit as much as matter without a sensation of it.

3.9.2.2.5. God and the Existence of Things

Is Berkeley saying that when you leave your room and cease to perceive your furniture and computer that these objects cease to exist? No. For another mind is still perceiving these objects, even when you have left the building. For even if you are not perceiving these objects, God is perceiving them. Berkley explains:

When I deny sensible things an existence out of my mind, I do not mean my mind in particular, but all minds. Now it is plain that things have an existence exterior to my mind, since I find them by experience to be independent of it. There is therefore some other mind wherein they exist, during the intervals between the time of my perceiving them.... There is an omnipresent eternal mind, which knows and comprehends all things, and exhibits them to our view in such a manner and according to such rules as he himself has ordained, and are termed by us The Laws of Nature.

The existence of things, therefore, depends upon the existence of God, and God is the cause of the orderliness of things in nature.

The order in nature is created and maintained by God, who secures the reality of all things by his perception.

3.9.2.3. The Nature of the Universe

3.9.2.3.1. The Nature of subjective spirit

Berkeley, while denying the existence of a material world and reducing it to a phenomenon of knowledge, did not deny the existence of the world of spirits. He believed that he had proved the existence of the subjective spirit from the very presence of ideas, for ideas can be produced only by a spirit.

Having thus assured himself of the existence of his own spirit, Berkeley devoted himself to determining its nature: the spirit is both active, a producer of ideas, and passive, a receptacle for ideas. Its activity is revealed in the imagination and in the memory, with which we produce or recall ideas, but more still in the coordination of ideas. Passivity, as we have said, is revealed in the fact that the spirit receives ideas that it has not produced. For example, it is not within my power to see or not to see the objects that are in my room.

3.9.2.3.2. Other spirits

The passivity of the spirit gave Berkeley the means of proving the existence of other finite spirits, independent of his own, and the existence of God. In fact, he asked, what is the origin of these ideas that are imposed on my spirit and of which I am not the origin -- for instance, the objects I mentioned before as being present in my room?

They are produced by the will of other spirits, since I perceive, besides my own spirit, other particular agents like myself, who participate with me in the production of many ideas. Besides, there are ideas that I perceive which are not only not produced by my spirit, but are not produced by any finite spirit -- for instance, the regularity of natural phenomena. Fire always burns, independently of any will. Such ideas presuppose a cause superior to all finite spirits -- God, who exists whole infinite, will produces the order and harmony and constancy of natural phenomena.

3.9.2.3.3. Ideas and Immaterialism

In a word, the phenomenal world of Berkeley is not unlike the phenomenal world that everyone knows, with this difference: while commonly it is believed that natural phenomena are the product of a physical, material world, for Berkeley this material world does not exist. That which we attribute to matter, he says, must be referred to God, the exciter and revealer of ideas corresponding to material things.

We are on the ground of the occasionalism of Malebranche: God presents to our souls -- produces in them -- the ideas that impress us. The constant relationship with which God determines the ideas of our spirits are the so-called laws of nature. They are the language with which God reveals Himself and speaks to us.

3.9.2.4. Philosophy of God

3.9.2.4.1. Mind and God

Locke had argued that the notions of spiritual substances and material substance stand or fall together, since we have no direct perception of either one, and since our notions of both are equally obscure; but rather than rejecting both for this reason, he accepted both notions, since he did not see how we could do without them. Berkeley on the other hand, hold that we can get along perfectly well without the notion of material substance, but not without notion of spiritual substance; for he too supposes that there must be *some* substance or ideas to inhere in - some being for them to be perceived by. And he denies that the notion of a spiritual substance is altogether meaningless, since he can say what he means by it, namely, that which thinks, wills, and perceives. A spirit is an active being, whose existence consists, not in being perceived, but in perceiving ideas and thinking.

If in fact we have some sort of meaningful notion of ourselves as spiritual being, however, then it would seem possible for us to have a meaningful notion of God as well, provided that he likewise is construed as a spiritual being (as he traditionally has been). Berkeley's account of how we come to form the notion of God thus is basically the same as Locke's.

But it is one thing to construe the notion of God as Berkeley does, and another to know that a being answering to that description exists. He gives two arguments for existence of God:

Nothing can be more evident to anyone that is capable of the least reflection than the existence of God, or a Spirit who is intimately present to our minds, producing in them all that variety of ideas or sensations which continually affect us.

The reason Berkeley supposes this to be so evident is that he takes it for granted that the perceptions we have which are not produced voluntarily by ourselves must have some cause outside of ourselves; that the great majority of these cannot plausibly be attributed to the actions of another human beings; and that, since this cause cannot be some independently existing material substance, it must be other sort of spiritual being.

The other argument is very astonishing in the history of modern philosophy:

Men commonly believe that all things are known or perceived by God, because they believe in the being of God; whereas I, on the other side, immediately and necessarily conclude the being of God, because all sensible things must be perceived by him. Supposing you were annihilated, cannot you conceive it possible that things perceivable by sense may still exist? I can, but then it must be another mind. It is plain that [sensible things] *have* an existence exterior to my mind. There is therefore some other mind wherein they exist, during the intervals between the times of my perceiving them; as likewise they did before my birth, and would do after my supposed annihilation. And, as the same is true with regard to all other finite created spirits, it necessarily follows there is an *omnipresent eternal Mind,* which knows and comprehends all things.

In short, by what has come to be known as an argument from design - an argument that is, based on the design and order and beauty of what we experience - Berkeley concludes, with respect to the spiritual being he supposes to be the cause of the things we perceive, that it has all those attributes traditionally predicated of God.

Berkeley does not use the argument from design to try to establish the existence of God, as some have. Rather he uses it to establish the nature of that non-human spiritual being whose existence he attempts to establish by a form of the cosmological argument, on the one hand, and by his argument from persistence and independence of sensible things, on the other.

God is a being of transcendence and unlimited perfections. His nature, therefore, is incomprehensible to finite spirits. It is not, therefore, to be expected, that any man should have exactly just notions of the Deity, His attributes, and ways of operation. However, his point is simply that we cannot have a very precise and adequate understanding of God's nature and various attributes, but rather only a general one - which, nonetheless, is enough to give one a pretty good idea of what he is like.

3.9.3. Critical Remarks

Berkeley believed that he had carried out the work he had set for himself: to justify theism against the attacks of incredulity; and to point out the emptiness of materialism by proving that the world as conceived by the materialist does not exist.

But did Berkeley really attain his goal? The existence of the (finite) spirit as something distinct from ideas implies the concept of spiritual substance; the activity and passivity of the spirit imply the concept of cause; the affirmation of the existence of God implies both the concepts of substance and of cause.

Now, all these concepts should have been established in a preliminary metaphysical study; this Berkeley did not do, and because of his empiricistic position, he could not do it. The development of Empiricism toward complete phenomenalism stops halfway in Berkeley.

It was David Hume who drew the logical consequences from Empiricism, and affirmed complete phenomenalism not only in reference to matter, as Berkeley had done, but also in reference to spiritual substance, the concept of cause, and the concept of God.

3.10. David Hume (1711–1776)

3.10.1. Life and Works

The most important philosopher ever to write in English, David Hume (1711-1776) — the last of the great triumvirate of "British empiricists" — was also well-known in his own time as an historian and essayist.

David Hume was a Scotsman. Born in Edinburgh, Hume spent his childhood at Ninewells, the family's modest estate on the Whitadder River in the border lowlands near Berwick. His father died just after David's second birthday.

Hume's family thought him suited for a career in the law, but he preferred reading classical authors, especially Cicero, whose *Offices* became his secular substitute for *The Whole Duty of Man* and his family's strict Calvinism. Pursuing the goal of becoming "a Scholar & Philosopher," he followed a rigorous program of reading and reflection for three years until "there seem'd to be open'd up to me a New Scene of Thought."

He moved to France, where he could live frugally, and finally settled in La Flèche, a sleepy village in Anjou best known for its Jesuit college. Here, where Descartes and Mersenne studied a century before, Hume read French and other continental authors, especially Malebranche, Dubos, and Bayle; he occasionally baited the Jesuits with iconoclastic arguments; and, between 1734 and 1737, he drafted *A Treatise of Human Nature*.

Hume returned to England in 1737 to ready the *Treatise* for the press. To curry favour with Bishop Butler, he "castrated" his manuscript, deleting his controversial discussion of miracles, along with other "nobler parts." Book I, *Of the Understanding*, and Book II, *Of the Passions*, was published anonymously in 1739. Book III, *Of Morals*, appeared in 1740, as well as an anonymous *Abstract* of the first two books. Although other candidates, especially Adam Smith, have occasionally been proposed as the *Abstract*'s author, scholars now agree that it is Hume's work. The *Abstract* features a clear, succinct account of "one simple argument" concerning causation and the formation of belief.

Hume's elegant summary presages his "recasting" of that argument in the first *Enquiry*.

The *Treatise* was no literary sensation, but it didn't fall "dead-born from the press," as Hume disappointedly described its reception. And despite his surgical deletions, the *Treatise* attracted enough of a "murmur among the zealots" to fuel his life-long reputation as an atheist and a sceptic.

In 1763, Hume accepted an invitation from Lord Hertford, the Ambassador to France, to serve as his Private Secretary. During his three years in Paris, Hume became Secretary to the Embassy and eventually its Chargè d'Affaires. Hume returned to England in 1766, accompanied by Jean-Jacques Rousseau, who was then fleeing persecution in Switzerland. Their friendship ended quickly and miserably when the paranoid Rousseau became convinced that Hume was masterminding an international conspiracy against him.

He retired to his native Edinburgh in 1769 and his autobiographical Essay: *My Own Life* was written shortly before his death in 1776.

Upon finding that he had intestinal cancer, Hume prepared for his death with the same peaceful cheer that characterized his life. He arranged for the posthumous publication of his most controversial work, the *Dialogues concerning Natural Religion*; it was seen through the press by his nephew and namesake in 1779, three years after his uncle's death.

A master stylist in any genre, Hume's major philosophical works — *A Treatise of Human Nature* (1739-1740), the *Enquiries concerning Human Understanding* (1748) and *concerning the Principles of Morals* (1751), as well as the posthumously published *Dialogues concerning Natural Religion* (1779) — remain widely and deeply influential. Although many of Hume's contemporaries denounced his writings as works of scepticism and atheism, his influence is evident in the moral philosophy and economic writings of his close friend Adam Smith. Hume also awakened Immanuel Kant from his "dogmatic slumbers" and "caused the scales to fall" from Jeremy Bentham's eyes. Charles Darwin counted Hume as a central influence, as did "Darwin's bulldog," Thomas Henry Huxley. The diverse directions in which these writers took what they gleaned from reading Hume reflect not only the richness of their sources but also the wide range of his empiricism. Today, philosophers recognize Hume as a precursor of contemporary cognitive science, as well as one of the most thoroughgoing exponents of philosophical naturalism.

3.10.2. Bibliography

3.10.2.1. Primary Sources

David Hume, 0n Human Understanding edited and with a new introduction by Antony Flew, New York, 1962.

_______, *Essays Moral and Political*, Oxford, 1961.

_______, *Dialogues Concerning Natural Religion*, edited by N K Smith, London, 1949 (this edition contains, among other essays, "My Own Life" by Hume).

_______, *Selections*, edited by Charles Handel, London, 1927 (Copious extracts from the Treaties of Human Nature; also, from An Enquiry Concerning Human Understanding, the

_______, *Principles of Morals*, the Natural Hisimy of Religions and the Dialogues Concerning Natural Religion.

_______, *On Religion*, selected and introduced by Richard Wellheim, New York, 1968.

3.10.2.2. Secondary Sources

A. H. Besson, *Hume*, Harinondsworth, 1958.

V.C. Chappell (editor), *A Collection of Critical Essays: Hume*, London, 1968.

Jonathan Harrison, *Hume's Moral Epistemology*, Oxford, 1976.

E. C. Mossner, *The Life of David Hume*, London, 1954.

N. K. Smith, *The Philosophy of Hume: A Critical Study of its Origins and Central Doctrines*, London, 1949.

3.10.3. Hume's Thought

3.10.3.1. Epistemology

3.10.3.1.1. Aim of the Treatise

The key to Hume's epistemology and, indeed, to his whole philosophical vision, is to be found in the introduction he wrote to his famous *Treatise of Human understanding.* There he tells us of his great desire to establish a science of human nature. After all, every science has to do with human nature in some way or the other. For some, logic, morals, politics and so on, it is obvious. For others, like mathematics and natural religion it is not quite obvious. But they are at least made by man and it is he who, ultimately, decides what is true and what is false in these disciplines. Thus, it is evident that human nature is the 'capital or centre' of the various sciences and should, therefore, serve as their focal point. Hume's aim will be, then, to explain the *principles of human nature,* so that all the various discipline may be able to build upon solid foundation, the only one upon which they can stand with any security.

3.10.3.2.2. Method

When Hume tells us of the method, he is advocating for us to establish this science, we are at once conscious of this Newtonian inspiration. For Hume will tell us that we can only make use of the method by means of which Sir Isaac Newton made of physics a full-blooded science, the *experimental method.* As the science of man is the only solid foundation for the other sciences, so that only solid foundation we can give to this science itself must be laid on experience and observation. We must make a close and accurate observation of man's psychological processes and moral behaviour and try to separate out from these the various laws according to which man works - just as is done in the natural sciences. Thus, rather than relying on supposed intellectual intuitions of the essence of the human mind through introspection, we shall make use of the more scientifically solid procedure of induction. And, where experiments of this kind judiciously collected and compared, we may hope to establish on them a science which will not be inferior in certainty, and will be much superior in utility, to any other of human comprehension.

3.10.3.1.3. On Ideas

As is the case with Locke, so with Hume it is necessary to have a clear grasp of his doctrine of ideas, to understand central theories built up by him. He too, subdivides ideas into two basic types: simple *idea* and simple *impression* or sensation. Now the basic difference between an idea and a sense impression of it is that the former is a faint image of the latter which is, by nature, more vivid. The difference between these consists in the degrees of force and liveliness with which they strike upon the mind and make their way into our thought or consciousness. These perceptions which enter with most force, and violence, we may name **impression**; and under this name I comprehend all our sensations, passion and emotions, as they make their first appearance in the soul. By **Ideas**, I mean the faint image of these in thinking and reasoning; such as, for example, are all the perceptions excited by the present discourse, excepting only those which arise from sight and touch, and excepting the immediate pleasure or uneasiness it may occasion. It is true that in a sleep, in a fever, in madness, or in any violent emotions of the soul, our ideas may approach impression; as on the other hand, it sometimes happens that our impressions are so faint and low that we cannot distinguish them from our ideas. Still, as a general rule, the distinction holds good and the most lively thought is still inferior to the dullest sensation.

3.10.3.1.4. Imagination and Memory

A past impression may be summoned up by the mind, as it were or - or to use Hume's expression - made to appear, in one of the two ways. First, it can be made to come back once again with a certain degree of vividness and this is done by the faculty of the memory. Or it could be made to reappear as a mere idea, that is, as a faint copy or image of the impression. This is done by imagination. The same degree of vividness / faintness is then used to distinguish memory, from imagination as was used to differentiate between impression and idea, more relevant to the present situation. Memory does not merely recall simple ideas, but makes them reappear faithfully in their original chronological order. The imagination, however, has freer rein. It can re-arrange the order of events by breaking down and re-combining, in a different way, the various complex ideas and can represent an event or events in a quite arbitrary fashion. This is what is done by novelists and poets, in a special way, but also by everyone. The imagination is, therefore, an important tool for our analytic study of human nature, for it is through the imagination that we re-cast our ideas.

3.10.3.1.5. Laws of the Association of Ideas

Are there any different patterns or laws, according to which the imagination goes about its job of disassociating ideas, or does it do so in a completely arbitrary manner? Hume's observations convinced him that there were a definite set of principles or association among the ideas themselves and the imagination is compelled by a strange 'gentle force' to work according to these norms. There is some uniting principle among the ideas themselves, some associating quality, by which one idea naturally introduces another. Hume is unable to say anything more precise about all those vague and mysterious forces and principle. They are there and they call for our obedience. Still, we can single out the qualities from which this association arise, and by which the mind is, after this manner, conveyed from one idea to the other, are three, namely, Resemblance, contiguity in time or place and cause and effect.

3.10.3.1.6. General Ideas

If all ideas, according to Hume, are reducible to simple ideas and their combinations, what about general ideas (we would prefer to say 'universal ideas' - a term which is non-sense to an empiricists)? Hume finds in Berkeley an answer to this question. A great philosopher disputed and received opinion into this particular area and had asserted that all general ideas are nothing but particular ones annexed to a certain term, which give them a mere extensive significance and makes them recall upon occasion other individuals, which are similar to them. "I look upon this to be one of the greatest and most valuable discoveries that have been made of late years in the republic of letters. When I see a particular thing, this particular table for instance, my memory calls to mind - more or less automatically - all particular objects similar to it that I have ever perceived (all the various tables of my past experience, in this case). This *'evocative power'* should, to be complete, actually summon up all tables I have ever seen. Now, to avoid the practical difficulties which this would entail, by a kind of mental or psychological short-cut, the tendency to summon them up is taken for the deed. This tendency or 'custom' or 'evocative power' is there. Why it should be there and what makes it operative is essentially a mystery: to explain the ultimate causes of our mental actions is impossible."

3.10.3.2. Cosmology - Relation of Ideas

So far, we have been studying ideas in themselves. We now turn ourselves to studying the various relations that there can exist between these ideas.

Now, rational knowledge or science is nothing but a study of the relations that exists between ideas. So, a critique of science will amount to a critique of the relations between ideas. This is what follows.

3.10.3.2.1. Relation between Ideas

There are two main subdivisions of relationship between ideas: intrinsic and extrinsic. Intrinsic relations are founded upon some property within, or intrinsic to, the very ideas concerned. Thus, an alteration in one of the ideas will destroy the original relationship. For instance, there is relation of similarity between two white walls. Were we to paint one of them black, the old relationship of similarity will cease to obtain. There are three intrinsic relations: contrariety, degree in quality and proportion in number. It is only the last one which creates difficulties, as we shall see. The three others (2 intrinsic + extrinsic) are 'discoverable at first sight and fall more properly under the province of intuition than demonstration'. As for extrinsic relations, they are not in any way impaired by altering one of the terms of relationship, since they are founded on qualities outside of, or extrinsic to, the terms as such. Thus, we have e.g. the carpenter, who is related to the table by efficient cause. In fact, this relationship is basic, because all others are founded on it and presupposes it. Some of these other extrinsic relationships are self-identity, objective existence, space and time.

3.10.3.2.2. Critique of Intrinsic Relations

The intrinsic relations of proportion in quantity or number cannot be so easily discovered as the other three, which can be 'intuited'. Of course, such intuition is possible when very small numbers are concerned. We can 'intuit' that there is a resemblance, or equality between '2+3+1' and '4+1+1'. Similarly, we can 'intuit' that in the ratio "2:4 : 3:X", the missing number is 6. But this is not immediately evident with bigger or more complex numbers. In such cases, as to equality or any exact proportion, we can only guess at it from single consideration, on which alone depends the validity of such relationship-knowledge. This demonstration will be either by arithmetic and algebra or by geometry. Since the basis of demonstration in each case is different, the results will not be of quite the same type. In the first two, the basis of demonstration is the unity of number, something absolutely accurate and always strictly applicable. In geometry, however the basis of demonstration is the unity of measurement and this only can be approximate. Thus, geometry falls short of that perfect precision and certainty which are particular to arithmetic and algebra, yet it excels the imperfect judgments of our sense and imagination. Hume means that you can count and give the exact number of persons in a room, but you cannot measure and give the exact length of a line to the ultimate decimal point.

3.10.3.2.2. Extrinsic Relation of Space and Time

The Newtonians, whose views dominated at the time, viewed Space and Time as absolute, as things-in-themselves and quite objective entities. Space was seen as a kind of container and time as a kind of stream; we would be situating the objects of our daily experience in those. Hume invites us to analyze how these ideas come to us in our minds. Thus, he says, we will realize that there are no such things as 'pure' space or 'pure time' which exists independent of objects and to which we can postulate a real extrinsic relationship. In the absence of extended bodies, it is the series of sensation perceived by the moving hand or eye, in exploring the gap left by them that gives us the feeling of emptiness or unoccupied distance. We then go beyond the immediate, simple impression and imagine an 'absolute space' which would be the *cause* of this distance, independent of our impressions. Thus, the validity of the concept of space, in the last analysis, depends on the objectivity of the principle of causality. The same can be said of time, *mutatis, mutandis.*

3.10.3.2.3. Extrinsic Relation of Objective Identity

According to Hume, the principle of individuation or principle of identity is nothing else than the invariability of an object during a certain lapse of time. We all, spontaneously assign a relationship of identity to the table which we last see in the classroom at 1:00p.m. and the same table which we find there again at, say 8:00a.m., the next day. What is the validity of this assumed relationship? When the lapse in time is short, there is no problem. We perceive immediately the identity of the idea of the table at, say, 1.30 p.m. with the table at 1.31 p.m. But when the lapse of time is longer, and when there are several long gaps in the actual perception of the idea, what happens? We fill in these gaps in perception by postulating a permanent substratum which, as a *cause* exterior to the idea, underlies it and is supposed to have caused this identity. This external cause, or substratum, we call substance. Hume extends this to *all* substances, to the spiritual substance of the Ego as well. Thus, one more time, is the objectivity of an extrinsic relation (here identity) reduced to the validity of the principle of causality.

3.10.3.2.4. Extrinsic Relation of Objective Existence

Here we are concerned with the relationship between 'immediate existence', the existence of an idea itself and 'exterior' existence, which is the existence, exterior (and anterior) to the idea, the existence of an object itself. If the latter concept has any valid meaning, it is as an assumed exterior and permanent *cause* of the former. Once again, analysis of an extrinsic relationship has brought us in confrontation with the principle of causality.

3.10.3.2.5. The Formation of the principle of Causality

By various paths, it has become evident to us, that we must make a bold and critical inquiry into the objectivity of the principle of causality. Hume, careful and precise observer as he was, noted that we speak of causality in two ways: one is when we pronounce it *necessary* that everything whose existence has a beginning, should also have a cause. This is the principle of causality used in metaphysics. The other is the type used by scientist (perhaps unconsciously) when he concludes that such particular cause *must* necessarily have such particular effects. For instance, that an electric current passed through a mixture of Hydrogen and Oxygen (causes) must produce water (effect). We should study each of this separately, for the former involves terms that do not fall within the limits of experience (we do not experience a thing beginning its existence, so easily - and never do we experience the necessary being). For this reason, Hume will call this 'transcendental principle' of causality (since it transcends experience). The other principle he calls 'empirical principle' of causality, for both terms, the cause and effect, or 'antecedent and consequent, to use a more neutral terminology- fall within the experience (in the example given, I can experience the hydrogen, oxygen and the electric current - which make up the cause or 'antecedent'; and also the water - the effect or 'consequent').

3.10.3.2.6. Critique of the Transcendental Principle of Causality

For what reason do we pronounce it *necessary* that everything whose existence has a beginning should also have a cause? There are those who, like Newtonians, claim that it rests on the principle of solid and sure demonstration. They argue that if anything were to exist without a cause, it would have to be either cause of itself or it would have to come from nothing. Now these alternatives are ridiculous. But rejoinders Hume - and rightly so - the charge of ridiculous holds good only if one presupposes what it is required to prove (namely that a thing that begins to be *must* have a cause, a real being other than itself). The demonstration is thus invalid, for it begs the point. As for those who claim that the principle can be intuited, Hume defies them to show how it can be. In their attempt to do so, they merely re-state the main points of the bogus of demonstration. In brief, none of the advocates of the Transcendental Principle of Causality is capable of exhibiting its validity.

3.10.3.2.7. Critique of the Empirical Principle of Causality

From the above, we can conclude that it is therefore by *experience* only that we can infer the existence of the one object from another. The empirical principle of causality established a necessary connection between two ideas (note the rationalistic prejudice still in force: two *ideas);* an 'antecedent' (literally 'something going before') and a 'consequent' (literally 'something coming after'), both of which were experienced in themselves. What is the basis of the 'necessary connection' that is made by us? If we make a study of the psychological genesis of the link, we note that this arise out of two preliminary steps. At first stage we note that the two ideas were *always de facto* connected in our past experience (Hydrogen and Oxygen always yielded water whenever we passed an electric current through them). Secondly, this 'always de facto' connection induces us to make an inference which is only practically necessary. That is, I have gotten so used to seeing that particular consequent coming after such a particular antecedent, that I as it were, automatically, conjure up in my mind the second idea, as soon as I experience the first. One could not attempt to reinforce the link by claiming that it is ultimately grounded on 'immutability of nature' or some principle. For this so-called principle cannot be demonstrated without reference to the principle of transcendent causality itself. – back to the vicious circle? No, there is no explanation possible, other than an inferred psychological necessity. When one particular series of events has always, in all instances, been conjoined with another, we make no longer any scruple of foretelling one upon the appearance of the other, and of employing that reasoning (viz. causal inferences) which alone can assure us of any matter of fact or existence. We then call one object *cause* and the other *effect.* The alleged validity of this principle is based on the mere supposition that future resembles the past. Nor this presupposition is 'not founded on arguments of any kind, but is derived from habit, by which we are determined to expect for the future the same train of objects to which we have been accustomed'. Thus, we must admit that it is not therefore, reason which is the guide of life, but custom. That alone determines the mind, in all instances, to suppose the future conformable to the past. However, easy this step may seem, reason would never, to all eternity, be able to make it.

3.10.3.2.8. Skepticism

Relations in space and time, identity, objective existence - all these are grounded on the so- called principle of causality which offers no objective foundation. So, metaphysics is uncertain and so are the natural sciences. We can only have knowledge of the concrete data simple, unrelated experiences. This amounts phenomenalism and skepticism.

3.10.3.3. Philosophy of Human Person

3.10.3.3.1. The Substantial Ego

The status of the substantial Ego is on a par with that of any other substance. The human ego is no more than a bundle of perceptions. If the only sure knowledge we can have is of concrete, unrelated perceptions, then the Ego is nothing more than the ever-increasing totality of perceptions that accumulated around it. "The question concerning the substance of the soul is absolutely unintelligible. All our perceptions are not susceptible of a local union, either with what is extended or unextended, there being some of them of one kind, and some of the other." That is why Ego cannot be anything more than a bundle of perceptions: nothing more unified or organic is possible.

3.10.3.3.2. Ethics and Politics

Hume's ethics could not but be based on instinctive feelings, since he refused to accept any such things as nature, natural law and so on. According to him, man seeks 'instinctively' what is useful to the common good. As regards his political, or rather sociological theory, he admits a kind of compromise, very much along the lines of Locke, but one that grows out of his introspective observation. As a midway position between the primitive individualism of Hobbes and the naive optimism of Rousseau, Hume - more realistically - admits that man has both egoistic and altruistic instincts. Now, the stability of society depends on the balance of these two, whence follows, also, the various rights and duties of man.

3.10.3.4. Philosophy of God

3.10.3.4.1. God's Existence

If it is right to assume - as many do - that the views of Cleanthes, one of the characters in the *Dialogues concerning Natural Religion,* are those of Hume, then we can say that the Scotsman was convinced of God's existence and this belief was founded on the argument from design. "By this argument *a posteriori,* and by this argument alone, we do prove at once the existence of a deity and his similarity to human mind and intelligence." so says Cleanthes. Yet, remembering Hume's view on the principle of causality, we cannot be sure that he views this argument as conclusive. Actually, it is more likely that Philo, the other character in the dialogues, expresses Hume's convictions, when he says: "The cause or causes of order in the universe probably bear some remote analogy to human intelligence." Such a probability demands of man no more than a "plain, philosophical assent", In other words, no conclusions can be drawn from this as to human conduct, religious or moral.

3.10.3.4.2. Religion

Hume's views on God's existence and the consequences of it are not at all clear and he seems to have wanted it to this way. Religion, especially organized religion, does not convey much to him. Writing on the history of religions, he asserts that a primitive polytheism was first practiced by man. This, in turn, gave way to anthropological monotheism which, finally developed into philosophical monotheism. Hume is also very much against all religions which, like Christianity, claim some special revelation and a kind of unique predilection from God. He has also very strong views against miracles, as is to be expected.

3.10.4. Critical Remarks

3.10.4.1. His Philosophy of Knowledge

3.10.4.1.1. The "Science of Human Nature"

This is what Hume hoped to achieve, through his famous Treatise. And his insight, which showed the centrality of man in the whole conspectus of the various sciences, is most welcome in a world where progress is conceived along very impersonal, if not inhuman, lines. Yet, he should have noticed, himself, that we cannot have a science of man as we can have a science of the plant world. There is more to man than in- immediately observable and he is a free agent to boot. Though Hume may have avoided to excesses that such an approach is prone to, not all of his followers know how not to. Finally, Hume returns to Descartes' old view, but from a new angle. He too was guilty of professional narrow-mindedness. Descartes wanted to use the mathematical method for the study of all the sciences. He wanted the empirical method. But each subject of study demands a method of approach proper to it alone!

3.10.4.1.2. Ideas

Hume shares in the contestable rationalists' presupposition that all we know directly are ideas and the relations between them. There is no need for us to repeat, here, what we have already remarked. His reduction of the difference between what he calls impressions and ideas (a more accurate terminology might prefer "images" and ideas) to a there a question of quantity is also open to question. Even accepting his point "of view, we note that an impression of, say, a loud voice has the necessary sensible connotations of loudness. On the other hand, the idea of a loud voice is neither loud not soft. This shows that the differences between the two is more than an accidental one! And there is another phenomenon which Hume was not unaware. of, and which contradicted his premises. Though he dismissed it in a rather cavalier fashion it is worth singling out here. Suppose the mind were presented with a spectrum of colour, say ranging from a light shade of blue and ending up with a deep version of-the same, advancing, as it were, along definite progressive lines. If one of the shades along the line were omitted, the mind would be able to supply it, though it had no previous experience of it before. This, as I have said, was known by Hume. Though he merely dubbed it an "insignificant exception" to his static conception of knowledge, had he taken it seriously he would have been constrained to recognise there an evidence of what White head termed "the tendential nature of a knowledge always in process." This, in turn, would have necessitated an overhauling of his basic understanding of knowledge! As for his ingenious attempt to account for the origin and existence of what he called 'general idea", this is rooted in his determination to reduce all knowledge to "simple" concrete ideas. That this is a questionable hypothesis in pointed out in the very first heading under this section.

3.10.4.1.3. The Imagination

It is interesting to note the progressively important rolẹ assigned by modern philosophy to a previously somewhat neglected faculty, the imagination. This inevitably results from the kind of elementarism encouraged by Locke. For, if all knowledge is to be reduced to some atomic concepts, there must be some means of bringing together these constituents and fashion them into a complex whole. And what faculty would be best suited for the work of dissociation and association of these than the imagination? Kant himself will devote a good deal of his work to studying the imagination and its workings. Even in recent times the work of the imagination is receiving considerable attention: witness the studies of Husserl, Sartre and various Kantian off-shoots.

3.10.4.1.4. Laws of Association

Most rationastically did Hume assume that the inner workings of the human mind follow a very logical procedure and that all people do their job of associating and dissociating ideas according to faithfully observed universal laws. Now it is certainly true that there are some discoverable patterns of association in human psychology: this is-borne out by psycho-analytical studies. Still, when all is said and done, it remains equally certain that often our minds follow an inner logic of their own and associate various ideas that seem logically quite "unconnectable". The notion of "traumatic experience' as well as the entire "stream of consciousness" tradition in contemporary literature would hear this out. The element of human spontaneity and individualism is grossly under-rated in Hume's introspective generalisations.

3.10.4.2. His Philosophy of the World

3.10.4.2.1. The Critique of Science

The leading exponent of empiricism is still labouring under the rationalistic prejudices of Descartes when he sees science as nothing more than a study of the relations between ideas! No end of pseudo-problems, calling for all manner of mental gymnastics, result from this uncritical presumption.

We cannot deny that Hume's scathing attack on the all to naively accepted "principle of causality" did spark of a lot of serious in depth reflection by later thinkers and we are all the richer for this. Marechal, for instance, would show that a good deal of the problem is due to a clumsy formulation of the principle. It is only a cautious statement such as "Every being that is not being by its essence depends for its total being on the being that is being by essence", that can be meaningfully defended. The usual expressions of the principle do, in fact, beg the question, as Hume had pointed out.

3.10.4.2.2. Hume's Sceptism

How seriously are we to take Hume's sceptical conclusions? I do not think we would be justified in claiming that all Hume wanted to do was to wake us out of our dogmatic slumber, make us realise that a lot of things we had taken for granted could be upon to serious doubts and that he never really meant to profess unabashed scepticism. Granting that there is some truth in all this and that critics have tended to overstress this destructive element in Hume, I think that there is no question that Hume was dead serious in claiming for himself "the privilege of a sceptic". Indeed, the sceptical conclusion to the Cartesian "bridge", coupled with Lockean elementarism is inevitable. Descartes, Leibniz and Spinoza were able to escape such an impasse because they could find an easy way out in theistic principles of unification, such as divine goodness, pie-established harmony and so on. But Hume refused to kow-tow to such a creaky *deus ex machina*. He showed his predecessors the logical conclusion of taking their own assumptions seriously: scepticism!

3.10.4.3. His Philosophy of Man: Disintegrated Man

Hume's difficulties with the substantial ego as well as the "permanence and self-identity" issue which admittedly trouble him no little bit are, once again, the consequence of his taking his predecessors more seriously than they took themselves. A distinguished, disassociated bundle of perceptions that 'calls itself a man and with precious little scope for anything to provide him with any real sense of identity was precisely what resulted from Locke and Berkeley's attack on substance. They lost heart in the process and turned back on their own logic. Hume, though fully aware of the unpleasant and alarming consequences of his inexorable logic, plunged boldly on.

3.10.4.4. His Philosophy of God: God and Religion

As we have seen, Hume's views on God's existence are not very clear. And if we grant his rejection of transcendental causality then, apart from blind faith, there is little basis for upholding the existence 'of God. As for his views on the evolution if religion, it is enough to point out that though Hume's theory seems very plausible, it has not been borne out by the more recent researches of anthropologists. Their studies nigh unanimously reveal. that a primitive monotheism stands at the beginning of the human quest for the absolute.

3.10.5. Conclusion

Rather than blaming Hume for his conclusion, we should blame his predecessors for their assumptions. After all, he was more logical and resolute than they.

However, had he been yet a bit more faithful to the logic of more than one indication of the phenomena he duly noted, he would have had to abandon his narrow and static prejudices about knowledge. The recognition, for instance, of the 'evocative power' of the intellect as well as our inevitable postulating of a 'permanent substrate' to supply the 'gaps in perception' would point in this direction.

3.11. Immanuel Kant (1724–1804)

3.11.1. Life

Immanuel Kant, the son of a master saddler in Konigsberg, an obscure town in Germany, was what we might call a self—made man. He rarely left his native town and never crossed the borders of the province of that same name. Yet he was the first German professor to teach physical geography and that with such consummate skill that an English visitor who heard his description of Westminster Bridge could hardly believe he had never set eyes on it. At various times, we find him lecturing oh physics, mathematics, pedagogy, anthropology, mineralogy, logic, metaphysics and moral philosophy. He wrote his doctoral dissertations on *fire*, proposed an original interpretation of Laplace's nebular hypothesis and, long before Darwin's time, suggested a bold theory of evolution.

A voracious reader, in his earlier days Kant had been steeped in the Wolffian brand of rationalism (he later described that worthy as "the greatest of dogmatic philosophers"). He delved deep into the speculations of contemporary British and Continental philosophers: Shaftesbury, Hutcheson, Hume, Rousseau. A close friendship developed between him and his professor, Martin Knutzen, who allowed his distinguished pupil the run of his library. Here it was that Kant was able to deepen an develop his scientific interests through the reading of Newton and other such writers.

For his family, Kant had imbibed a thorough grounding in Pietism, a strict religious current of the German *Aufklarung* or Enlightenment. We might link to this his profound sense of duty and discipline. Later, at the Collegium Fredericanum his pietism was given, if anything, a more solid foundation. Here, too, he picked up his fluency in Latin and a familiarity with. classical literature - a flair evident even in his most technical works.

Soon after graduation, he taught for a while in his alma mater, numbering among his pupils the great German philosopher, Herder, who left a glowing eulogy of his master's lively and interesting classes. Kant ever insisted that his students learn to think for themselves and stressed, too, the importance of scientific subjects as a sure means of helping them realise the central role of experience in knowledge. Somewhere round 1770, the memory of what he had read in Hume led Kant to abandon his erstwhile rationalistic convictions. "I frankly admit", he was to write later in his *Prolegomena* to *Any Future Metaphysics*, "it was David Hume's remark that first, many years ago, interrupted my dogmatic slumber and gave a completely different direction to my enquiries in the field of Speculative philosophy." That "remark" originally had been aimed at the naive acceptance of the principle of causality. In the scientific sphere, this meant that the laws of physics, for one thing, were based on nothing more solid than subjective, psychological associationism. This was something that the scientist Kant could hardly rejoice over. Besides, did it not disrupt the very foundations of experience itself? This set him thinking very hard.

So, for Kant, as for a great number of outstanding personalities, "life began at sixty." He published his first major work, *The Critique of Pure Reason*, at the age of 55 - an age at which Descartes had already completed his life's work and spent one year in his grave. Ten years of amazing productivity followed, during which the first Critique saw a new edition and a brilliant study came off the press at the rate of almost one per year. But Kant's title to posterity will always be for his famous trilogy: in addition to the above-mentioned *Kritik*, there was the *Critique of Practical Reason* and the *Critique of Judgment*.

This sudden burst of research and study, combined with his regular teaching schedule, forced Kant to husband his time very strictly. This earned him the reputation of having lived a cold and aloof, clockwork existence - in short, the typical professor of caricature. But nothing could be further from the truth. His rich and popular social life suffered not one whit. He enjoyed his card games, played billiards quite proficiently and was much sought after at dinner parties on account of his enchanting conversation.

By 1790, we are told, reading and/discussing Kant had become quite the fashion (though we may be quite sure few went beyond the table of contents and the opening chapter). Yet, when he died, in 1804, but a few blocks from his birth-place, he was reverently laid to rest in the Professor's Vault of the local University and Germany scarcely noted the passing of her illustrious son.

3.11.2. Bibliography

3.11.2.1. Primary Sources

Immanuel Kant, *Critique of Pure Reason* (trans Norman Kemp Smith), London, Macmillan, 1963 (reprint). The Standard text of the first critique today.

_______, *Critique of Practical Reason and Other Works on the Theory of Ethics* (trans T. K. Abbott), London, Longmans, 1948 (reprint). The "Other Works" included in this edition are the following: *Fundamental Principles of the Metaphysics of Morals*, *Introduction to the Metaphysics of Morals*, *Preface to the Metaphysical Elements of Ethics* and *First Part of the Philosophical Theory of Religion*. There is an appendix of two short essays by Kant, "On a supposed Right to Tell Lies from Benevolent Motives" and "On the Saying," 'Necessity has no Law.

_______, *The Critique of Judgment* (trans J C Meredith), Oxford, The Clarendon Press, 1952. This edition does not contain any introduction or commentary of note, but it has some useful analytical indexes.

_______, *The Prolegomena to Any Future Metaphysics* (trans J H Bernard), London, Macmillan, 1915. This edition carries an excellent appendix and extensive notes. There is also a very good later edition with an even more readable translation by P. G. Lucas, brought out by the Manchester University press, 1959.

_______, *On Perpetual Peace* (trans M C Smith), London, Allen and Unwin, 1903. An English translation, with introduction and notes, of a not too well-known but very topical Kantian reflection.

_______, *On History*, (ed L W Beck), New York, Library of Liberal Arts, 1963. An eminent Kantian scholars' edition of various essays of Kant on sundry topics touching on the philosophy of history. Translations of the essays by various scholars. Beck has prefixed an excellent introduction.

_______, *Observations on the Feeling of the Beautiful and the Sublime* (trans J T Goldtheait), California, University of California Press, 1960. With a fine introduction and notes. An important text for those interested in Kantian Aesthetics.

_______, *Religion within the Bounds of Reason Alone* (trans Greene and Hudson), New York, Harper, 1960. An edition, with a very good introduction and notes, of an interesting and topical (though controversial) Kantian text.

Blankey, R.B., *An Immanuel Kant Reader*, New York, Harper, 1960. Choice selections from the three Critiques as well as the Metaphysical Foundations of Morals. Excellent summing—up introductions to each section together with a very readable text — the selections from the first critique are rendered into a more flowing English than Professor Smith's version.

Greene, T. M., *Kant Selections*, London, Scribner's 1929. Selections from the three Critiques.

3.11.2.2. Secondary Sources

This is an extremely select bibliography. I am listing only the best and latest books from among those we have here and for obvious reasons, am confirming myself to works in English only.

Bonnet, J., *Kant 's Analytic*, London, Cambridge University Press, 1966. A study of the first part of the Critique of Pure Reason.

_______, *Kant 's Dialectic*, London, Cambridge University Press, 1977. A study of the second part of the first Critique. This volume (which treats of the many interesting and relevant themes raised by Kant in the latter part of this book), together with the first, constitutes an excellent hand-book for one who would like to go a bit deeper into Kant's views on knowledge.

Cassirer, H. W., *Kant's First Critique*, London, Allen and Unwin, 1957. One of the classical English commentaries. Detailed.

Smith, N K, *A Commentary on the Critique of Pure Reason*, London, Macmillan, 1918. A rather old study, but the work of a painstaking and devoted Kantian scholar. Very detailed.

Wilkerson, T E., *Kant 's Critique of Pure Reason*, Oxford, Clarendon Press, 1976. A handy and excellent commentary for students. Not too abstruse.

Beck. L.W., *A Commentary on Kant 's Critique of Practical Reason*, Chicago, University of Chicago press, 1960. A must for any serious work on the second critique.

Duncan, A., *Practical Reason and Morality*, London, Nelson, 1957. A shorter study.

Raschke, C.A., *Moral Action God and History in the Thought of Immanuel Kant*, University of Montana Press, 1975. A useful dissertation, gathering together a critical review of Kent's ideas on these various topics.

Ward, K, *The Development of Kant's Views on Ethics*, London, Blackwell, 1972.

Action, H.B., *Kant 's Moral Philosophy*, London, Macmillans, 1970. Brief and to the point (only 65 pp).

Beck. L.W. (ed), *Kant 's Studies Today*, Illinois, Open Court Publication, 1969. Assembles some 20 critical essays on contemporary and relevant themes in Kant by a group of international scholars.

Gram, M.S. (ed.), *Kant: Disputed Questions*, Chicago, Quadrangle Books, 1967. Ten core essays by international scholars.

Wolff, R. P., *Kant*, London, Macmillan 1967. A selection of the critical essays by international scholars Includes an appendix of a bibliography of works on Kant 1945- 1965.

3.11.3. Kant's Philosophy

3.11.3.1. His Philosophy of Knowledge

3.11.3.1.1. The Plight of Metaphysics

Like Descartes before him, Kant noted the sad state of affairs in philosophy. "So far. are the students of metaphysics from exhibiting any kind of unanimity in their contentions, that metaphysics had become rather to be regarded as battle-ground quite particularly suited for those who desire to exercise themselves in mock combats, and in which no participant has ever succeeded in gaining even so much as an inch of territory, not at least in such a manner as to secure him its permanent possession. This shows, beyond all questioning, that the procedure of metaphysics has hitherto been a merely random groping, and, what is worst of all, a groping among more concepts.' In short, metaphysics, "though it is older than all the rest (of disciplines, such as physics and astronomy) . . . has not yet had the good fortune to enter upon the secure path of a science."

(*Critique of Pure Reason*, Smith's Trans. By Convention "A" & "B" refer to the text of the first and second editions of the first critique).

3.11.3.1.2. Science vs Natural Disposition

Kant would whole-heartedly agree with Emerich Coreth that "man is a metaphysical animal." He can't help asking the question of being. "Thus, in all men," Kant writes, "as soon as their reason has become ripe for speculation, there has always existed and will always continue to exist, some kind of metaphysics." (Pure Reason, B 21, Smith). This "metaphysics as a natural disposition", as Kant calls it, would survive "even if all the rest (of disciplines) were swallowed up in the abyss of an all-destroying barbarism." (B xiv) This is because metaphysics, in itself, stems not from "an idle desire for extent and variety of knowledge, (but) proceeds impetuously, driven on by an inward need, to questions such as cannot be answered by empirical employment of reason, or by principles thence derived" (B 21). Of course, this brand of "metaphysics" has little to recommend; part opinion and part prejudice, it is highly, tinged with dogmatism and illogic. It is not worthy of the name of science, for it lacks that precision, that clarity and that certitude that are the hall—marks of any science, such as physics and mathematics (Kant's preferred terms of comparison).

3.11.3.1.3. The Response

Kant refuses to admit that the sure path of metaphysics to science is no-existent. Why would nature have visited us with a relentless desire for what is impossible, he asks. So, realistically, he suggests that the only reason why man has hitherto failed to establish metaphysics on a sure footing is because he has been following the wrong path. But how to find the right path? Kant feels we can learn a lesson from the ancients and the beginnings of scientific astronomy. Once upon a time astronomy was in as confused a mess as metaphysics is now. That was because the ancient systems of astronomy (Ptolemaic) had wrongly assumed that the sun and planets revolved round the earth. Once they accepted Copernicus' hypothesis that it is the other way round: the earth and planets move round the sun - there was no problem. May be, what is required in metaphysics is the same kind of radical re-ordering of our presuppositions. "Hitherto it has been assumed that all our knowledge must conform to objects. But all attempts to extend our knowledge by establishing something in regard to them a priori, by means of concepts, have, on this assumption, ended in failure. We must, therefore, make trial whether we may not have more success in the tasks of metaphysics if we suppose that objects must conform to our knowledge…" (B xvi) This is quite a radical and revolutionary view!

3.11.3.1.4. The "a priori" and "a posteriori"

Let us try to clarify the meaning of these terms which we have already heard Kant use. For he gives them a very specific meaning. "There can be no doubt that all our knowledge begins with experience," states Kant early in the first critique (B 1) but, he hastens to add, this should not make us mistakenly assume that all knowledge arises out of experience. There could well be a contributory element from ourselves, from the understanding, to be precise. Experience would, then, furnish us with the occasion for a knowledge that arises from out of ourselves! From this observation, Kant derives his famous distinction between *a priori* and *a posteriori*. The former is the name he will give to "any knowledge that is independent of experience and even experience of the senses." (B 2) This is to be opposed to 'the empirical, which has its source *a posteriori*, that is, in experience." (1b) we should not misunderstand Kent's distinction, though. For any knowledge to be called *a priori* according to his conception, it is not sufficient for it to be "independent of this or that experience, but . . . absolutely independent of all experience." (B 3) I know that if I leave a hot iron on my shirt, the latter will burn. I might be inclined to call this *a priori* knowledge. But Kant would not agree. For this knowledge is dependent on my experience of other shirts and what happens to then when left under other hot irons. This knowledge, then, is not independent of "absolutely . . . all experience." So, it is not *a priori* in the Kantian sense of the term. But, one may ask, is there any such knowledge at all? Kant certainly thinks so. He would point to the famous twelve categories of the understanding and the two *a priori* forms of the senses. But about these, more later,

3.11.3.1.5. The Call for a Critique

From the above, it is evident why we find ourselves faced with a call to reason to undertake anew the most difficult of all its tasks, namely, that of self—knowledge, and to institute a tribunal which will assure to reason its lawful claims, and dismiss all groundless pretensions, not by despotic decrees, but in accordance with its own eternal and unalterable laws. This tribunal is none other than the *Critique of Pure Reason* (A xii). Indeed, there is a call for other critiques, too, For, "our age is, in especial degree, the age of criticism, and to criticism everything must submit. Religion, through its sanctity, and law—giving through its majesty, may seek to exempt themselves from it. But then they awaken just suspicion, and cannot claim the sincere respect which reason accords only to that which has been able to sustain the test of free and open examination" (A xi, ped a). In 1791, ten years after the publication of the first critique, Kant made an important clarification about its intent. "The transcendental philosophy," he wrote, "that is, the teaching concerning the possibility of all *a priori* knowledge which is the *Critique of Pure Reason* has as its purpose the establishment of metaphysics."

3.11.3.1.6. Analytic and Synthetic Judgments

In his Introduction to the first critique, Kant poses what he calls "the proper problem of pure reason", viz., "How are *a priori* synthetic judgment possible?" (B 19) He goes on to remark that the whole edifice of his philosophy stands or falls with his answer to that question. But what exactly is an a priori synthetic judgment?

A judgment, first of all (the term is here used in its epistemological sense), according to Kant is a union of Subject and Predicate. Now this union may be of two kinds. "Either the predicate, B, belongs to the subject, A, as something which is (covertly) contained in this concept A, or B lies outside the concept A, although it does indeed stand in connection with it." (A 6) In the former case we have an analytic judgment; in the latter, we have a synthetic judgment.

In simple language, an analytic judgment is one in which the predicate is pre—contained in the subject, though in. a hidden way. Kant gives, as example, the judgment, "All bodies are extended." (B 11 – B 12). Here, the predicate "extend" is implied in the very meaning of the subject "body." To formulate such a judgment, all one needs to know is understand the meaning of the subject, here, "body" and he will see that "extended" belongs to its as one of its necessary implications. Such a judgment is called "analytic by Kant it is formed by breaking up (Greek analysis) the subject term into its constituent implications. Analytic judgments, remarks Kant, are "thought through identity" and he suggests that. we could also call them "explicative" (Latin explicate, to unfold, root of the English "to explain") because "they add nothing through the predicate to the concept of the subject, but merely break it up into its constituent parts that have already been thought in it, although confusedly." (A 7) Analytic judgments are tautological (that is, repeat themselves,- don't add any new knowledge to the subject).

But let us take some other examples: "All bodies have weight" (Kant's example) or "John was born on January 1"). In both these cases, the predicate is in no way implied in the subject and no amount of analysis of the meaning of "bodies" or of "John" will yield us the predicates "having weight" and "birth on January 1st" respectively. The judgment is not the result of analysing or breaking up the subject into its implicit constituents, but is due to one real linking up or joining together (Greek, synthesis) of two distinct terms: "the predicate is something quite different from the mere concept of body in general (in the case of the first example); and the addition of such a predicate yields a synthetic judgment." (A 7) Synthetic judgments, Kant remarks, could be described as "ampliative." This is because they yield new knowledge and thus increase of amplify our fund of information.

3.11.3.1.7. The Two Types of Synthetic Judgments

Analytic judgments are purely conceptual and so need no experience for their formulation. "Since in framing the (analytic) judgment, I must not go outside of my concept, there is no need to appeal to the testimony of experience in its support." (A 7) They are, therefore, *a priori* judgments. Synthetic judgments require experience to provide the link between a particular subject and a particular predicate. In this sense they are *a posteriori*, dependent on experience. Kant, however, further subdivides synthetic judgments into two types: Synthetic *a priori* judgments and synthetic *a posteriori* judgment is singular and contingent. Take the famous principle of judgments. The former name sounds a contradiction and the latter merely redundant. What does he mean? Putting it simply, a synthetic *a priori* judgment is a synthetic judgment which involves strict universality and necessity. A synthetic *a posteriori* causality (Kant's example), which he formulates as follows, 'Everything which happens has its cause." There is the element of universality here, for the statement is not about an isolated, single thing but about all things that happen or begin to be. And the force of the principle is that all that begins to be must necessarily have a cause. But take the other example (my example) "John was born on January 1st." This judgment is made only about John (singular, not universal) and it merely states a fact. It does not try to affirm that John had to be born on January 1st with a strict necessity of nature. There is no universality and necessity here. Yet this is a synthetic judgment. It is a synthetic *a posteriori* judgment. 'But why call judgments like the principle of causality *a priori* synthetic? Because, according to Kant, Experience teaches us that a thing is so and so, but not that it cannot be otherwise. (B 3) In other words, experience, cannot yield true and strict universality (and necessity), "but only an assumed and comparative universality through induction." (*Ibid.*)

If, then, I discover true and strict universality and necessity in a judgment (as in the principle of causality), this could not have come from experience. Hence it comes to the judgments *a priori* (independent of experience). An *a priori* synthetic judgment is synthetic or dependent on experience from the point of view of the linkage of a particular predicate to a particular subject; it is an *a priori* or independent or experience from another point of view: from the point of view of the universality and necessity contained therein. This, according to Kant, is the only way to explain how "*a priori* synthetic judgments are possible." And our "Copernican revolution" is a great help here. For, if we assume our knowledge has to conform to experience, we can never explain how universality and necessity get into our judgments, granted that experience cannot yield us these qualities. But if objects have to conform to our mind in knowledge, then it is easy to see how we contribute the elements of universality and necessity to them. It remains to show (and we will, presently) just how this happens.

3.11.3.1.8. Metaphysics as a Strict Science Impossibles

Any science, to be worthy of its name, must need advance through its use of universal necessary judgments based on experience. For science is not interested in analysing concepts or giving information about isolated and singular objects. It seeks to make generalisations, draw universal laws and so on. Now, if metaphysics is to be a science, it will have to base itself on the progress offered through *a priori* synthetic judgments. After all, its business "is not merely to analyse concepts which we make for ourselves *a priori* of things, but to extend our *a priori* knowledge." (B 18) However, as we have seen, *a priori* synthetic judgments, by their very nature, are intimately bound up with experience. Indeed, they cannot transcend it as regards their content. But metaphysics, on the other hand "soars far above the teachings of experience" and makes judgments about, for instance, God, immortality and freedom (B xiv). Metaphysics, then, in trying to be a strict science and, thereby, use *a priori* synthetic judgments to go beyond the limits of experience, is engaged in a self-defeating, impossible quest. So, metaphysics, as a strict science, is quite impossible.

BUT...

Metaphysics, as a strict science, is impossible. But his does not mean that for Kant no more metaphysics is possible. We have already referred to his remark in 1791 that the first critique had "as its purpose the establishment of metaphysics." So, what Kant really meant was to say that traditional metaphysics (which went beyond the bounds of sense—experience and tried to give us knowledge of the supra—experimental world) was no longer possible. But a new kind of metaphysics, one which would concern itself with a critical investigation of the a priori contribution of the mind to knowledge, could now begin. And this is, in fact, the type of metaphysics that the first critique will inaugurate. However, in his second critique, Kant will treat of God, immortality and freedom and claim to extend our knowledge of these very things which, he had earlier claimed, we can have no real metaphysical knowledge about. But there he would be making use of practical reason, not pure reason, Kant would point out. Thus, he was not contradicting himself for what he had earlier said was that the traditional metaphysics, elaborated by pure reason, was no longer possible!

3.11.3.1.9. The Structure of the First Critique

The first critique is divided into two main parts, the "Transcendental Doctrine of the Elements" and "The Transcendental Doctrine of Method." The first part — by far the largest — inquires into, and explicitates, the *a priori*, set up of our knowledge process. This, in turn, is sub-divided into two sections: the "Transcendental Aesthetic", wherein the *a priori* contribution of sensation to knowledge is studied (Greek, *aesthemi* = to feel, to sense), and the "Transcendental Logic", which busies itself with going into the *a priori* of the understanding. The latter part of the book is taken up with the proper usage of these tools of knowledge.

3.11.3.1.10. The Process of Knowledge

Kant had noted the extremist positions of his rationalist and empiricist contemporaries. From their excesses he learnt to hold that knowledge requires both sensation and understanding working together, the former supplying the latter the data for knowledge. "Objects are given to us by means of sensibility (sensation), and it alone yields us intuitions; they are thought through understanding, and from the understanding arise concepts" (A 19) Or, as he clinches his theory, "Thoughts without content are empty, intuitions without concepts are blind." (A 51) The understanding is incapable of intuiting and senses are incapable of thinking. It is only from the united action of the two that knowledge can arise. The only valid use of the understanding, consists of its 'thinking data' supplied to it by sensation. Using the understanding to go beyond the data of sensation is an illegitimate use of the understanding, a "paralogism" as Kant calls it. (A 340ff).

3.11.3.1.11. The Contribution of Sensation

The "Transcendental Aesthetic" opens with a series of definitions which are worth noting. Intuition is "that through which (knowledge) is in immediate relation to (objects)." (A 19) Sensibility (sensation) is "the capacity (receptivity) for receiving representations through the mode in which we are affected by objects." (Ibid.) This alone yields us intuitions. The raw sense data, if we may call then such, comes to us through the various sense organs and present themselves to us in a confused and unconnected manner. Kant calls these the *matter* of sensation. This "manifold of appearance" must needs be properly ordered in certain relations. In sensation there are two a priori forms which provide this ordering – space and time. Space is "nothing but the form all appearance of our outer sense" (a 26). This is "the determinate form in which alone the intuition of inner states is possible" (A 33) Neither space nor time as such, are derived from experience, nor do they represent any property of things is themselves. They are *a priori* forms according to which we organise and perceive sense data. This is what Kant means when he says that we may maintain their "transcendental ideality as well as their empirical reality") (A 37). That is, aside from experience (hence, "transcendental"), they are not real ("ideal", in effect), though it is perfectly true that the objects of our sense experience are represented as being spatio-temporal (so, "empirical reality").

3.11.3.1.12. The Contribution of Understanding

The erstwhile confused sense-data, now organised according to the a priori forms of space and time are now passed on to the understanding to be "thought" by it through concepts. Now there are twelve basic categories (fundamental concepts) according to which these are thought. Each of these is linked to a type of judgment for, after all, judgments are nothing but "functions of unity between concepts." (A 68) Now "the function of thought in judgment can be brought under four heads" - quantity, quality, relation and modality. Each of these heads "contains three moments" (A 70), such that the last "moment" under each head is a kind of synthesis or reconciliation of the opposing tendencies of the first two. We have thus the twelve basic judgments, illustrated below with an example. To each we append its derived concept. The examples, let it be stressed, are taken from Blakney, not Kant, but they help us to understand the table of judgments more clearly.

	Table of Judgments	**Illustrations**	**Derived Concepts**
Quantity	Universal	All men are mortal.	Unity
	Particular	Some men are short.	Plurality
	Singular	I am short	Totality
Quality	Affirmative	Man is mortal.	Reality
	Negative	The soul is not mortal.	Negation
	Infinite	The soul is immortal.	Limitation
Relation	Categorical	God is just.	Sustenance – Attribute
	Hypothetical	If God is just, he will punish sinners.	Cause – effect
	Disjunctive	God is either just or unjust.	Reciprocity of Agent – patient
Modality	Problematic	If you were present, you would have known.	Possibility – impossibility
	Assertoric	You were present.	Existence – non-existence
	Apodeictic (certain)	You must be knowing.	Necessity – contingency

Knowledge for Kant is the process of taking the confused sense data through the senses, organising them according to the a priori forms of space and time and assigning to this a "category."

On the one had we have confused "manifold intuition", duly ordered according to the *a priori* forms of space and time; on the other hand, we have the twelve categories. How do we know which is the appropriate category for thinking this particular sense data? The answer is provided by the faculty of the imagination, through function of schematism, as Kant calls it, and of which it is the bearer, if not the producer. Schematism, in Kant's words, is "the representation of a universal procedure of imagination in providing an image for a concept." (A 140) Or, as Copleston puts it, "A Schema is, in general, a rule or procedure for the production of images which schematize or delimit, so to speak, a category, so as to permit its application to appearance." (History, VI, pp. 256-257) But just how does the schema work? Just how does it come about that the schema determines the conditions under which a particular category is to be used. By determining the temporal conditions according to which the category is to be applied to appearances. "The schema of necessity is existence of an object at all times… the schema of relation is the connection of perceptions with one another at all times, according to a rule of time-determination" (A 143 - 144) and so on.

3.11.3.1.13. Noumena and Phenomena

Though Kant is quite in emphatic in asserting that we can never go beyond the level of appearance of phenomena, he does not go so far as to say that nothing exists in itself, apart from the realm of appearances and manifestations. It is in this connection that he makes his famous distinction between phenomena (things perceived) and noumena (things thought). The noumenon is the 'thing-in-itself', in effect. The phenomenon is the "thing—as-we-know—it." What we "know is the appearance, clothed under the a priori forms of space and time and invested with a category. We-can never know anything in its pure state, divested of forms and category.

3.11.3.1.14. Conclusion

We have, admittedly, gone into quite a bit of detail over this aspect of Kant's philosophy. This is unavoidable, since it is a very well-thought out, complex and influential theory of knowledge. We may note, incidentally, how Kant has made good use of his Copernican revolution. Knowledge is getting objects to conform to the forms and categories of the mind. The universality and necessity of cause-and-effect relationships, weakened by Hume, is now restored in strictness (albeit subjectively).

3.11.3.2. His Philosophy of Man

3.11.3.2.1. The Theme of the Second Critique

If the first critique took off with the question about *a priori* synthetic speculative judgments, the second critique draws our attention to the *a priori* practical judgments which we all have. These ethical directives have a universal and necessary connotation. "Do not steal", "Respect your parents", are examples. These laws, Kant observes, would continue to be in force even if no one observed them at all. In other words, they are not *a posteriori,* based on experience, though we may need the help of experience to elaborate the terms of the law - "men", "property" and so on. The second critique, then busies itself with the groundwork or metaphysics of ethics and asks, "How are *a priori* synthetic moral judgments possible?"

3.11.3.2.2. Heteronomous Solutions Rejected

The first part of the second critique is negative. Kant reviews the various ways in which men have tried to answer the question he poses about the basis of morality. He rejects them all, because, in effect, they propose a heteronomous basis of morality. For instance, there are those who would ground morality on the will of God. But this will hardly serve to give a solid grounding to the moral order for were one to deny God's existence, the moral order would have no basis for him! As for alternative views proposed by thinkers like Montaigne or Epicurus, they are no help either, for there are perfectly sound men who would seem to be quite deficient in that very quality upon which they would have us base the moral law - and yet many of these self-same people observe a very high moral code! Thus, Kant concludes that the only valid basis of obligation can be found *"a priori* simply in the conceptions of pure reason."

3.11.3.2.3. The Good Will

"Nothing can possibly be conceived in the world or even out of it, which can be called good, without qualification, except a Good Will." This sentence, which opens *Kant's Groundwork of Metaphysics of Morals* (which Abbot, in his translation, renders "Fundamental Principle of the Metaphysics of the Morals"), gives his answer to the foundation of ethics, namely, the good will. Nothing else can be described as unqualifiedly good: health, wealth and so on can all be misused. Only a good will is good simply. But what is a good will? A good will is to be called good not because of something extrinsic to it, as when we speak of a "good" punishment, it is good because of the extrinsic results which come from it. A good will is good because of some intrinsic property. In short, we can say that a will which acts for the sake of duty is a good will. For this reason, it is best to call God's will a holy will, rather than a good will. Calling God's will a good will would imply that he does his duty faithfully.

Now, as Kant will show, doing "duty" necessarily means overcoming obstacles - and we can hardly say that of God!

3.11.3.2.4. The Categorical Imperative

This "duty" may be expressed in the form of maxims or practical expressions of the will, such as, "I must not steal", or "I must not tell lies." All of these may be summed up or resolved into one general law or "Categorical Imperative", one statement of which is, "Act so that the maxim of thy will can always at the same time hold good as a principle of universal legislation." *(Practical Reason,* Abbot, 119) Another formulation, even more well-known runs, "So act as to treat humanity, whether in thine own person or in that of any others in every case as an end withal, never as means only." *(Groundwork,* Abbot, p.47) The general law is called a categorical imperative because it is a law (imperative) that admits of no exceptions (so categorical), as opposed to what Kant would call a hypothetical imperative. If you wish to be a doctor, then you must do your B.Sc. The imperative to do your B. Sc. is enjoined on one if he wishes to be a doctor. Otherwise no. But the categorical imperative, the basis of morality allows for no "ifs" or buts": no exceptions and no concessions. Even if one were to ignore or disregard it, that would in no wise and no concessions. Even if one were to ignore or disregard it, that would in no wise weaken the force of the categorical imperative. Thus, the autonomy of the will is made the basis of all morality.

3.11.3.2.5. Man is Free

From the categorical imperative, we can derive three important postulates or necessary implications. The first of these is that man is free. An imperative, command or obligation means that there is a possibility of disobeying, that is, it implies freedom to say no. Else it would be superfluous to give such a command. 'I ought; therefore, I am free", is how Kant would put it.

3.11.3.2.6. Man has a Soul

"The immortality of the soul as a postulate of pure practical reason" *(Practical Reason,* Abbot p. 218ft) follows next. The categorical imperative enjoins a very high ideal in us: nothing short of an absolute conformity with the law that is holiness in the technical sense. But holiness is "a perfection of which no rational being of the sensible world is capable at any moment of his existence." *(Practical Reason,* Abbot, p. 218) Yet, since such holiness "is required as practically necessary" the only course left is that of an indefinite process, an everlasting tending to it as a remote goal, so near and yet so far. "Now, this endless progress is only possible on the suppositions of an *endless* duration of the existence and personality of the same rational being - which is called the immortality of the soul." *(Ibid.)* Thus, the immortality of the soul, as a postulate of practical reason, is established.

3.11.3.3. His Philosophy of God

3.11.3.3.1. Negative part: Old Proofs rejected

Before we go on to showing how according to Kant, the existence of God is the third postulate of practical reason, we need to review briefly his consideration of the traditional proofs for God's existence which he takes up towards the end of the first critique. According to Kant, there are only three possible approaches to establishing God's existence through reason and they are all illusory. "All the paths leading to this goal begin either from determinate experience and the specific constitution of the world of sense as thereby known, and ascend from it, in accordance with laws of causality, to the supreme cause outside the world; or they start from experience which is purely indeterminate, that is, from experience of existence in general; or finally they abstract from all experience, and argue completely *a priori,* from mere concepts, to the existence of a supreme cause. The first proof is the physico-theological, the second the cosmological, the third the ontological. There are, and there can be, no others."

3.11.3.3.2. The "ontological" Proof

This is the name that Kant gives to all those proofs for God's existence which take, as their starting-point, the notion of the most perfect being. St. Anselm, as we have seen, was perhaps the first to propose it. From time to time, other thinkers returned to it and tried to touch it up (e.g. Descartes, Leibniz, Spinoza and even Hegel). Yet, it must be admitted, that Kant's criticism of it is one of the most devastating. It is also pertinent to note that, in Kant's view, all the other proofs have to return to it in some way or the other, as their basis. Kant's essential point is that we cannot treat existence as an attribute. The concept of the necessary being necessarily includes all its attributes. But existence is not an attribute. Hence, to find whether we must grant existence to the necessary being - as for all beings - we must go out of the concept to experience. "The small word 'is' adds no new predicate, but only serves to posit the predicate in its relation to the subject ... the concept expresses merely what is possible ... the real contains no more than the merely possible. A hundred real dollars do not contain the least coin more than a hundred possible dollars... Otherwise it would not be the same thing that exists, but something more than what had been thought in the concept; and we could not, therefore, say that the exact object of my concept exists ... Whatever, therefore, and however much, our concept of an object may contain, we must go outside of it, if we are to ascribe existence to the object."

3.11.3.3.3. The "cosmological proof"

This proof is so called because it begins with the cosmos and thence proceeds to the existence of a creator. It thereby enters upon "a course of reasoning which ... is at any rate natural, and the most convincing, not only for common sense, but even for the speculative understanding." Yet, Kant observes, it more pseudo-rational than rational and, at bottom is but a disguised form of the first in a mere change of dress and voice, as he so colourfully puts it. The typical form of the proof, according to Kant, runs, "If anything exists, an absolutely necessary being must also exist. Now I, at least, exist. Therefore, an absolutely necessary being exists." That done, reason proceeds to "abandon experience altogether and endeavours to discover from mere concepts what properties an absolute being must have." After detailing these, it is then asserted that such properties are "nowhere to be found except in the concept of an *ens realissimum* (Latin, most real being); and the conclusion is therefore drawn, that the *ens realissimum* is the absolutely necessary being." And this takes us back to the contestable ontological argument.

3.11.3.3.4. The "physico-theological" Proof

The proof that Kant so styles might be likened to the famous fifth way of Aquinas, 'the argument from design' or 'the proof from order or finality' as it is sometimes called. It cannot fail to strike a responsive chord in the heart of the unprejudiced scientist-believer, Kant. "This proof always deserves to be mentioned with respect", says Kant. "It is the oldest, the dearest, and the most accordant with the common reason of mankind. It enlivens the study of nature, just as it itself derives its existence and gains ever new vigour from that source." But even this proof is not without defects. First, what it proves is a mere architect of the world and not its creator (that is, it attempts to discover, at most, one who planned and ordered this world - not one who brought it into being!). Secondly, this *finite* world, with its *finite* order, is insufficient grounds to demand an *infinite* being to account for it. At most we may "argue to the existence of a cause proportioned to it." To get out of this and show that, in the last analysis, we must have recourse to an infinite being, we are constrained to "abandon the argument from empirical grounds and fall back upon ... contingency." "Thus, the physico-theological proof of the existence of an original or supreme being rests upon the cosmological proof, and the cosmological upon the ontological" - and we know haw valid that is!

3.11.3.4. His Philosophy of the World

3.11.3.4.1. The Reality of the World

As we have seen, Kant never denied that there is a real "thing-in-itself", even if we can know only its 'appearance'. For the same reason, he will hold that all we can know of ourselves is the existence of the "phenomenal ego" - the living body that I refer to as 'myself in my daily life. But we cannot assert that there is something like a substantial (or noumenal) ego, for we have no sense data about it. Still, we can't help "postulating" a common centre of our activity, a "transcendental" ego. But this is not objectively grounded.

3.11.3.4.2. Causality

As we have seen, Kant is quite willing to grant empirical causality, as against Hume. Furthermore, he maintains that the universality and necessity that we encounter these are not due to mere psychological associationism, as Hume had said. It is rooted in the very constitution of the mind - the *a priori* categories of the understanding. Transcendental causality, of course, is quite out of the question. Nevertheless, Kant felt he had quite safely saved science form the radical scepticism of Hume.

3.11.3.4.3. Kant on Aesthetics

In his third great work, *The Critique of Judgment,* Kant takes up, among other things, the whole controversial theory of Aesthetics. The perennial point of dispute among thinkers is whether beauty is objective or subjective Is it a real property inherent in the thing considered or is "beauty in the eye of the beholder"? After reviewing various positions, he finally opts for a subjectivist answer, as well as we might expect, His conclusion is based on an analysis of the aesthetic feeling of beauty. Such an analysis reveals a sense of pleasure coupled with no connotation of the object concerned being in any way useful to me. This is the unique peculiarity of the aesthetic feeling. I perceive, say a rose. The sight gives me delight while the rose does not, in any way, present itself to me as being useful to me, here and now. It is this disinterested aesthetic delight that makes me feel it would be universally shared by everyone. In reality the "universality" of "a judgment of taste" is based, Kant says, on subjective, not objective considerations.

3.11.4. Critical Remarks

3.11.4.1. His Philosophy of Knowledge

3.11.4.1.1. A Basic Realism

That a certain basic realism underlies Kant's whole outlook cannot be denied. His starting-point is always a recognition of what cannot be denied. Then he goes out to investigate how it is possible that such be the case, that is, he seeks out the necessary pre-conditions for undeniable facts. This is, in essence, what constitutes the "transcendental philosophy", so valuable a tool in the hands of the contemporary metaphysician. This is the basic methodology that Fr. Joseph Marechal (1878 - 1944), the Belgian Jesuit would use in "waking up some members of the almost monolithic Scholastic camp to the philosophic value of the transcendental method of Kant. His treatment was a kind of baptism, somewhat similar to the baptism St. Thomas conferred on Aristotle." (Donceel)

3.11.4.1.2. The Copernican Revolution

Kant's Copernican revolution would hardly be borne out by experimental psychology today. And it would seem to show scant respect for the world. From this stance is a small step to doctoring reality to make it fit our own preferences - whence arises much of the inauthentic pluralism of our times. Still, we can't help admiring the radical mentality of a mind that such a completely new approach. Most of us - including the most vociferous revolutionaries - can only, at best, tinker here and there with old machines and nothing more. Kant struck out boldly in a completely new direction. Even if he was wrong, mistakes are the privilege of the pioneer and his work sparked of a lot of valuable research.

3.11.4.1.3. Analysis and Synthesis

No one would deny that there are certain *a priori* elements in knowledge, in the sense that there are certain necessary dispositions and faculties required of the subject to be before knowledge can take place - for instance, healthy sense-organs, attentiveness and so on. But can we meaningfully speak of having knowledge independent of ail sense experience? Before we can even become aware of what these *a priori* are, we must needs undergo a sense experience. And though it is true that mere sense experience does not present us with necessary connections and true universality. This would not rule out the possibility of the senses providing the intellect with information that the latter might discover to contain indications of a universal and necessary connection. Again, is a judgment nothing but a link between two concepts, as Kant thought - though such a position is understandable, given his subservience to the Cartesian problem of the bridge? Is this not, rather, a pre-condition to a judgment which is formed only when one asserts that this intramental link is verified in reality? Finally, it is not quite fair to dismiss analytic judgments as "merely tautological", as Kant did. The statement, "being is being" really means "Being is always and necessarily being." In other words, what is asserted is something more than what is contained in the subject!

3.11.4.1.4. Kant on Metaphysics

Much of Kant's difficulties with metaphysics lose weight with the clarifications culled from the preceding section. In addition, it might also be necessary to point out that it is not quite correct to say, with him, that metaphysics "soars beyond the teachings of experience." It is, of courses, true that some of the conclusions of metaphysics touch upon aspects of reality that are beyond the ambit of sense-experience. But his should not be understood to mean that after a while, metaphysics turns its back on sense experience and ventures off onto an arbitrary flight into the unknown, quite according to its own whims and fancies. Though it may be claimed that some metaphysics - and especially the Wolffian school known to Kant - do this, this is an abuse of metaphysics. Authentic metaphysics is anchored in experience and aims at no more than a plunge into the deepest depths of reality, always checked and guided by what experience dictates. In the last analysis, metaphysics is dependent on experience - it has to be!

3.11.4.1.5. The Process of Knowledge

A common (and valid) criticism of Kantian epistemology is that is rather static vision of what is, essentially, a very dynamic act. Knowledge is not something that merely "happens to us" from outside. It is the result of a dynamic thrust from within. Kant sees sensation as the more passive aspect of knowledge, but even this questionable. No sensation takes place unless and until there is a positive decision to pay attention, an active *reaction* to the more or less spontaneous and passive reception of sense data. His view on the *a priori* nature of space and time are interesting and have gone a long way to dispel certain naive views which are the heritage of Newtonian physics. Einstein's theory of relativity would seem to favour Kant's views on time and space though Bergson reminds us that there seems to be something like fundamental space and time in reality that also provokes us to see things in space and time." For Kant, the understanding and its work provides the more active element of knowledge. But in the last analysis, it is a very poor "activity" indeed - a mere pigeon-holing of phenomenon in category slots! Of course, the whole thing is quite consistent in terms of his Copernican revolution, but that, too, is also to be linked with his uncritical acceptance of the Cartesian doctrine that what we know immediately is not the reality of our experience, but our idea of it.

3.11.4.1.6. Phenomena and Noumena

This is, perhaps, the most dangerous aspect of Kant's epistemology. His own basic realism saved him, as we have said, from the pitfalls of idealism. But not everyone was like him. Soon after Kant, there came a man like Fichte who said that, if it is true that we can't know the famous, "thing-in-itself", then it would be best to leave it out of our philosophy altogether ad seek to explain the whole of knowledge solely in terms of, and from the part of, the subjects. And from here it is a short step to the idealist thesis that we make, if not the object itself, at least all of our knowledge!

3.11.4.2. His Philosophy of Man

3.11.4.2.1. Duty and the Categorical Imperative

Firstly, we might question Kant's rather uncritical acceptance of the Categorical Imperative's various expressions. Now that we know how much of our so-called "autonomous values" are due to heredity and environment, as psychology has shown, we might pause a bit for feeling too sure that what we have put our fingers on its valid enough to be taken as a staring-point for an overly confident non-heteronomous system of morality. As for Kant's stem ethics of duty for duty's sake, it may be true that its impersonal formalism an inhumanity has been exaggerated by unsympathetic critics (Cf. Azzopadi, *Ethics,* Cyclostyled notes, Pune, JDV, pp. 29-30). On the other hand, we cannot deny that Kant's writings lend themselves to such an interpretation. Indeed, they seem to fit in well with a certain iron tradition of disciplinarianism that would, more or less, establish itself as part of the Germany ways of life. It is not too much of an exaggeration to see a chain of development from Luther, via Kant, through Nietzsche - right up to Hitler! Kant has had an undeniable influence on German Protestant thought and we may legitimately view the sort of Situation Ethics championed by men like Barth and Tillich to be a kind of reaction to Kantian legalism which they had inherited. Furthermore, one could make out a pretty good case for saying that it is not unfair to judge Kantian morality in this light, whatever, his defenders may say. Especially when we read his lyrical rhapsodies on duty such as the following horrific lines, "Duty, thou sublime and mighty name that dost embrace nothing charming or insinuating, but requirest submission, and yet seekest not to move the will by aught that would arouse natural aversion or terror, but merely holdest forth a law which of itself finds entrance into mind, and yet gains reluctant reverence (though not always obedience), a law before which all inclinations are dumb, even though they secretly counterwork it; what origin is there worthy of thee, and where is to be found the root of the noble descent which proudly rejects all kindred with the inclinations; a root to be derived from which is the indispensable condition of the only worth which men can give themselves." This is no to deny that even these lines can be defended in the sense that sometimes justice or honesty (duties!) could conflict with other values and yet should be given pride of place.

3.11.4.2.2. Freedom and Immortality

The weakening of the force of the "categorical imperative" is not, of course, without its repercussions on its postulates. Still, there seems to be good insight in the introspection that reveals a basic inner freedom at the heart of the sense of the "ought." This may be a very valid way to demonstrate human freedom today. The postulate of immortality does not rest on so impressive a foundation.

Finally, contemporary humanism would not agree that God is required to prop up the moral order!

3.11.4.3. His Philosophy of God

3.11.4.3.1. Kant on the Traditional Proofs

Many a successor of Kant overlooked the positive aspect of his thinking on God. For such, Kant was the man who well and truly refuted all the old proofs for God's existence. That done, they were assured that troublesome notion could be dispensed with. But Kant's view was that pure reason could not establish God's existence. And, in his handling of the proofs for God's existence, that he was encountering but pretty garbled - Wolffian - version of these. However, the critique of Hume and Kant of the principle of causality admittedly do undermine the proofs of Aquinas, all of which rest on the presumed validity of it. It is only a transcendental analysis of the direct judgment a la Marechal that can save the situation.

3.11.4.3.2. Kant's 'Proof'

This is perhaps one of the most unsatisfactory elements in all of Kant's philosophy. One can be quite sure that Kant's own belief in God was not grounded on this kind of thing. In the first place, one might question Kant's definition of happiness, a convenient one which very easily ties in a belief in god with the whole moral order. To round off this section, we may mention that Kant has frequent biblical references throughout his writings, though his interpretation of many a Christian dogma is hardly orthodox - by Catholic or Lutheran standards.

3.11.4.4. His Philosophy of the World

3.11.4.4.1. The Reality of the World

Ever since Descartes created the famous pseudo-problem of the bridge, philosophers have been labouring to assure the reality of "the external" with little success. Kant's basic realism coupled with his ultimate agnosticism is perhaps the most logical and the least far-fetched of all such responses. For after all, the only satisfactory way out of the impasse is to question the very validity of the problem itself.

3.11.4.4.2. Causality

Kant himself formulated the principle rather carelessly. Such a wording can scarce be defended without begging the point. Nor does his solution restore any appreciable level of objectivity to even the empirical statement. It was left to Marechal - especially in his fifth cahier of *The Starting-Point of Metaphysics* – to provide a more serious and solid response. Marechal belonged to a whole stream of progressive Catholic thinking which numbered among its leaders such luminaries as Pierre Rousselot SJ and Maurice Blondel. He complemented these with a leaf from Kant's own book and, with his theory of "Intellectual dynamism" was able to find, in the very insights and method of the sage of Konigsberg, a way to vindicate the transcendental principle of causality, establish the existence of God as also the reality of the external world. Thereby he laid the foundations for the "transcendental Philosophy" of men like Karl Rahner, Bernard Lonergan and Emerich Coreth – to mention just a few writers we cannot afford to ignore.

3.11.5. Conclusion: A Man We Can't Ignore

The great German poet, Heinrich Heine, contemptuously dismissed Kant as 'petty tradesman" whom nature intended "to weigh out tea and sugar" whereas Kant perversely applied such a temperament to philosophy and gave to the world a thought that was "subversive, world- bruising." Heine's assessment is hardly fair, though we can understand the reaction of a poet and it must be admitted that Kant is perhaps a bit too given to dividing up, categorising, separating out and mixing up.

None would contest, however, James Collins hailing Kant as "our contemporary." He is truly the Father of Contemporary Thought. Some of the most well-known thinkers of our times - Heidegger and Jaspers to mention but two - derived their philosophical insights from rethinking his positions. Indeed, as Jaspers himself observed, "Everyone who wishes to philosophise, at o nee on his own original ground and within the historical tradition, must open-mindedly immerse himself in Kant to see what ideas come to him in the process." John E Smith traces the perennial value of Kant's approach "chiefly in his having established the *reflective* approach. The older cosmology and the philosophy of nature gave way, under the impact of positions influenced by him, to the study of matter as of the concept of matter and not so much of levels or forms in nature as of the role played by principles in theory construction. In this regard, the 'critical' philosophy is still very much alive." Be that as it may, there is no doubt that Kant is a man we can't ignore.

> Our age is, in especial degree, the age of criticism, and to criticism everything must submit. Religion through its sanctity, and law-giving through its majesty, may seek to exempt themselves from it. But they then awaken just suspicion, and cannot claim the sincere respect which reason accords only to that which has been able to sustain the test of free and open examination.
>
> (Immanuel Kant, *Critique of Pure Reasons* (A xii, N K Smith's Edition, p. 9))